赢在高考

——基于学科素养的主题语境策略解读

李新定◎编著

文化发展出版社
Cultural Development Press

图书在版编目（CIP）数据

赢在高考：基于学科素养的主题语境策略解读 / 李新定编著. — 北京：文化发展出版社，2020.4

ISBN 978-7-5142-2963-9

Ⅰ. ①赢… Ⅱ. ①李… Ⅲ. ①英语课—教学研究—高中 Ⅳ. ①G633.412

中国版本图书馆CIP数据核字（2020）第032630号

赢在高考：基于学科素养的主题语境策略解读

编　　著：李新定

责任编辑：张　琪　　　　责任校对：岳智勇

责任印制：刘贝贝　　　　责任设计：侯　铮

出版发行：文化发展出版社（北京市翠微路2号 邮编：100036）

网　　址：www.wenhuafazhan.com　　www.printhome.com　　www.keyin.cn

经　　销：各地新华书店

印　　刷：北京政采印刷服务有限公司

开　　本：787mm × 1092mm 1/16

字　　数：293千字

印　　张：16.25

印　　次：2022年6月第1版　　2022年6月第1次印刷

定　　价：45.00元

ISBN：978-7-5142-2963-9

前言

FOREWORD

一期一会，高考英语备战过程中，总会遇到很多困惑，要想赢在高考，势必要有策略与技巧。从英语学科素养角度去解读主题语境，就会产生许多智慧，形成教学策略。鉴于此，编撰《赢在高考——基于学科素养的主题语境策略解读》一书，期望在高考英语备考的征途上，为一线教师和考生点燃心灵的薪火，为其照亮明天的旅程。

避开生硬简单的说教，于简练的语言中引发出策略指导，旨在引导考生如何迎接高考的挑战、如何在备考训练中获得自信。梳理试卷，高效备考，针对高考英语题型和复习板块提出合理化建议，进行策略指导和应试技巧指导，短时间内迅速调适备考心态，提高解题能力，正是作者编著此书的目的。

本书按照英语新课标卷特点编排，共分为七大专题：听力、阅读理解、阅读理解七选五、完形填空、语法填空、改错和书面表达专题。旨在指导高中英语教师精确解读高考大纲、考试说明和新课标要求，明确新课标主体语境考查点，从学科素养考核角度进行试题分析、题型解读，精准解析近三年高考真题，快速提高高考英语备考效率。同时，收集分析近几年全国卷及各省市优秀模拟卷，为来年高考英语学科素养主题语境备考提供专题训练。教师可以随时查阅，掌握备考策略，授予学生实战技巧，合理组题并有针对性地训练，形成技巧与策略。

纵览高考英语全国卷各套试卷可以发现，高考英语命题体现高考评价体系“一核四层四翼”的总体要求（一核：立德树人，服务选拔，导向教学；四层：第一层——必备知识，第二层——关键能力，第三层——学科素养，第四层——核心价值；四翼：基础性，综合性，应用性，创新性），围绕立德树人的教育根本任务，紧扣全国统一考试大纲，以考查学生关键能力和学科素养为主要目标，坚持稳定中求发展。

最后，愿《赢在高考——基于学科素养的主题语境策略解读》能够指引一线教师和考生的备考方向，带来解题思路和调适备战心态的启迪！用心品读，相信每一个人会受益匪浅，高效复习，赢在高考！

目录 CONTENTS

专题一 听力训练

专题二 阅读理解

专题三 阅读理解七选五

专题四 完形填空

专题五 语法填空

专题六 短文改错

专题七 书面表达

专题一 听力训练

一、题型特点

听力部分分为两节：第一节共5小题，第二节共15小题。考生将听到5段简短的对话（一般为一问一答的形式）和5段较长的对话或独白，从每小题所给的三个选项中选出最佳选项。第一节的5个小题主要考查考生理解简单的事实性信息和进行简单的推理判断和计算的能力；第二节的15个小题主要考查考生对材料的整体理解能力，要求考生理解对话或独白的主旨、要义，获取事实性的具体信息，对对话的背景、说话者之间的关系等能做出简单的推理判断，理解说话者的意图、观点或态度等。

二、题材范围

高考的听力材料多样化，其内容主要涉及日常生活、文化教育、风土人情、时事、人物和科普常识等方面。常见的关于日常生活的话题有：就餐、问候、邀请、约会、购物、通知、问路、打电话、旅游、住宿、谈论天气、询问时间、寻求/提供帮助、安排、病痛、看法、自然灾害、新闻报道等。

三、听力录音特点

1. 语速特点

听力部分的朗读速度约为每分钟42 ~ 45个单词，低于或相当于高中英语教学大纲中规定的语速。

2. 语音特点

在高考英语的考试说明中，并没有对听力部分的语音做出任何规定。这两年高考英语听力试题一般都是英音。但是语言学习一定要体现出其真实性、交际性和实用性。所以，以后的听力部分肯定也会出现美音、澳大利亚式英语发音，甚至还会有背景音。

四、考查的知识点

1. 时间数字题

此类试题，主要考查考生根据读音辨认时间、数字的能力以及了解多个数据之间的关系并进行计算的能力。对话中出现的数字有可能是价格、日期、时间、数量、年龄、门牌号等。

（1）设问方式

What time is it now?/When will the train leave?/What's the price of...?/How long...?/How much does...cost? / How many...? 等。

（2）解题技巧

关键是听清并记录对话中的数字与相关运算信息。具体步骤是在听到数字后立即将其记下或在选项中找到，并在旁边记录相关信息；熟知各个数字之间的关系，然后根据提问快速运用相应的加减乘除运算得出正确答案。具体说来，如出现电话号码、门牌号、航班号、车牌号等，考生可在听的过程中记录所需数字；对于判断类数字题，需要在听到的两个或两个以上数字中判断符合题意的数字；对于推断类数字题，则通常涉及简单的数学四则运算，需稍加计算，才能得出正确答案。

2. 对话场景题

此类试题主要考查有关地点的信息，要求考生判断对话发生的地点。有些地点是对话中直接提到的，有些是需要根据对话的内容来判断的，还有的是两者兼而有之。常见的对话场景：学校(教室)、医院(诊所)、机场、车站、餐馆、商店、图书馆、书店、邮局、警察局等。

（1）设问方式

Where does the conversation most probably take place?/Where are the two speakers?/Where does the man(woman) work?/Where is the man going?等。

（2）解题技巧

熟悉、积累常用地名，如国家、首都、大城市、著名的标志性建筑以及山川河流的名称等；熟悉、积累与各个地点场所有关的单词、短语、句型和场景。

3. 人物关系及身份题

此类题的选项一般为表示职业或身份的名词或由两个名词构成的表示人物关系的并列词组。对话中不会直接提到某人的职业或对话者的关系，通常只用一些相关词作为暗示。主要考查考生能否根据对话内容、说话者的语气及态度等判断对话者之间的关系或说话人的职业、身份。

常考查的人物关系：师生、朋友、夫妻、父女、母子、同事、同学、邻居、老板与职员、医生与病人、司机与乘客等。

（1）设问方式

Who are the speakers?/ What's the probable relationship between the two speakers? What is the man's (woman's) job(occupation, profession)?/ What is the person's probable job? / Who is the woman(man) speaking to? / What's the profession of the man?/ Who is the woman most probably speaking to? / Who is the speaker? / What is his(her) job?/ What does he(she) do?

常考查的人物职业：医生、工人、教师、司机、秘书、服务员、售货员、图书管理员、警察、工作人员、作家、经理、学生等。

（2）解题技巧

抓住职业相关词，也就等于抓住了关键词；通过不同人物身份及人物关系所对应的单词、短语、句型和场景，结合生活常识进行判断；通过关键词并结合对话的语气判断对话者的身份和关系；通过不同语音语调所表达的不同意思，以及特定单词、短语和句型所表达的隐含信息，进行准确判断。

4. 观点态度题

此类题要求考生根据对话者说话的语音、语调、语气以及谈话内容，判断出说话者对某人、某事物的看法或态度。

（1）设问方式

What does the man(woman) say about/think of...? / How does the man(woman) feel about/like...?/What's the man's(woman's) opinion about... / What is the man's(woman's) attitude towards the conversation?/How does the man(woman) feel?/The man's(woman's) feeling toward the subject can be best described as...等。

（2）解题技巧

语调有升调、降调两种：降调（尤其是在一般疑问句和反义疑问句中）通常表示说话人的态度是肯定、赞同的，而升调(特别是在陈述句和特殊疑问句中)表示对事物的怀疑、惊讶或否定。注意提示词和关键词，表示否定、转折和虚拟等含义的指示词。在听的过程中，要从字里行间把握关键词，其透露出说话者的观点态度。

五、解题策略与技巧

（一）听力三步法

（1）听前：略读题目，切入话题，划出重点，预测内容(确定人物身份)。

（2）听中：捕捉信息速记要点(短文独白，首末为主旨句，注意5个W、1个H)。

（3）听后：连贯记忆，前后联系，综合考虑，一锤定音。

（二）保持良好状态，变预览为预测

调节情绪，保持良好的心理状态。进入考场前，听一些舒缓的音乐或往年高考听力真题，灌耳音，调节考前情绪。

拿到试题后，先预览后预测，变被动为主动。拿到试卷，在填涂完姓名及准考证号后的剩余时间预览；在播放试音小乐曲及试音材料时预览；在介绍第一节试题的做法时预览；在每段对话或独白播放前的5秒钟时间预览。

（三）驾驭预测策略与技巧

1. 标题预测策略

根据文章或所给材料的标题进行预测。标题是语篇的导向，统领着语篇的中心思想，从中可预测到语篇的体裁和大体内容，甚至还可以预测出语篇的用词范围。在听音之前，教师可引导学生有意识地注意文章的标题，启发学生对即将听到的内容进行积极预测。

Sample：Healthy Eating Habits

遇到这样的标题时，教师可预先就标题引导学生根据各自所掌握的有关“Healthy Eating Habits”的内容进行预测。教师可以提问：“By skimming the title, what can you predict?”该标题可能预测的内容如下：healthy eating habits，vegetables and fruits，less meat，drink milk，a balanced diet，nutrition，junk food，breakfast等，预测出这一话题即将涉及的关键词（key words）和内容。

2. 答题预测策略

根据文章或试题设置的问题进行预测。问题的设置都与文章或材料的内容有关，通过所给的问题仔细推理，就可以预测出即将谈论的内容。一般来说提出的问题有：

Who are the two speakers?

What does the man think of the book?

When did they have the conversation?

Why did he/she...?

社会语言学研究揭示，人们在进行语言交际时都会遵循“合作原则”，即在一般情况下，人们不会说不符合逻辑、不符合常规的话语，也不会从一个话题突然跳到另一个完全不相干的话题，而且语篇发展形势通常都是从已知信息到新信息这一模式展开的。因此，在听力活动之前，我们可以利用题项及相关背景知识对即将听到材料的主题和内容做出合乎逻辑的预测，以帮助对语篇的理解。

Sample 1：

Why did the woman choose the restaurant?

A. She wants to eat fish.

B. It got good reviews online.

C. She knows the waiter from the Internet.

原文：

M: Have you decided what you will order?

W: I've never eaten sushi.What do you recommend? What is the best item on your menu? I only know that your restaurant is highly rated on the Internet.

M: Everything is good here. We have 12 different...

浏览答题选项后，我们便可以利用所掌握的有关知识进行分析预测（By scanning the question, what can you predict）。Sample 1谈及的是吃饭预定餐馆问题。由于事先对材料的主题以及答案进行了积极预测，这样听的过程实际上就是对事先预测的验证过程，答题准确性也就大大提高了。

Sample 2：

(1) What is the most probable relationship between the two speakers?

A. Father and daughter.

B. Teacher and student.

C. Doctor and patient.

(2) What are the speakers now talking about?

A. The woman's bad cough.

B. The woman's bad cold.

C. The woman's stomach trouble.

原文：

M: Hi, pretty girl, how are you feeling today?

W: Not so good.

M: I understand, you've got stomachache?

W: Yeah, it's pretty bad...

M: When did it start?

W: During the night.

M: How long have you had the trouble?

W: About three days, at first, it was not so serious as it is now.

M: Does your stomachache come before or after meals?

W: It hurts after meals.

M: Well, take the medicine, you'll feel better soon.

以上例子说明学生可以根据试题中已给的选项在听前进行预测。题中所给的三个选项往往就包含了已知信息，只要细心推断，不难从选项中预测出即将给出的信息。

3. 主题句预测法

根据文章的主题句进行预测。主题句所起的作用与标题类似，往往代表该段的议题和中心思想，它大都出现在文章的开头或结尾。因此，学生应集中注意力听懂主题句，并通过主题句对文章内容进行预测。

Sample：

What are the two speakers mainly talking about?

A. Eco-tour.

B. Popular sports.

C. Famous countries.

原文：

M: Welcome to our program “eco-tour”. Today we are honored to invite Hannah to be our special guest. Welcome Hannah.

W: Thanks. Today I’m going to suggest some eco-tours to you...

学生应该很自然地预测到此文谈论的是生态旅游的话题。因而，在听的过程中，应特别注意文中出现的时间、地点、人物以及事件等。若是由几个段落组成的较长篇幅的文章，还可以把每段的主题句连接起来，得到整个语篇的梗概，以帮助理解整个语篇。

4. 文化背景知识预测法

以往的知识水平、背景知识对听力材料的预测也起到关键作用。历史、地理、信息、政治、军事、文艺、文化等常识对预测的帮助很大。

Sample 1：

What does the man think of Picasso?

A. He thinks that he is the greatest Spanish painter.

B. He doesn’t consider him the best Spanish painter.

C. He is sure that he can become famous.

原文：

M: How do you like these paintings in the museum?

W: Not too bad.

M: In my opinion, Picasso is the greatest Spanish painter. Do you think so?

W: Well, I’m not sure.

对毕加索的相关背景知识的了解，就有助于通过选项，做出合理的预测。

5. 关键词预测法

利用文中的关键词进行预测。学生在听力理解过程中应学会捕捉关键词，通过关键词激活有关图式，预测所听内容。就语言而言，最基本的图式是语义图式，每个图式都可以被某个单词或某些提示所激活，被激活的某个图式又可诱导几个相关联的图式。例如，我们的记忆图式中都有关于“医院”的知识，当听到“hospital”一词时，就会很自然地去预料将要听到的主要话题及相关意义，联想到与医院有关的词汇，如medicine、nurse、doctor、patient、operation、injection等。学生可以根据这种联想积极地预测和筛选所听材料。

Sample 1：

What does the girl think about Mr. Yang's idea?

A. It's interesting.

B. It's worth trying.

C. It's impractical.

原文：

M: Air pollution is so bad in this city. I think the government should stop people from driving cars on certain days.

W: I see your point, Mr. Yang, but I still think it wouldn't be possible to stop people from driving...

从中听到的pollution，wouldn't be possible等关键词就能预测出文章接下来要谈论的话题。

6. 功能词预测法

根据语篇中的功能词进行预测。人们在谈话中，有相当一部分词语是用来传递说话人的心理态度，表示转折、过渡、开始、结束等，如I'd like to...; but; in a word; to sum up; that is to say; as a matter of fact; to begin with; because; so; since; however; seeing that; considering that; now that; so that; in order that; thus; therefore; as a result; result in; result from; occur from; that is to say; for example; in a word等，这些功能词在很大程度上为考生预测内容提供了方向。

Sample 1：

What did Paul do this morning?

A. He had a history lesson.

B. He had a chemistry lesson.

C. He attended a meeting.

原文：

W: What about your chemistry class this morning, Paul?

M: We were supposed to have a chemistry class, but Mr. Anderson was out of town for a meeting. So we had a history lesson instead.

（四）抓大放小，紧盯关键词句

1. 透露说话人身份的关键词

通过关键词很快判断对话者的关系和身份，有助于有目的地集中注意力，并在脑海中搜索相关背景知识，进一步加深对听力材料的理解。只要捕捉到关键的词句就能找出问题的答案，不要盲目地逐词逐句地听。

例如：I just can't believe you are a police officer，Kay. I remember in high school, you always wanted to be a lawyer.如果考生意识到该对话中的关键词为in high school，那么考生马上会意识到这是两个老同学之间的对话。

再比如：Good morning, ladies and gentlemen. Welcome to Universal Studio. I'd like to guide you all the way in the amazing park and share the wonderful moments with you.这段话的关键词是guide、park，从中考生可以推断说话人是导游。

常见的对话者关系：husband & wife；teacher & student；boss & employee；waiter & customer；doctor & patient；parents & kid；classmates; roommates；shop assistant & customer。

2. 透露地点/场合的关键词

善于捕捉听力材料中关于地点或场合（即语言环境）的关键词，也有助于判断听力材料的主题、说话人之间关系等。如果对话中出现special price，那么对话很可能发生在商店；treatment，therapy等词可以透露出医患关系；以下是有关机场和旅馆的关键词：check in入住登记，check out结账，porter搬运工，luggage行李，book a room预订房间，double room双人房，passenger乘客，economy class经济舱，business class公务舱，runway跑道，passport护照，flight航班，stewardess乘务员。

3. 捕捉数字

许多听力材料中涉及数字，例如年代、日期、价格、数量等，并且会以基数词、序数词、分数、小数、百分比等形式出现，这就要求考生既要辨别各种形式的数字，还要熟悉数字之间的关系。例如：

减价：20% off，special offer，special price，25% discount，sale

原价：regular price，normal price

增长：10% increase in... 1/3 climb in...

下降：23% fall in... 5.5% decrease in...

4. 熟悉听力常见词汇，形成思维定势，对症下药

高考英语听力的设疑方式是相对稳定的。比如说，常在故事情境发生的主要要素上设疑。一般来说，特定场景的用语和关键词是基本固定的，考生在平时的训练中应多加留意。

许多考生可能有这样的经历：听的过程中整个句子中仅仅因为一个单词未理解，使得考生对整个句子甚至语篇的理解产生误解，所以高三考生需要掌握尽可能多的词汇，以备不时之需。

做好听力题是一个不断实践的学习过程。听力对语言综合运用能力提出很高的要求，高三考生须本着循序渐进、持之以恒的训练方针，在语法、词汇、听力技巧、心理素质等各个方面进行操练。平时还要注意积累相关基础词汇，比如：时间表达方式；学科的名称；表示数目的单词；年代表达方式；十二个月份、日期、星期；四个季节；金钱的表达方式；常见地名的拼写；国家和国籍等。

5. 多感官协调，把握速记要领，运用速记符号，增加得分空间

高考听力的第二部分Longer Conversation所占时间相对较长，如果考生能够培养一定的速记技巧，有助于获得听力内容，帮助记忆。毕竟高考的长篇对话时间并不算太长，高三考生只要进行初级的入门速记锻炼，不必把听到的所有内容写下来，只要捕捉一些关键性问题即可，比如时间、地点、数字以及相关信息等。考生可以尝试以下技巧：

例如：↑up，↓down，←left，→right，=equal。

发明并运用字母的缩写形式。考生可以在平时训练时，本着便于记忆、快速、容易联想的原则，发明一些只需自己明白的字母搭配来表示相应的信息。

例如：ex—expensive；lg—large；eq—earthquake；ys—yesterday等，通过运用这些字母和符号，帮助考生储存信息，帮助回忆。

6. 学会放弃，避难就易，不放过任何可得分

高考英语属于能力选拔型考试，考生不一定能顺利完成所有的题目。再加之英语听力的语速、语音、语调的特点，在交际中出现的连读、爆破、辅音浊化等一系列语言现象以及材料中可能涉及的语法，如部分否定、虚拟语气，表示转折、让步等的特殊句型和情态动词的特殊用法等，使得一部分考生应接不暇，难以听懂，这是很正常的。遇到这种情况，考生要学会放弃，避难就易，不放过任何可得分。

真题回顾·典例·2018新课标全国卷II & III

第一节（共5小题；每小题1.5分，满分7.5分）

听下面5段对话。每段对话后有一个小题，从题中所给的A、B、C三个选项中选出最佳选项。听完每段对话后，你都有10秒钟的时间来回答有关小题和阅读下一小题。每段对话仅读一遍。

例：How much is the shirt?

A. 19.15.　　B. 9.18.　　C. 9.15.

答案是C。

1. What does John find difficult in learning German?

A. Pronunciation.　　B. Vocabulary.　　C. Grammar.

2. What is the probable relationship between the speakers?

A. Colleagues.　　B. Brother and sister.　　C. Teacher and student.

3. Where does the conversation probably take place?

A. In a bank. B. At a ticket office. C. On a train.

4. What are the speakers talking about?

A. A restaurant. B. A street. C. A dish.

5. What does the woman think of her interview?

A. It was tough. B. It was interesting. C. It was successful.

第二节（共15小题；每小题1.5分，满分22.5分）

听下面5段对话或独白。每段对话或独白后有几个小题，从题中所给的A、B、C三个选项中选出最佳选项。听每段对话或独白前，你将有时间阅读各个小题，每小题5秒钟；听完后，各小题将给出5秒钟的作答时间。每段对话或独白读两遍。

听第6段材料，回答第6、7题。

6. When will Judy go to a party?

A. On Monday. B. On Tuesday. C. On Wednesday.

7. What will Max do next?

A. Fly a kite. B. Read a magazine. C. Do his homework.

听第7段材料，回答第8、9题。

8. What does the man suggest doing at first?

A. Going to a concert.

B. Watching a movie.

C. Playing a computer game.

9. What do the speakers decide to do?

A. Visit Mike. B. Go boating. C. Take a walk.

听第8段材料，回答第10至12题。

10. Which color do cats see better than humans?

A. Red. B. Green. C. Blue.

11. Why do cats bring dead birds home?

A. To eat them in a safe place.

B. To show off their hunting skills.

C. To make their owners happy.

12. How does the man sound at the end of the conversation?

A. Grateful. B. Humorous. C. Curious.

听第9段材料，回答第13至16题。

13. Who is Macy?

A. Ed's mother. B. Ed's teacher. C. Ed's friend.

14. How does Ed usually go to kindergarten?

A. By car.　　B. On foot.　　C. By bus.

15.What does Ed enjoy doing at the kindergarten?

A. Telling stories.　　B. Singing songs.　　C. Playing with others.

16. What do the teachers say about Ed?

A. He's clever.　　B. He's quiet.　　C. He's brave.

听第10段材料，回答第17至20题。

17. At what age did Emily start learning ballet?

A. Five.　　B. Six.　　C. Nine.

18. Why did Emily move to Toronto?

A. To work for a dance school.

B. To perform at a dance theater.

C. To learn contemporary dance.

19. Why did Emily quit dancing?

A. She was too old to dance.

B. She failed to get a scholarship.

C. She lost interest in it.

20. How does Emily feel about stopping training?

A. She's pleased.　　B. She's regretful.　　C. She's upset.

参考答案

1. C　2. A　3. B　4. A　5. C　6. B　7. B　8. A　9. C　10. C　11. A　12. B

13. A　14. B　15. C　16. A　17. B　18. C　19. C　20. A

听力试题详细分析：

听力部分要求考生听懂有关日常生活中所熟悉的话题，如德语学习、是否参加聚会、买火车票、饭店、工作面试、放风筝计划、周日下午计划、猫的习性、孩子在幼儿园的表现、学习舞蹈的经历。与往常相同，听力部分中有 10段听力材料，其中的 5 段较短，另 5 段则较长。话题覆盖面广，对话内容逻辑清楚，话语流畅。所考查的听力微技能包括：理解主旨和要义，获取事实性的具体信息，对所听内容做出简单推断，理解谈话人的意图、观点和态度。问题涉及多个方面，多个角度，采用 where-、when-、why-、how-、what- 等多种特殊疑问句。

录音人：男：Kris Chung; 女：Laura Estelles

口　音：美音（没变）

词　数：773（比2017年少111词）

时　间：5分22秒

语　速：144词/分（比2017年每分钟慢22词）

难　度：难度整体与2017年持平

考　点：2018年全国II&III卷高考英语听力的 20 个小题中，考查理解主旨与要义的有1道题，获取事实性的具体信息的有12道题，对所听内容做出推断的有4道题，理解说话者的意图、观点和态度的有3道题，较好地体现了考试大纲和考试说明对考生的要求。

第一节

Text 1:

W: So, how is your German class going, John?

M: Well, not bad. The pronunciation is fine with me, and its vocabulary is similar to English. But I'm finding the grammar awful.

W: Well, it takes a while to get it right.

（词数：39；时间：17″；语速：138词/分）

1. What does John find difficult in learning German?

A. Pronunciation.　　B. Vocabulary.　　C. Grammar.

【分析】考查考生获取事实性具体信息的能力。

由男士所说的I'm finding the grammar awful可知，他觉得学习德语的语法有困难。

【答案】C

【语音】

连读：Well, it takes a while to get it right.

Text 2:

W: I hope you can come to the party on Saturday.

M: I didn't know I was invited.

W: Sure you are. Everyone in our office is invited.

（词数：25；时间：10″；语速：150词/分）

2. What is the probable relationship between the speakers?

A. Colleagues. B. Brother and sister. C. Teacher and student.

【分析】考查考生对所听内容做出简单推断的能力。

男士说他不知道自己被邀请参加宴会了，女士回答说Sure you are. Everyone in our office is invited.由此可知说话双方应该是在同一个办公室工作，是同事关系。

【答案】A

【语音】

（1）重读

I hope you can come to the party on Saturday.

（2）连读

Everyone in our office is invited.

Text 3：

W: May I help you?

M: Yes. When is the next train to London?

W: Oh, let me check. It leaves in twenty minutes.

M: One ticket, please.

（词数：24；时间：11″；语速：131词/分）

3. Where does the conversation probably take place?

A. In a bank. B. At a ticket office. C. On a train.

【分析】考查考生对所听内容做出简单推断的能力。

男士问去伦敦的下一班火车是几点，女士查看之后告知他是在二十分钟后，男士紧接着对女士说"请给我一张票"，由此可知男士在售票处买票。

【点拨】对话中能提示是在售票处的关键信息有When is the next train，let me check和One ticket, please.这些都是买车票时的常用语。

【答案】B

Text 4：

W: Charlie, do you know a restaurant called Bravo?

M: Bravo ... I know the name.But I'm not sure where it is.

W: It's on George Street.The food there is excellent.

（词数：30；时间：13″；语速：138词/分）

4. What are the speakers talking about?

A. A restaurant.　　B. A street.　　C. A dish.

【分析】考查考生理解主旨与要义的能力。

女士所说的do you know a restaurant called Bravo点明对话主题，接下来的对话谈论该餐馆在什么地方、饭菜如何，都是围绕该餐馆展开的。

【答案】A

Text 5：

W: Brian, I just had an interview.They said they would make a decision soon.

M: What are your chances of getting the job?

W: Quite good.I think the interview went very well.

（词数：31；时间：13″；语速：143词/分）

5. What does the woman think of her interview?

A. It was tough.　　B. It was interesting.　　C. It was successful.

【分析】考查考生对说话者观点的理解能力。

男士问女士得到这份工作的可能性有多大，女士回答说挺好的，她觉得面试进行得很顺利，由此可知，她认为面试很成功。

【答案】C

【语言知识】

chance *n*. 可能性

【语音】

冠词the的发音。I think the interview went very well.

第二节　听第6段材料，回答第6、7题。

Text 6：

M: Let's go kite flying, Judy.It's such a lovely day.

W: Okay, but let me finish my chemistry homework first.Would you mind waiting for half an hour, Max? There are a few sports magazines on the table.

M: Isn't the chemistry homework due next Wednesday?

W: Yeah, but I have a full day of classes on Monday and a birthday party to attend on Tuesday.

M: All right, then.You go ahead, and I'll catch up on some sports news while waiting.

（词数：79；时间：33″；语速：144词/分）

材料内容涉及日常活动，主要谈论写完作业后去放风筝。

6. When will Judy go to a party?

A. On Monday. B. On Tuesday. C. On Wednesday.

【分析】考查考生获取事实性具体信息的能力。

由女士的话but I have a full day of classes on Monday and a birthday party to attend on Tuesday可知女士周二要去参加一个生日聚会。

【答案】B

7. What will Max do next?

A. Fly a kite. B. Read a magazine. C. Do his homework.

【分析】考查考生获取事实性具体信息的能力。

由女士的话There are a few sports magazines on the table和最后男士的话I'll catch up on some sports news while waiting可知男士接下来要看体育杂志。

【答案】B

【语言知识】

catch up on (sth.) 了解（某事）

You go ahead, and I'll catch up on some sports news while waiting.

【语音】

（1）同化

Would you mind waiting for half an hour, Max?

（2）连读

Yeah, but I have a full day of classes on Monday and a birthday party to (w)attend on Tuesday.

You go (w)ahead, and I'll catch up on some sports news while waiting.

听第7段材料，回答第8、9题。

Text 7:

W: We've been on the computer all the time lately.Why don't we do something different Sunday afternoon?

M: Well, we could go to a concert.

W: But I don't think we can get the tickets this late.

M: Then what about playing a computer game? There's a really cool new one we could download.

W: Hmm, I don't know.I feel like I need to do some exercise.We could probably just walk by the lake, and I'll ask Mike to join us.

M: That sounds like fun. Let's do it!

（词数：86；时间：35″ ；语速：147词/分）

材料内容涉及节假日活动，主要是商量周日下午做什么。

8. What does the man suggest doing at first?

A. Going to a concert.

B. Watching a movie.

C. Playing a computer game.

【分析】考查考生获取事实性具体信息的能力。

由男士的话we could go to a concert可知男士一开始建议去听音乐会。

【答案】A

9. What do the speakers decide to do?

A. Visit Mike.　　B. Go boating.　　C. Take a walk.

【分析】考查考生获取事实性具体信息的能力。

女士建议去湖边散步，叫上迈克一起去，男士说That sounds like fun. Let's do it! 可知他们决定去湖边走一走。

【答案】C

【语言知识】

this *adv.* 这么；这样

But I don't think we can get the tickets this late.

【语音】

（1）失去爆破

But I don'(t) think we can ge(t) the tickets this late.

（2）弱读

I feel like I need to do some exercise.

听第8段材料，回答第10至12题。

Text 8：

W: Welcome to our program, Dr.Peterson.Let's see what questions we've got for you today.Here's one: Can cats see color?

M: Sort of.In the wild, many cats hunt at night because their eyes are designed for low light.Your cat can't see bright colors such as red and green.But it picks up more shades of blue, yellow, and grey than humans do.

W: And why do cats give dead birds to their owners?

M: When your cat drops a dead bird at your feet, she isn't bringing you a present. Most cats just drag food home because it's a safe place to eat.A cat's mom also brings home things to her children to help them practice hunting.So, a female cat without children may bring these "treats" to her owner instead.You may not like them, but at least you don't have to write her a thank-you note.

（词数：149；时间：1′；语速：149词/分）

材料为一段访谈节目，主要是谈论猫的特点和习性。

10. Which color do cats see better than humans?

A. Red.　　B. Green.　　C. Blue.

【分析】考查考生获取事实性具体信息的能力。

由男士所说的Your cat can't see bright colors such as red and green.But it picks up more shades of blue, yellow, and grey than humans do.可知，猫识别蓝色、黄色、灰色的能力比人强。

【点拨】题干中的see better than humans与材料中的pick up more shades of ... than humans do呼应。

【答案】C

11.Why do cats bring dead birds home?

A. To eat them in a safe place.

B. To show off their hunting skills.

C. To make their owners happy.

【分析】考查考生获取事实性具体信息的能力。

女士问男士为什么猫把死鸟带回给主人，男士回答，它并不是要给主人带回来礼物，大多数猫把死鸟拖回家，只是因为家里是吃食物的安全地点。由此可知，本题选择A。

【答案】A

12. How does the man sound at the end of the conversation?

A. Grateful.　　　　B. Humorous.　　　　C. Curious.

【分析】考查考生理解说话者态度的能力。

最后男士说虽然没有小猫的母猫会把这些"美味的食物"送给主人，主人可能不喜欢，但至少不用给猫写感谢信。给猫写感谢信，这是一种幽默的表达。

【答案】B

【语言知识】

（1）pick up 辨认；识别出

（2）shade *n.* 浓淡；深浅；色度

（3）treat *n.*（尤指不常吃的）美味食物

【语音】

（1）意群与停顿

In the wild, many cats hunt at night | because their eyes are designed for low light.

（2）失去爆破

Your ca(t) can'(t) see brigh(t) colors such as red an(d) green.

You may no(t) li(ke) them, but a(t) least you don'(t) have to wri(te) her a thank-you note.

（3）同化＋失去爆破

When your ca(t) drops a dea(d) bird at your feet, she isn'(t) bringing you a present.

听第9段材料，回答第13至16题。

Text 9:

W: How is little Ed doing at the kindergarten, Jack?

M: Oh, he's doing fairly well. It's been three weeks since he first started going, so Macy and I are pretty used to it now. You should have seen Macy cry when Ed was about to set off on the first day, though.

W: I think that's a normal reaction for mothers.You live quite close to the kindergarten, don't you? How does he get there?

M: Macy walks there with him every morning unless the weather is bad.When it rains, they'll drive.

W: And is Ed enjoying kindergarten?

M: Yeah, he loves to have other kids to play with.He keeps telling us things they do together.

W: What do the teachers at the kindergarten say about him?

M: They said he's bright, and that he's starting to learn how to tell time. Isn't that fantastic?

W: That is fantastic.It sounds like everything goes well.

（词数：149；时间：57″；语速：155词/分）

材料内容主要是谈论孩子上幼儿园的情况。

13. Who is Macy?

A. Ed's mother.　　B. Ed's teacher.　　C. Ed's friend.

【分析】考查考生对所听内容做出简单推断的能力。

由男士所说You should have seen Macy cry when Ed was about to set off on the first day, though.及女士所说 I think that's a normal reaction for mothers.可知Macy在Ed上学的第一天哭了，而女士说这是作为妈妈的正常反应，由此可知Macy是Ed的妈妈。

【答案】A

14. How does Ed usually go to kindergarten?

A. By car.　　B. On foot.　　C. By bus.

【分析】考查考生获取事实性具体信息的能力。

根据男士所说Macy walks there with him every morning unless the weather is bad.可知Ed通常是步行去幼儿园。

【答案】B

15. What does Ed enjoy doing at the kindergarten?

A. Telling stories.　　B. Singing songs.　　C. Playing with others.

【分析】考查考生获取事实性具体信息的能力。

由男士的话he loves to have other kids to play with.可知Ed喜欢和其他孩子一起玩。

【答案】C

16. What do the teachers say about Ed?

A. He's clever.　　B. He's quiet.　　C. He's brave.

【分析】考查考生获取事实性具体信息的能力。

由男士的话They said he's bright, and that he's starting to learn how to tell time. 说明老师认为Ed很聪明。clever是bright的同义转述。

【答案】A

【语言知识】

（1）be used to sth. 习惯某事情

（2）set off 出发；动身；启程

【语音】

（1）失去爆破

How is little E(d) doing a(t) the kindergarten, Jack?

（2）意群与停顿

Macy walks there with him every morning | unless the weather is bad.

听第10段材料，回答第17至20题。

Text 10：

W: My name is Emily.I had been a dancer for quite a long time.I started studying ballet when I was six years old.By the time I was nine, I was dancing five days a week. When I was eighteen, I decided that I really preferred contemporary dance and that I wanted to do it professionally.So I applied successfully for the training program at the School of Toronto Dance Theater, and moved to Toronto to attend the program. That was the period of time I enjoyed most in Toronto.I graduated on scholarship and danced professionally for ten years.But after all those years, I found that dance was gradually becoming something that felt like more of a burden than a joy.I found myself increasingly unwilling to drag myself to dance performances, so I quit.I do miss dance often.But it makes me happy to think that I'll never have to go to another training session again.

（词数：161；时间：1′13″；语速：132词/分）

材料内容与说话者的个人经历有关。说话者通过讲述自己的舞蹈生涯告诉我们：放弃有时也是一种不错的选择。

17. At what age did Emily start learning ballet?

A. Five.　　B. Six.　　C. Nine.

【分析】考查考生获取事实性具体信息的能力。

由I started studying ballet when I was six years old.可知，埃米莉6岁时开始学芭蕾舞。

【答案】B

18. Why did Emily move to Toronto?

A. To work for a dance school.

B. To perform at a dance theater.

C. To learn contemporary dance.

【分析】考查考生获取事实性具体信息的能力。

由I decided that I really preferred contemporary dance ... 及So I applied successfully for the training program at the School of Toronto Dance Theater, and moved to Toronto to attend the program.可知，埃米莉18岁的时候确定自己更喜欢现代舞蹈，而且想成为专业的现代舞蹈演员，就这样她成功地申请到了多伦多舞蹈剧院的培训项目，因此她搬到了多伦多。

【答案】C

19. Why did Emily quit dancing?

A. She was too old to dance.

B. She failed to get a scholarship.

C. She lost interest in it.

【分析】考查考生对所听内容做出简单推断的能力。

由 I found that dance was gradually becoming something that felt like more of a burden than a joy.I found myself increasingly unwilling to drag myself to dance performances, so I quit.可知，埃米莉渐渐发现舞蹈对她来说更像是一种负担而不是乐趣，自己越来越不愿意勉强自己去参加舞蹈表演了，所以她放弃了。

【点拨】C项中的lose interest in（对……失去兴趣）与材料中的drag呼应。

【答案】C

20. How does Emily feel about stopping training?

A. She's pleased. B. She's regretful. C. She's upset.

【分析】考查考生理解说话者态度的能力。

由I do miss dance often.But it makes me happy to think that I'll never have to go to another training session again.可知埃米莉确实很怀念以前的跳舞时光，但是想到自己再也不用去参加训练了，还是很高兴。

【点拨】But it makes me happy to think that I'll never have to go to another training session again.是说话者真正的感受。

【答案】A

【语言知识】

（1）contemporary *adj.* 当代的; 现代的

（2）professionally *adv.* 专业地

（3）apply for 申请

（4）increasingly *adv.* 越来越多地; 不断增加地

（5）drag *vt.* 拖; 拽

（6）session *n.* 一段时间

【语音】

（1）意群与停顿

I started studying ballet | when I was six years old.

When I was eighteen, | I decided that I really preferred contemporary dance | and that I wanted to do it professionally.

（2）重读

I found myself increasingly unwilling to drag myself to dance performances, so I quit.

2017、2018新课标全国卷Ⅱ & Ⅲ 听力试题简析：

考点统计表

年 份	理解主旨和要义	获取事实性的具体信息	对所听内容做出简单推断	理解说话者的意图、观点和态度
2018	1	12	4	3
2017	1	9	9	1

录音数据统计表

年 份	词数			累计时间（一遍）	平均语速（词/分）
	第一节	第二节	合计		
2018	149	624	773	5′ 22″	144
2017	183	701	884	5′ 20″	166

话题统计表

年份	第一节					第二节				
	Text 1	Text 2	Text 3	Text 4	Text 5	Text 6	Text 7	Text 8	Text 9	Text 10
2018	德语学习	是否参加聚会	买火车票	饭店	工作面试	放风筝计划	周日下午计划	猫的习性	孩子在幼儿园的表现	学习舞蹈的经历
2017	活动计划	更改会面时间	存钱买车	请假	天气	购物	工作变动	为课程准备书	旅游计划	实验室须知

答案分布表

年 份	答案邻近分布	答案总数分布		
		A	B	C
2018	CABAC BBACC ABABC ABCCA	7	6	7

续 表

年 份	答案邻近分布	答案总数分布		
		A	B	C
2017	BCACB ACCBA ABCAB BACAB	7	7	6

六、2019年高考备考之听力训练篇

真题回顾 · Practice 1 · 2018新课标全国卷Ⅰ

第一部分　听力(共两节，满分30分)

做题时，先将答案标在试卷上。录音内容结束后，你将有2分钟的时间将试卷上的答案转涂到答题卡上。

第一节（共5小题；每小题1.5分，满分7.5分）

听下面5段对话。每段对话后有一个小题，从题中所给的A、B、C三个选项中选出最佳选项。听完每段对话后，你都有10秒钟的时间来回答有关小题和阅读下一小题。每段对话仅读一遍。

例：How much is the shirt?

A. 19.15.　　B. 9.18.　　C. 9.15.

答案是 C。

1. What will James do tomorrow?

A. Watch a TV program.　　B. Give a talk.　　C. Write a report.

2. What can we say about the woman?

A. She's generous.　　B. She's curious.　　C. She's helpful.

3.When does the train leave?

A. At 6: 30.　　B. At 8: 30.　　C. At 10: 30.

4. How does the woman go to work?

A. By car.　　B. On foot.　　C. By bike.

5. What is the probable relationship between the speakers?

A. Classmates.　　B. Teacher and student.　　C. Doctor and patient.

第二节（共15小题；每小题1.5分，满分22.5分）

听下面5段对话或独白。每段对话或独白后有几个小题，从题中所给的A、B、C三个选项中选出最佳选项。听每段对话或独白前，你将有时间阅读各个小题，每

小题5秒钟；听完后，各小题将给出5秒钟的作答时间。每段对话或独白读两遍。

听第6段材料，回答第6、7题。

6. What does the woman regret?

A. Giving up her research.

B. Dropping out of college.

C. Changing her major.

7. What is the woman interested in studying now?

A. Ecology. B. Education. C. Chemistry.

听第7段材料，回答第8、9题。

8. What is the man?

A. A hotel manager. B. A tour guide. C. A taxi driver.

9. What is the man doing for the woman?

A. Looking for some local foods.

B. Showing her around the seaside.

C. Offering information about a hotel.

听第8段材料，回答第10至12题。

10. Where does the conversation probably take place?

A. In an office. B. At home C. At a restaurant.

11. What will the speakers do tomorrow evening?

A. Go to a concert. B. Visit a friend. C. Work extra hours.

12. Who is Alice going to call?

A. Mike. B. Joan. C. Catherine.

听第9段材料，回答第13至16题。

13. Why does the woman meet the man?

A. To look at an apartment.

B. To deliver some furniture.

C. To have a meal together.

14. What does the woman like about the carpet?

A. Its color. B. Its design. C. Its quality.

15. What does the man say about the kitchen?

A. It's a good size.

B. It's newly painted.

C. It's adequately equipped.

16. What will the woman probably do next?

A. Go downtown. B. Talk with her friend. C. Make payment.

听第10段材料，回答第17至20题。

17. Who is the speaker probably talking to?

A. Movie fans. B. News reporters. C. College students.

18. When did the speaker take English classes?

A. Before he left his hometown.

B. After he came to America.

C. When he was 15 years old.

19. How does the speaker feel about his teacher?

A. He's proud. B. He's sympathetic. C. He's grateful.

20. What does the speaker mainly talk about ?

A. How education shaped his life.

B. How his language skills improved.

C. How he managed his business well.

真题回顾·Practice 2·2017新课标全国卷I

第一部分 听力(共两节，满分30分)

第一节（共5小题；每小题1.5分，满分7.5分）

听下面5段对话。每段对话后有一个小题，从题中所给的A、B、C三个选项中选出最佳选项。听完每段对话后，你都有10秒钟的时间来回答有关小题和阅读下一小题。每段对话仅读一遍。

1. What does the woman think of the movie?

A. It's amusing. B. It's exciting. C. It's disappointing.

2. How will Susan spend most of her time in France?

A. Traveling around. B. Studying at a school. C. Looking after her aunt.

3. What are the speakers talking about?

A. Going out. B. Ordering drinks. C. Preparing for a party.

4. Where are the speakers?

A. In a classroom. B. In a library. C. In a bookstore.

5. What is the man going to do?

A. Go on the Internet. B. Make a phone call. C. Take a train trip.

第二节（共15小题；每小题1.5分，满分22.5分）

听下面5段对话或独白。每段对话或独白后有几个小题，从题中所给的A、B、C三个选项中选出最佳选项。听每段对话或独白前，你将有时间阅读各个小题，每小题5秒钟；听完后，各小题将给出5秒钟的作答时间。每段对话或独白读两遍。

听第6段材料，回答第6、7题。

6. What is the woman looking for?

A. An information office. B. A police station. C. A shoe repair shop.

7. What is the Town Guide according to the man?

A. A brochure. B. A newspaper. C. A map.

听第7段材料，回答第8、9题。

8. What does the man say about the restaurant?

A. It's the biggest one around.

B. It offers many tasty dishes.

C. It's famous for its seafood.

9. What will the woman probably order?

A. Fried fish. B. Roast chicken. C. Beef steak.

听第8段材料，回答第10至12题。

10. Where will Mr.White be at 11 o'clock?

A. At the office. B. At the airport. C. At the restaurant.

11. What will Mr.White probably do at one in the afternoon?

A. Receive a guest. B. Have a meeting. C. Read a report.

12. When will Miss Wilson see Mr.White?

A. At lunch time. B. Late in the afternoon. C. The next morning.

听第9段材料，回答第13至16题。

13. Why is Bill going to Germany?

A. To work on a project.

B. To study German.

C. To start a new company.

14. What did the woman dislike about Germany?

A. The weather. B. The food. C. The schools.

15. What does Bill hope to do about his family?

A. Bring them to Germany.

B. Leave them in England.

C. Visit them in a few months.

16. What is the probable relationship between the speakers?

A. Fellow-travelers. B. Colleagues. C. Classmates.

听第10段材料，回答第17至20题。

17. When did it rain last time in Juárez?

A. Three days ago. B. A month ago. C. A year ago.

18. What season is it now in Juárez?

A. Spring. B. Summer. C. Autumn.

19. What are the elderly advised to do?

A. Take a walk in the afternoon.

B. Keep their homes cool.

C. Drink plenty of water.

20. What is the speaker doing?

A. Hosting a radio program.

B. Conducting a seminar.

C. Forecasting the weather.

真题回顾 · Practice 3 · 2017新课标全国卷II&III

第一节（共5小题；每小题1.5分，满分7.5分）

听下面5段对话，每段对话后有一个小题。从题中所给的A、B、C三个选项中选出最佳选项。听完每段对话后，你都有10秒钟的时间来回答有关小题和阅读下一小题。每段对话仅读一遍。

1. What will the woman do this afternoon?

A. Do some exercise. B. Go shopping. C. Wash her clothes.

2. Why does the woman call the man?

A. To cancel a flight. B. To make an apology. C. To put off a meeting.

3. How much more does David need for the car?

A. \$ 5,000. B. \$ 20,000. C. \$ 25,000.

4. What is Jane doing?

A. Planning a tour. B. Calling her father. C. Asking for leave.

5. How does the man feel?

A. Travel. B. Dizzy. C. Thirsty.

第二节（共5小题；每小题1.5分，满分7.5分）

听下面5段对话或独白。每段对话或独白后有几个小题，从题中所给的A、B、

C三个选项中选出最佳选项。听每段对话或独白前，你将有时间阅读各个小题，每小题5秒钟；听完后，各小题将给出5秒钟的作答时间。每段对话或独白读两遍。

听第6段材料，回答第6、7题。

6. What does Jack want to do?

A. Watch TV. B. Play outside. C. Go to the zoo.

7. Where does the conversation probably take place?

A. At home. B. In a cinema. C. In a supermarket.

听第7段材料，回答第8至10题。

8. What does Richard do?

A. He's a newsman. B. He's a manager. C. He's a researcher.

9. Where is Richard going next week?

A. Birmingham. B. Mexico City. C. Shanghai.

10. What will the speakers do tomorrow?

A. Eat out together. B. Visit a university. C. See Professor Hayes.

听第8段材料，回答第11至13题。

11. What is the probable relationship between the speakers?

A. School friends.

B. Teacher and student.

C. Librarian and library user.

12. Why does Jim suggest Mary buy the book?

A. It's sold at a discount price.

B. It's important for her study.

C. It's written by Professor Lee.

13. What will Jim do for Mary?

A. Share his book with her.

B. Lend her some money.

C. Ask Henry for help.

听第9段材料，回答第14至16题。

14. Where does Stella live?

A. In Memphis. B. In Boston. C. In St Louis.

15.What would Peter and his family like to do on Beale Street?

A. Visit a museum. B. Listen to music. C. Have dinner.

16. What kind of hotel does Peter prefer?

A. A big one. B. A quiet one. C. A modern one.

听第10段材料，回答第17至20题。

17. How many lab sessions will the students have every week?

A. One. B. Two. C. Three.

18. What are the students allowed to wear in the lab?

A. Long scarves. B. Loose clothes. C. Tennis shoes.

19.Why should the students avoid mixing liquid with paper?

A. It may cause a fire.

B. It may create waste.

C. It may produce pollution.

20. What does the speaker mainly talk about?

A. Grades the student will receive.

B. Rules the students should follow.

C. Experiments the students will do.

参考答案及听力原文

真题回顾·Practice 1·2018新课标全国卷I

参考答案：

1. B 2. C 3. C 4. B 5. A 6. B 7. A 8. B 9. C 10. C 11. A
12. B 13. A 14. A 15. C 16. B 17. C 18. B 19. C 20. A

听力原文：

Text 1

W: James, you've been watching TV for the whole evening.What's on?

M: It's a science program on the origin of the universe.I'll give a presentation on it in my class tomorrow.

Text 2

M: Hello, do you have "The Best of Mozart"?

W: Um, sorry, we've just sold out. But we can order one for you.If you give us your number, we'll call you when the CD arrives.

Text 3

W: W'd better be going now, or we'll be late for the train.

M: No rush.It's 8: 30 now.We still have two hours.

Text 4

M: I am so tired of driving all those hours to work.

W: Yeah.I know what you mean.I used to drive two hours to work each way.But now, I live within walking distance of my office.I don't even need a bike.

Text 5

W: Hi, Andy.I didn't see you in Professor Smith's class yesterday.What happened?

M: Well, I had a headache.So, I called him and asked for sick leave.

听第6段材料，回答第6、7题。

Text 6

W: The biggest mistake I made, uh...was leaving college in my last year and not completing my education.So, I'm thinking of going back to school.

M: School? To study what?

W: Ecology.I'm interested in the relationship between humans and nature.

M: Cool. Is it what you studied years ago?

W: No, I majored in chemistry then.

听第7段材料，回答第8、9题。

Text 7

M: Good morning, madam.I am your guide for this trip.

W: How lovely! Could you tell me about the hotel I'm going to stay at?

M: Yes, of course. The Grand Hotel opened in 1990. And it sits on the seaside along the South Coast Highway. It is the most beautiful hotel here.

W: That sounds great.

M: And there are some restaurants outside. So, at dinnertime, you'd have a lot of choices.

W: That's really nice. I like to have some local foods while traveling.What about the scenery around it?

M: The hotel has the best views of the Pacific Ocean.

W: Oh, I think I will love this hotel.

听第8段材料，回答第10至12题。

Text 8

W: Hi, Mike.

M: Hi, Alice.Nice to see you.You don't often come here.

W: I usually have fast food delivered to my office. Just came here for a change today.

M: The environment here is good — clean and relatively quiet.

W: Yeah, and I heard the food is tasty. By the way, are you going to the concert tomorrow evening?

M: Yes, are you?

W: Yeah. Catherine was supposed to go with me. But she may have to work extra hours tomorrow. Do you know anyone who might like to go?

M: No. But if you like, I can ask around.Uh, Joan might want to go.

W: Oh, yes. She's a great fan of classical music.I'll give her a ring after lunch.

听第9段材料，回答第13至16题。

Text 9

W: Hi, I've only just arrived.

M: Oh, good.Now,here are the keys.Let's go in.There are two apartments.The one for rent is on the right.Do come in.

W: Thank you.I like the carpet.The color is nice, isn't it?

M: Yes, and this apartment is in good condition.Here is your lounge.

W: Where would we eat?

M: There is this corner here, or you can use your kitchen.Come and see.

W: The kitchen is quite small.

M: Yes, but it has everything — cooker, fridge,even a dishwasher.

W: And there are lots of cupboards.

M: Let me show you the bedrooms.This is the smaller one.

W: It's a good size, though.

M: Now come into the other bedroom.You can see the bathroom, too.

W: Yes.It is very nice, but I will have to ask my friend first.And we will come together.I understand it is $800 a month.

M: Yes, but a few blocks downtown would be much more expensive.

W: Well, thank you.I will be in touch.

听第10段材料，回答第17至20题。

Text 10

Thank you very much.Thank you, Dr.Johnson.Well, it is really great to be back at university again.The thing that I wanted to tell you today is this: Education is important. When I came to the US, I was only thinking about being a carpenter, but I could not read the newspaper. And I could not understand the news on television or movies or anything like this.So, I entered the city college to take English classes for foreign students.I was very proud that I was going to a college because no one in my family ever went to any college or to any university.You know, when you're 15 years old in my country, you finish school and then you learn a trade. And that's exactly what I did.When I was 15 years old, I learned how to be a carpenter.A year later, I came to America.Luckily, I met a very good teacher who encouraged me to take some math classes, business classes, and history classes, and I became a full-time college student.And today, when I look back, I'm so happy because you never know where life will take you.All of a sudden, I started making money because I was really good at math.You know, how work out everything with math is so important. This is something that I learned when I started my own business, which is doing really well.

真题回顾·Practice 2·2017新课标全国卷I

参考答案:

1. C　2. A　3. C　4. B　5. A　6. C　7. A　8. B　9. C　10. B

11. B　12. C　13. A　14. B　15. A　16. B　17. C　18. A　19. C　20. A

听力原文:

Text 1

W: Have you seen the movie "Hangover"? We went to see it last night.

M: How was it?

W: Jason thought it was extremely amusing, but I was a bit disappointed.

Text 2

M: Susan, I heard you are going to France.How long will you be staying there?

W: A whole year.My aunt lives there. I'm going to do a one-month course at a language school and spend the rest of the time traveling.

Text 3

M: Let's see what drinks you've got for the party tonight.

W: Everything! Beer, wine, soft drinks like Coke, 7-Up... You name it, I've got it! Have you ordered the cake?

M: Of course.

Text 4

M: I don't have a library card. Do I need one?

W: You have to have one only to take books out.You're okay if you just sit in one of the rooms reading.

M: Well then, I'll just read here.Thank you.

Text 5

W: I wish I knew the times of the trains to London.But our phone's out of order.

M: Don't worry, Grandma. I'll find out for you on the Internet.

W: Thank you!

Text 6

W: Excuse me.I wonder if you could tell me how to find a place to have my shoes mended. I'm new in town.

M: Ah, there is a good shop not far from here.Go straight ahead and walk about three blocks. I can't remember the name of the shop, but you'll find it. It's near the police station. By the way, you know about the Town Guide? It's a thin book and has all kinds of useful information. You'll find one in any bookstore.

W: Thanks a lot! You've been so helpful. Let's see. Did you say the repair shop was three blocks away from here?

M: Exactly.

W: Thanks again.

Text 7

M: I've been here many times. There are quite a lot of delicious dishes to choose from. What are you thinking of ordering?

W: Well, I haven't decided yet. What are you going to order?

M: I think I'll have the roast chicken.They really make it well here.

W: I had roast chicken yesterday when I ate out with Shelly.

M: Their beef steak is good, too.You can have it served with beans and mushrooms.

W: But I'm not that hungry. Is the fried fish or the seafood salad good?

M: Never had them before. Maybe if you get the steak, we could share.

W: That sounds like a good idea.

Text 8

W: Hello, Mr.White.Do you think it's possible for us to talk sometime today?

M: I'd love to, Miss Wilson, but I've got a pretty tight schedule today. I've got to finish reading the yearly financial report by 10. Then I have to drive to the airport to pick up an advertiser at 11. After that, I'll have a meeting with him over lunch.

W: Can I see you after lunch?

M: Well, let me see... After lunch, I have to attend a senior staff meeting, which may last about two hours.Can you come at 3? We can talk for an hour before I meet my sales team at 4.

W: I'm afraid an hour is too short.What about tomorrow morning?

M: 9 to 11, then. I'll wait for you at the office.

W: OK, see you then.

Text 9

W: Hey, Bill.I hear they're going to send you to Germany for the new project.

M: Boy, news travels fast around here! I only got the orders a couple of hours ago.Rachel doesn't even know...

W: Oh, no? So, what are you waiting for? When do you plan to tell her?

M: Well, she is at work at the moment.She doesn't finish until 5. I'll have to wait until tonight now, I suppose.

W: Well, I was posted there before, back in 2008. It's OK — a bit like England, really. At least the weather is similar, and the people aren't much different.The only thing I didn't like is the food, especially the sausages.What do you intend to do about the family? Are you going to take them with you?

M: Well, I'd like to, but I don't know much about the situation at the moment... You know, about schools and all that.But I hope to move the family out there in a couple of months' time. I don't think I want to spend a year and a half out there on my own...I mean, without Rachel and the kids. I mean, I don't see that much of them now as it is.

W: Yeah.Well, that's the way it is normally in our company, I suppose.

M: Yeah.Well, we'll see.Let me pay for the coffee.

W: No, no. I'll pay.

Text 10

W: Hello, everyone.Welcome to our program. I'm Jenny Jackson.The weather here in Juárez has become unbearable.With no rains for over a year, the city is suffering from unusually hot weather.Some light showers have been forecast since last month, but all of them have been effective in surrounding areas.Summer has not even started yet, but temperatures have reached 40 degrees centigrade in the past three days.And people have been warned not to go out of their homes — not if you walk on foot, at least — between 11 in the morning and 7 in the evening. Little kids and the elderly are the ones who have suffered the most from this extreme heat wave.They must drink water all the time.To help our audience have a better understanding of this extreme weather, we have invited Prof.Torres from University of Mexico to our studio this evening.

真题回顾·Practice 3·2017新课标全国卷II&III

参考答案：

1. B　2. C　3. A　4. C　5. B　6. A　7. C　8. C　9. B　10. A

11. A　12. B　13. C　14. A　15. B　16. B　17. A.　18. C　19. A　20. B

听力原文：

Text 1

M: Let's go for a nice walk into the country this afternoon.

W: I certainly could enjoy the exercise, but I've agreed to go with Alice to buy some clothes.

Text 2

W: Hello, Mr.Smith. I'm afraid Dr.Brown won't be able to see you today. He's still waiting for a flight out of New York.He said he would meet you tomorrow afternoon. Is it OK?

M: Sounds good. Thank you for calling.

Text 3

W: David, have you saved enough for the car?

M: I have $20,000 now, and the car cost 25,000.My parents said they would like to help, but I don't want to use their money.

Text 4

W: Dr.Block, I need to take a few days off because my father is coming over to visit.And I need to show him around the city.

M: OK, Jane.But be sure to come back to work next week.

Text 5

M: Amy, my head is spinning.It must be a touch of the sun.

W: You'd better lie back still for a while. Take it easy for the rest of the day and stay in the shade. It's too hot today.

Text 6

M: Mum, this is going to take forever. *Animal World* will be on in twenty minutes. It's my favorite program. You know I can't miss it.

W: I know, honey, but we have to wait in line to pay for these things we need.

M: You promise we'd be home in time.

W: Be a little patient, Jack.We'll get out of here soon.

Text 7

M: Hi, Samantha, do you have a minute?

W: Hi, Richard, come in, please.

M: I've been trying to get hold of you all afternoon.

W: I was at the weekly managers' meeting. How were things?

M: Oh, splendid.I have some news.

W: Good news?

M: Wonderful news, to me, anyway. I've been offered a job for three years as an assistant to Professor Hayes from Birmingham University. I'll join him in Mexico City.What do you think about that?

W: Wonderful, Richard.Just what you've always wanted, isn't it? Doesn't mean that you'll leave soon?

M: Next week.But before I go, I'd like to invite you out for dinner.Just thank you for all the help you gave me during my three-month research work here.Would tomorrow evening be a good time for you? We can go to the Shanghai Restaurant in Chinatown.

W: Fine with me.

Text 8

M: What's that book you just picked up, Mary?

W: The one Professor Lee uses in his course.

M: Oh, I see.You'd better have it if you want to pass that course.

W: But it costs $30.I simply can't afford it.

M: Did you check the used-book section here? Maybe they have it.

W: No, they don't.I asked.

M: Why don't you get it from the library?

W: I've been trying for a month and it's always out.There are over 50 students in the course, and every single one wants the book.

M: Listen, you know my roommate, Henry, don't you? He took the same course last year. And I remember he owes a copy. I can borrow it from him for you.

W: Oh, that would be great.Thank you, Jim.

Text 9

W: Hello.

M: Hello, Stella.This is Peter.

W: Hi, Peter.Fancy hearing your voice.How are you?

M: Couldn't be better. I'm planning a trip to Memphis with my family this summer.

W: Great, I'd love to host you here.When are you coming?

M: We'll leave Boston on June 20th.Stay in St Louis Missouri for a week, and then fly to your city.We'd probably stay for five days with you and come back. For it's a two-week vacation.

W: Is there anything special you'd like to do here?

M: We'd love to explore Beale Street, the official home of the blues, where we'd listen to live music.We'd also like to visit Graceland, the popular museum in memory of Elvis Presley.

But above all, we want to spend some time with you and your family.

W: Of course, it's been ages since we met last time. Let's have a dinner party in my garden.

M: Lovely. Oh, could you find for us a hotel near where you live? It doesn't have to be big, but I can't stand noisy at bedtime.

W: Sure.

M: Thank you.See you soon.

Text 10

Hello, everyone.My name is John. I'm the teaching assistant for this lab session.Let me explain a little about it.As you may know already, it's a required meeting once a week. I expect you to do all the experiments and keep the results in your lab notebook. I'll collect the notebooks every two weeks. You'll be graded on lab notebooks and quizzes.But the most important information I want to give you now is about safety.First of all, you must wear shoes that cover your feet in the lab.Tennis shoes are OK; also don't wear loose clothes, long scarves, big necklaces or loose belts.They get cut in something or fall into liquid. Another thing to do for safety is cleaning up. Be sure to put the waste in the correct containers.We can't mix liquid with paper.This is extremely important.I don't want any fires in this room. You are responsible for washing out your own lab equipment and putting it away.If you don't do this, I will take away points from your grade.Nobody is going to clean up after you. OK, any questions?

专题二 阅读理解

一、《新课标》与考纲要求

普通高中英语课程强调对学生学科核心素养的综合培养，英语学科核心素养主要包括语言能力、文化意识、思维品质和学习能力。

英语学科核心素养的基础，包括六个要素：主题语境、语篇类型、语言知识、文化知识、语言技能和学习策略。主题语境涵盖人与自我、人与社会和人与自然。人与自我涉及"生活与学习""做人与做事"两个主题群下的9项子主题；人与社会涉及"社会服务与人际沟通""文学、艺术与体育""历史、社会与文化""科学与技术"四个主题群下的16项子主题；人与自然涉及"自然生态""环境保护""灾害防范""宇宙探索"四个主题群下的7项子主题。所有主题语境都应包含中外文化的范畴。

高考考纲和《新课标》是统一的，因此2019年的高考备考应该依据考纲，结合《新课标》的学科素养要求进行。高考英语的阅读理解，应该以主题语境为引领，分类训练各种主题内容的阅读语篇。学生通过学习语篇，不断提高自己的语言能力。

二、试题特点

选用的命题材料新颖，主要选用原汁原味的英语国家的材料，试题全新自创。凡与网上或纸质的同类资料雷同的试题、高考真题、四六级考题、考研题及大学教材教辅题一概不予采用。

记叙文、说明文、议论文、广告类应用文都有，话题广泛；科普、社会、财经、文体、人物等都有，不要出现任何宗教色彩的内容或背景，阅读内容要给人以美的感受。少出或不出残疾人之类的话题，对残疾相关细节的描述就更不能出现了(近年高考阅读几乎没有关于残疾人的话题)。

考查内容全面，每组20个题中主旨大意2 ~ 3个，事实细节8 ~ 9个，猜测词义1个，推理判断5 ~ 6个，文章结构1个，观点态度1 ~ 2个。

材料长度平均每篇220 ~ 350词，四篇文章总词数1100 ~ 1150词。材料难度以中档为主，很少出现超纲词，如有就进行了改写，影响理解的生词加了汉语注释，每篇不超过3个。试题涉及的材料信息分布均匀，不要太集中或大片信息无题。所有试题及选项都基于材料内容设计，不要设计超出材料范围的"漫游题"。

题干形式以问题式为主，约占五分之四，完成句子形式为辅约占五分之一，但决不能在题干中间设空或在材料中间设空。题干和选项都比较简洁，选项为同类形式，长短基本一致，正确选项唯一，错误选项有干扰性，正确答案一般不是文中的原句，而是改写后的句子。

特别注意：阅读理解出题形式严格参照高考英语新课标卷，杜绝出现Which of the following is (not) true? Which... except that...? 等设问方式。

三、题型解读

阅读理解题型在新课标卷高考英语试题中占30分，是整张卷的五分之一，其比重之大，可想而知，做好阅读理解，其他试题也就会相应地做得很好。

2016—2018年阅读理解命题情况

试卷类型	年份		体裁	词数	话题	考点分布
卷I	2016	A	记叙文	267	主要介绍几位著名的女性，她们在各自的领域做出了非凡的贡献	细节理解题10 推理判断题3 词义猜测题1 主旨大意题1
		B	议论文	287	介绍社会上很多老年人搬到离子女近的地方居住的一种趋势	
		C	记叙文	262	作者在一次运送造血干细胞途中的一段经历	
		D	说明文	327	沉默在不同文化背景下的不同内涵	
	2017	A	应用文	231	购物中心Pacific Science Center	细节理解题6 推理判断题5 观点态度题1 词义猜测题1 主旨大意题1 写作意图题1
		B	记叙文	296	救助一只小猫头鹰的故事	
		C	说明文	352	爵士乐问题	
		D	说明文	315	自制太阳能蒸馏器的方法	
	2018	A	应用文	270	Washington, D. C. 旅游的四种路线	细节理解题8 推理判断题2 词义猜测题1 观点态度题1 主旨大意题2 写作意图题1
		B	说明文	270	介绍了一档英国系列电视节目	
		C	说明文	304	随着社会的发展人类语言越来越少及其原因	
		D	说明文	363	新旧电子设备的差别	

续 表

试卷类型	年份		体裁	词数	话题	考点分布
卷II	2016	A	应用文	281	四则广告的具体内容及细节信息	细节理解题8 推理判断题4 代词指代题1 词义猜测题1 主旨大意题1
		B	记叙文	280	通过让学生拼装玩具发现并鼓励学生的创造性和想象力	
		C	说明文	249	Book Crossing. com所进行的分享图书活动的目的及具体过程	
		D	记叙文	278	Frank的图片记录了一次海难	
	2017	A	应用文	306	莎士比亚剧本翻译及上演	细节理解题5 推理判断题5 代词指代题1 写作意图题1 主旨大意题2 词义猜测题1
		B	记叙文	289	作者与Paul的友谊	
		C	说明文	307	Terrafugia 公司研制出飞行汽车	
		D	说明文	293	植物在受到昆虫的攻击时自我保护	
	2018	A	应用文	284	家长和孩子一起挑选可以参加的活动	细节理解题6 推理判断题5 文章出处题1 词义猜测题1 主旨大意题2
		B	说明文	268	水果营养丰富且对人体有益	
		C	说明文	300	青少年和年幼的孩子们读书的乐趣减少	
		D	议论文	330	减少手机使用、增加与人谈话	
卷III	2016	A	应用文	195	介绍五个与音乐有关的活动	细节理解题7 推理判断题4 写作意图题1 词义猜测题1 代词指代题1 主旨大意题1
		B	记叙文	325	一位女作家请纽约的朋友吃饭时发生的故事	
		C	说明文	278	介绍了一个节日——Apple Day	
		D	说明文	346	好消息比坏消息传得更快、更远，越积极乐观的消息越容易被大众分享	
	2017	A	应用文	52	美国旧金山的四个旅游活动和路线	细节理解题5 推理判断题7 词义猜测题1 主旨大意题2
		B	记叙文	282	一家具有75年历史的剧院因为不利的地理位置和现代剧院的竞争而被转售	
		C	说明文	295	美国黄石公园重新引进灰狼的故事	
		D	说明文	334	科研人员研制出DriveLAB，目的是能够帮助他们延长驾龄，从而保持积极、健康的生活方式	
	2018	A	应用文	197	去Holker Hall& Garden 旅游的相关信息	细节理解题10 推理判断题2 词义猜测题1 主旨大意题2
		B	说明文	316	Dawson城市的发展原因、过程与现状	
		C	新闻报道	372	中国建筑设计师王澍获得了建筑界的诺贝尔奖——普利策奖	
		D	说明文	307	引导孩子主动捐献玩具，并从玩耍简单的玩具中获得快乐的做法	

近三年全国新课标卷阅读选材地道，贴近学生实际，体裁多样。在选材上保持了知识性、趣味性强，信息量不是很大，语篇长度适中，题材与体裁广泛的特点，彰显了文化特色，考查考生快速获取、处理、分析信息的能力。4篇文章按难度渐进排列，阅读总量1100～1200词（不含选项），细节题略多于或相当于推断题试题数量。

四、解题策略与技巧

（一）细节理解题

1. 如何解决事实细节题

做事实细节题最基本也最常用的方法是题干定位法。一般在原文中找到相关的句子，然后进行比较和分析，便可确定答案。此类题通常用一些疑问词来提问，或者是判断正误。

2. 如何解决细节转换题

细节理解题也叫间接理解题，包括语意转换题、图文转换题和是非判断题。

（1）语意转换题。需要将题目信息与原文相关信息进行语意上的转换，两者存在表述上的差异。解答这类题目时可带着问题，有针对性地扫读全文，迅速锁定相关语句，再对相关部分进行分析对比，找出答案。

（2）图文转换题。在阅读理解题中，有的图表、图画出现在阅读理解题的正文中。在解答这类题时，可采用"文字锁定法"，找出描述图形中的句段，采用按图寻找答案的方法，按图索骥，图文互相参照、互相验证，便可确定正确答案。

3. 如何解决数字计算题

先理解文章的大意，然后经过对比、分析、计算等就能够得出正确的答案。

（1）仔细阅读文字说明部分，准确把握图表信息。

（2）仔细分析题干，抓牢关键词。

（3）运用数学公式计算，注意巧算。

4. 如何解决细节排序题

做此类题目可采用"首尾定位法"，即先找出第一个事件和最后一个事件，这样可以迅速缩小选择范围，从而迅速找到答案。阅读理解的文章如果是记叙文，排序题通常以事件发生的时间为线索；如果是说明文，排序题通常以说明的先后顺序为线索；如果是议论文，排序题通常以逻辑顺序为线索。从近几年高考试题来看，这类试题主要出现在记叙文和说明文中。

真题回顾·典例1·2018新课标全国卷Ⅰ·A

Washington, D.C. Bicycle Tours

Cherry Blossom Bike Tour in Washington, D.C.

Duration: 3 hours

This small group bike tour is a fantastic way to see the world-famous cherry trees with beautiful flowers of Washington, D.C. Your guide will provide a history lesson about the trees and the famous monuments where they blossom. Reserve your spot before availability—and the cherry blossoms—disappear!

Washington Capital Monuments Bicycle Tour

Duration: 3 hours (4 miles)

Join a guided bike tour and view some of the most popular monuments in Washington, D.C. Explore the monuments and memorials on the National Mall as your guide shares unique facts and history at each stop. Guided tour includes bike, helmet, cookies and bottled water.

Capital City Bike Tour in Washington, D.C.

Duration: 3 hours

Morning or afternoon, this bike tour is the perfect tour for D.C. newcomers and locals looking to experience Washington, D.C. in a healthy way with minimum effort. Knowledgeable guides will entertain you with the most interesting stories about Presidents, Congress, memorials, and parks. Comfortable bikes and a smooth tour route (路线) make cycling between the sites fun and relaxing.

Washington Capital Sites at Night Bicycle Tour

Duration: 3 hours (7 miles)

Join a small group bike tour for an evening of exploration in the heart of Washington, D.C. Get up close to the monuments and memorials as you bike the sites of Capital Hill and the National Mall. Frequent stops are made for photo taking as your guide offers unique facts and history. Tour includes bike, helmet, and bottled water. All riders are equipped with reflective vests and safety lights.

21. Which tour do you need to book in advance?

A. Cherry Blossom Bike Tour in Washington, D.C.

B. Washington Capital Monuments Bicycle Tour.

C. Capital City Bike Tour in Washington, D.C.

D. Washington Capital Sites at Night Bicycle Tour.

22. What will you do on the Capital City Bike Tour?

A. Meet famous people. B. Go to a national park.

C. Visit well-known museums. D. Enjoy interesting stories.

23. Which of the following does the bicycle tour at night provide?

A. City maps. B. Cameras.

C. Meals. D. Safety lights.

语篇解读：

本文是一篇广告应用文。文章介绍了骑自行车到Washington, D.C.旅游的四种路线的相关行程及注意事项。

答案解析：

21. A 细节理解题。根据文章Cherry Blossom Bike Tour in Washington, D.C.中的Reserve your spot before availability可知，这个骑行项目需要提前预约。故选A。

22. D 细节理解题。根据文章 Capital City Bike Tour in Washington, D.C. 中的Knowledgeable guides will entertain you with the most interesting stories about Presidents, Congress, memorials, and parks. 可知，在这个活动中，你可以享受有趣的故事。故选D。

23. D 细节理解题。根据文章Washington Capital Sites at Night Bicycle Tour中的All riders are equipped with reflective vests and safety lights.可知，所有骑行者都要装备反光背心和安全手电筒。故选D。

真题回顾·典例2·2017新课标全国卷II·A

In the coming months, we are bringing together artists from all over the globe, to enjoy speaking Shakespeare's plays in their own language, in our Globe, within the architecture Shakespeare wrote for. Please come and join us.

National Theatre of China Beijing Chinese

This great occasion(盛会) will be the National Theatre of China's first visit to the UK. The company's productions show the new face of 21st century Chinese theatre. This production of Shakespeare's *Richard III* will be directed by the National's Associate Director, Wang Xiaoying.

Date & Time: Saturday 28 April,2.30 p.m. & Sunday 29 April,1.30 p.m. & 6.30 p.m.

Marjanishvili Theatre Tbilisi | Georgian

One of the most famous theatres in Georgia, the Marjanishvili, founded in 1928, appears regularly at theatre festivals all over the world. This new production of *As You Like It* is helmed（指导）by the company's Artistic Director Levan Tsuladze.

Date & Time: Friday 18 May, 2.30 p.m. & Saturday 19 May,7.30 p.m.

Deafinitely Theatre London | British Sign Language（BSL）

By translating the rich and humourous text of *Love's Labour's Lost* into the physical language of BSL, Deafinitely Theatre creates a new interpretation of Shakespeare's comedy and aims to build a bridge between deaf and hearing worlds by performing to both groups as one audience.

Date & Time: Tuesday 22 May, 2.30 p.m. & Wednesday 23 May,7.30 p.m.

Habima National Theatre Tel Aviv| Hebrew

The Habima is the centre of Hebrew-language theatre worldwide. Founded in Moscow after the 1905 revolution, the company eventually settled in Tel Aviv in the late 1920s. Since 1958, they have been recognised as the national theatre of Israel. This production of Shakespeare's *The Merchant of Venice* marks their first visit to the UK.

Date & Time: Monday 28 May,7.30 p.m. & Tuesday 29 May, 7.30 p.m.

21. Which play will be performed by the National Theatre of China?

A. *Richard* Ⅲ. B. *Love's Labour's Lost*.

C. *As You Like It*. D. *The Merchant of Venice*.

22. What is special about Deafinitely Theatre?

A. It has two groups of actors.

B. It is the leading theatre in London.

C. It performs plays in BSL.

D. It is good at producing comedies.

23. When can you see a play in Hebrew?

A. On Saturday 28 April. B. On Sunday 29 April.

C. On Tuesday 22 May. D. On Tuesday 29 May.

语篇解读：

本文是一篇应用文。主要介绍了莎士比亚的戏剧被翻译成几个国家的语言，并将在这些国家的大剧院上映的有关情况。

答案解析：

21. A 细节理解题。根据“This great occasion（盛会）will be the National Theatre of China's first visit to the UK. 以及This production of Shakespeare's *Richard III* will be directed by the National's Associate Director,Wang Xiaoying”，可知*Richard III*将要在中国国家大剧院上映。故选A。

22. C　细节理解题。根据“By translating the rich and humourous text of *Love's Labour's Lost* into the physical language of BSL, Deafinitely Theatre creates a new interpretation of Shakespeare's comedy and aims to build a bridge between deaf and hearing worlds”，可知选C。

23. D　细节理解题。根据“Date & Time: Monday 28 May,7.30 p.m. & Tuesday 29 May,7.30 p.m.”可知，可以在5月29日星期二这一天，观看希伯来语戏剧。故选D。

（二）推理判断题

推理判断题的设题形式有很多，不同的题型对应不同的技巧。

推理判断题的解题技巧

推断内容	考查点	解题方法
推断隐含含义	考查考生通过词语的字面意思去理解作者的言外之意或弦外之音的能力	1. 跳读，找到相关信息点(推理的依据)。 2. 细读，理解相关信息点的字面意义。 3. 结合语境和常识，在字面意义的基础上进行符合逻辑的推断，理解作者的言外之意
推断写作意图	考查考生根据短文内容推断作者写该文章的目的的能力	根据文体的特点和用途来推断作者的写作目的： 1. 记叙文，特别是个人的有趣经历或幽默故事类的文章——娱乐读者。 2. 夹叙夹议文——让读者得到某种启示或教育。 3. 广告和议论文——说服读者接受某种产品、服务或接受某种观点。 4. 科普说明文或新闻报道——告知读者某些信息
推断下段内容、文章出处	考查考生通过阅读材料，预测内容及推断材料的来源的能力	1.根据文章的内容或结构来推断。 2.根据各种文体的特征来判断其出处，如广告的用词和格式非常特殊，因此容易辨认。 3.报纸的前面会出现日期、地点或通讯社名称。 4.产品说明的特点也比较明显，一般会介绍其名称、作用、操作方式等
推断目标读者	考查考生根据短文内容推断此篇文章主要是写给谁看的能力	根据文章内容，特别是从作者使用的词语和语气来判断

真题回顾·典例1·2018新课标Ⅱ卷·C

Teens and younger children are reading a lot less for fun, according to a Common Sense Media report published Monday.

While the decline over the past decade is steep for teen readers, some data in the report shows that reading remains a big part of many children's lives, and indicates how parents might help encourage more reading.

According to the report's key findings, "the proportion (比例) who say they 'hardly ever' read for fun has gone from 8 percent of 13-year-olds and 9 percent of 17-year-olds in 1984 to 22 percent and 27 percent respectively today."

The report data shows that pleasure reading levels for younger children, ages 2—8, remain largely the same. But the amount of time spent in reading each session has declined, from closer to an hour or more to closer to a half hour per session.

When it comes to technology and reading, the report does little to counsel(建议) parents looking for data about the effect of e-readers and tablets on reading. It does point out that many parents still limit electronic reading, mainly due to concerns about increased screen time.

The most hopeful data shared in the report shows clear evidence of parents serving as examples and important guides for their kids when it comes to reading. Data shows that kids and teens who do read frequently, compared to infrequent readers, have more books in the home, more books purchased for them, parents who read more often, and parents who set aside time for them to read.

As the end of school approaches, and school vacation reading lists loom(逼近) ahead, parents might take this chance to step in and make their own summer reading list and plan a family trip to the library or bookstore.

28. What is the Common Sense Media report probably about?

A. Children's reading habits. B. Quality of children's books.

C. Children's after-class activities. D. Parent-child relationships.

29. Where can you find the data that best supports "children are reading a lot less for fun"?

A. In paragraph 2. B. In paragraph 3.

C. In paragraph 4. D. In paragraph 5.

30. Why do many parents limit electronic reading?

A. E-books are of poor quality. B. It could be a waste of time.

C. It may harm children's health. D. E-readers are expensive.

语篇解读：

本周一公布的一份报告显示，青少年和年幼的孩子们读书的乐趣大大减少。文中从阅读的乐趣、阅读的时间、阅读方式和父母对孩子阅读的影响等角度展示了该报告的内容。

答案解析：

28. A　推理判断题。题干问的是这篇报道可能是关于什么内容。根据整篇文章，我们可以看出这篇报道讲述了孩子们阅读的乐趣，孩子们阅读的时间，孩子们阅读方式和父母对孩子阅读的影响。A项意为：孩子们的阅读习惯；B项意为：孩子们所读书籍的质量；C项意为：孩子们的课后活动；D项意为：父母与孩子的关系。故选A。

29. B　推理判断题。根据第三段"the proportion (比例) who say they 'hardly ever' read for fun has gone from 8 percent of 13-year-olds and 9 percent of 17-year-olds in 1984 to 22 percent and 27 percent respectively today."可知，很少为乐趣而阅读的人的比例已经分别从1984年的13岁的8%和17岁的9%上升到现在的22%和27%，也就是说，为乐趣而读书的人越来越少。故选B。

30. C　推理判断题。根据倒数第三段最后一句"many parents still limit electronic reading, mainly due to concerns about increased screen time"可知，许多家长仍然限制电子阅读，主要是由于担心看一些电子屏幕的时间越来越多，也就是担心会伤害孩子们的健康。故选C。

真题回顾·典例2·2017新课标全国卷II·B

Minutes after the last movie ended yesterday at the Plaza Theater, employees were busy sweeping up popcorns and gathering coke cups. It was a scene that had been repeated many times in the theater's 75-year history. This time, however, the cleanup was a little different. As one group of workers carried out the rubbish, another group began removing seats and other theater equipment in preparation for the building's end.

The film classic *The Last Picture Show* was the last movie shown in the old theater. Though the movie is 30 years old, most of the 250 seats were filled with teary-eyed audience wanting to say good-bye to the old building. Theater owner Ed Bradford said he chose the movie because it seemed appropriate. The movie is set in a small town where the only movie theater is preparing to close down.

Bradford said that large modern theaters in the city made it impossible for the Plaza to compete. He added that the theater's location（位置）was also a reason. "This used to be the center of town," he said. "Now the area is mostly office buildings and warehouses."

Last week some city officials suggested the city might be interested in turning the old theater into a museum and public meeting place. However, these plans were abandoned because of financial problems. Bradford sold the building and land to a local development firm, which plans to build a shopping complex on the land where the theater is located.

The theater audience said good-bye as Bradford locked the doors for the last time. After 75 years the Plaza Theater had shown its last movie. The theater will be missed.

25. Why was *The Last Picture Show* put on?

A. It was an all-time classic.

B. It was about the history of the town.

C. The audience requested it.

D. The theater owner found it suitable.

26. What will probably happen to the building?

A. It will be repaired.

B. It will be turned into a museum.

C. It will be knocked down.

D. It will be sold to the city government.

27. What can we infer about the audience?

A. They are disappointed with Bradford.

B. They are sad to part with the old theater.

C. They are supportive of the city officials.

D. They are eager to have a shopping center.

语篇解读：

本文是一篇记叙文，讲述了一家具有75年历史的剧院因为不利的地理位置和现代剧院的竞争而被转售的故事。

答案解析：

25. D　推理判断题。根据第二段最后两句可知，剧院老板选择这部电影是因为这部电影本身讲述的就是小镇上唯一的电影院准备关门停业的故事，与Plaza Theater的现状一样。

26. C　推理判断题。根据第四段末句中的“which plans to build a shopping complex on the land where the theater is located”可以推断出这个剧院将被拆除，取而代之的是一个现代化的购物中心。

27. B　推理判断题。根据第二段中的“most of the 250 seats were filled with teary-eyed audience wanting to say good-bye to the old building”可知，人们非常难过，不愿意看到老剧院被拆掉。

（三）词义猜测题

猜词是应用英语的重要能力，也是高考中常用的题型。它不但需要准确无误地理解上下文，而且要有较大的泛读量，掌握或认识较多的课外词汇。词义猜测题要根据词、词组、句子所在的上下文语境来判断其意义，我们要特别注意熟词生义，切不可脱离语境主观臆断。我们要学会"顺藤摸瓜"，通过构词、语法、定义、同位、对比、因果、常识、上下文等线索确定词义。

1. 定义法

(1) Annealing is a way of making metal softer by heating it and then letting it cool very slowly.

句子给予annealing 以明确的定义，即"退火"。

(2) It will be very hard but also very brittle — that is, it will break easily.

从后面的解释中我们可以了解到brittle 是"脆"的意思。

(3) The herdsman, who looks after sheep, earns about 650 yuan a year.

定语从句中 looks after sheep 就表明了 herdsman 的词义为"牧人"。

2. 同位法

(1) They traveled a long way and at last got to a castle, a large building in old times.

同位语部分a large building in old times 给出了 castle 的确切词义，即"城堡"。

(2) We are on the night shift—from midnight to 8 a.m.—this week.

两个破折号之间的短语很清楚地表明night shift 是"夜班"的意思。

3. 对比法

She is usually prompt for all her class, but today she arrived in the middle of her first class.

"But"一词表转折，因此but 前后的意思正相反。后半句的意思是"她今天第一节上了一半才来"，因此反向推理，可得出她平时一向"准时"的结论。

4. 构词法（前缀、后缀、复合、派生等）

Perhaps, we can see some possibilities for next fifty years. But the next hundred?

Possibility 是 possible 的同根名词,据此可以判断 possibility 的意思是"可能性"。

5. 因果法

The lack of movement caused the muscles to weaken. Sometimes the weakness was permanent. So the player could never play the sport again.

从后面的结果"永远不能再运动"中，可以推测 permanent 的意思为"永远的，永久的"。

真题回顾 · 典例1 · 2018新课标全国卷Ⅰ · C

Languages have been coming and going for thousands of years, but in recent times there has been less coming and a lot more going. When the world was still populated by hunter-gatherers, small, tightly knit（联系）groups developed their own patterns of speech independent of each other.Some language experts believe that 10,000 years ago, when the world had just five to ten million people, they spoke perhaps 12,000 languages between them.

Soon afterwards, many of those people started settling down to become farmers, and their languages too became more settled and fewer in number. In recent centuries, trade, industrialization, the development of the nation-state and the spread of universal compulsory education, especially globalisation and better communications in the past few decades, all have caused many languages to disappear, and dominant languages such as English, Spanish and Chinese are increasingly taking over.

At present, the world has about 6,800 languages. The distribution of these languages is hugely uneven. The general rule is that mild zones have relatively few languages, often spoken by many people, while hot, wet zones have lots, often spoken by small numbers. Europe has only around 200 languages; the Americas about 1,000; Africa 2,400; and Asia and the Pacific perhaps 3,200, of which Papua New Guinea alone accounts for well over 800. The median number（中位数）of speakers is a mere 6,000, which means that half the world's languages are spoken by fewer people than that.

Already well over 400 of the total of 6,800 languages are close to extinction（消亡）, with only a few elderly speakers left. Pick, at random, Busuu in Cameroon (eight remaining speakers),Chiapaneco in Mexico(150), Lipan Apache in the United States(two or three) or Wadjigu in Australia (one, with a question-mark): none of these seems to have much chance of survival.

29. Which of the following best explains "dominant" underlined in paragraph 2?

A. Complex. B. Advanced.

C. Powerful. D. Modern.

语篇解读：

本文是一篇议论文。文章讲述了随着社会的发展人类语言越来越少及其原因。

答案解析：

29. C 猜测词义题。根据文章第二段中的"dominant languages such as English, Spanish and Chinese are increasingly taking over"可知，英语、西班牙语和汉语正在替代其他语言。由此推知dominant languages意为：强有力的语言。故选C。

真题回顾·典例2·2017新课标全国卷Ⅲ·C

After years of heated debate, gray wolves were reintroduced to Yellowstone National Park. Fourteen wolves were caught in Canada and transported to the park. By last year, the Yellowstone wolf population had grown to more than 170 wolves.

Gray wolves once were seen here and there in the Yellowstone area and much of the continental United States, but they were gradually displaced by human development. By the 1920s, wolves had practically disappeared from the Yellowstone area. They went farther north into the deep forests of Canada, where there were fewer humans around.

The disappearance of the wolves had many unexpected results. Deer and elk populations — major food sources（来源）for the wolf — grew rapidly. These animals consumed large amounts of vegetation（植被）, which reduced plant diversity in the park. In the absence of wolves, coyote populations also grew quickly. The coyotes killed a large percentage of the park's red foxes, and completely drove away the park's beavers.

As early as 1966, biologists asked the government to consider reintroducing wolves to Yellowstone Park. They hoped that wolves would be able to control the elk and coyote problems. Many farmers opposed the plan because they feared that wolves would kill their farm animals or pets.

The government spent nearly 30 years coming up with a plan to reintroduce the wolves. The U.S. Fish and Wildlife Service carefully monitors and manages the wolf packs in Yellowstone. Today, the debate continues over how well the gray wolf is fitting in at Yellowstone. Elk, deer, and coyote populations are down, while beavers and red foxes have made a comeback. The Yellowstone wolf project has been a valuable experiment to help biologists decide whether to reintroduce wolves to other parts of the country as well.

29. What does the underlined word "displaced" in paragraph 2 mean?

A. Tested. B. Separated.

C. Forced out. D. Tracked down.

语篇解读：

本文是一篇说明文，介绍了美国黄石公园重新引进灰狼的事情。因为人类活动的影响，灰狼数量逐渐减少，鹿群数量逐渐增加，从而造成植被遭到大量破坏。

答案解析：

29. 词义猜测题，答案为C。根据本段后两句可知，因为人类的发展，侵占了灰狼的领域，灰狼逐渐向北迁徙，由此推断灰狼被人类排挤走了。词义猜测题是高考英语阅读理解中常见的题型，一般考查考生对生词的猜测、熟词生义的猜测、短语的猜测、代词的指代以及句子的理解。要求考生掌握构词法，还要学会利用上下文语境、定义、解释、举例和对比转折等线索来进行判断推测。而构词法也是一种猜词的办法，比如通过前缀dis-、un-、im-等，如本题中的displace。

（四）观点态度题

高考阅读测试中有些题目考查学生对文章作者的主导思想、被描写人物语气、言谈话语中流露的情绪、性格倾向和作用或文中人物的态度、观点等方面的理解。做这一类题时一定要注意：

1. 技巧方法一

由表及里地准确把握字里行间的意思，切勿用自己的主观想法或观点代替作者的思想观点。不要把自己的态度揉入其中，还要注意区分题目问的是作者的态度还是别人的态度。

2. 技巧方法二

特别注意那些描写环境气氛的语言，以及表达感情、态度观点的词语。要特别注意作者在文章中的措辞，尤其是表示感情色彩的形容词。还要特别留意那些描写环境气氛的语言以及表达感情、态度或观点的词语。当作者的态度没有明确表明时，要学会根据作者在文章中所运用的具有褒贬含义的语言去判断作者的态度。

作者的观点态度大致分为三种：①褒义——支持或赞同；②中立或客观；③贬义——怀疑、批评或反对。作者的观点态度还可以从词的内涵中判断。如果作者对某个话题、事件、行为持肯定的态度或观点，那么他肯定用褒义词；相反，则用贬义词。

作者的观点态度

表示贬义	negative, doubtful, disgust, critical, disappointed, disapproval, pessimistic, subjective, sarcastic, hostile等
表示褒义	positive, enthusiastic, supportive, approval, optimistic, objective, satisfied, friendly等
表示中立	neutral, indifferent, impassive, uninterested等

3. 技巧方法三

问作者对某事物的态度时，表示“客观”的词多为正确选项，如objective、impartial、unbiased 等；问作者对文中提到的人/物或其观点态度时，答案多是肯定或否定、支持或反对。

4. 技巧方法四

能结合自己平时积累的有关英语国家的文化传统、风俗习惯等知识来判断评价。

真题回顾·典例·2018新课标全国卷Ⅰ·D

We may think we're a culture that gets rid of our worn technology at the first sight of something shiny and new, but a new study shows that we keep using our old devices（装置）well after they go out of style. That's bad news for the environment—and our wallets—as these outdated devices consume much more energy than the newer ones that do the same things.

To figure out how much power these devices are using, Callie Babbitt and her colleagues at the Rochester Institute of Technology in New York tracked the environmental costs for each product throughout its life—from when its minerals are mined to when we stop using the device. This method provided a readout for how home energy use has evolved since the early 1990s. Devices were grouped by generation. Desktop computers, basic mobile phones, and box-set TVs defined 1992. Digital cameras arrived on the scene in 1997. And MP3 players, smart phones, and LCD TVs entered homes in 2002, before tablets and e-readers showed up in 2007.

As we accumulated more devices, however, we didn't throw out our old ones. "The living-room television is replaced and gets planted in the kids' room, and suddenly one day, you have a TV in every room of the house," said one researcher. The average number of electronic devices rose from four per household in 1992 to 13 in 2007. We're not just keeping these old devices—we continue to use them. According to the analysis of Babbitt's team, old desktop monitors and box TVs with cathode ray tubes are the worst devices with their energy consumption and contribution to greenhouse gas emissions (排放) more than doubling during the 1992 to 2007 window.

So what's the solution (解决方案)? The team's data only went up to 2007, but the researchers also explored what would happen if consumers replaced old products with new electronics that serve more than one function, such as a tablet for word processing and TV viewing. They found that more on-demand entertainment viewing on tablets instead of TVs and desktop computers could cut energy consumption by 44%.

32. What does the author think of new devices?

A. They are environment-friendly. B. They are no better than the old.

C. They cost more to use at home. D. They go out of style quickly.

语篇解读：

本文是一篇科普说明文。文章讲述了新旧电子设备的差别，旧电子设备耗能高、不环保。所以作者主张使用新电子设备。

答案解析：

31. A 观点态度题。根据文章第一段中的That's bad news for the environment—and our wallets—as these outdated devices consume much more energy than the newer ones that do the same things.可知，使用旧的电子设备对环境和我们的钱包都是坏消息。这些过时的设备做相同的事情要消耗比新设备更多的能量。由此推知作者认为新电子设备环保、节能。故选A。

（五）主旨大意题

1. 如何概括语篇解读

做概括语篇解读题时，有效的方法就是辨认主题句。主题句具有简洁性、概括性的特点，文章的中心思想往往是每段主题句的综合。若文章无主题句，这就需要我们依据文中的事实、细节、观点去进行分析、推断和归纳，从而概括出语篇解读。

在选择答案时，根据自己总结的大意，就可以用排除法将干扰项逐个排除。

2. 如何总结段落大意

段落大意即一段的中心思想，通常中心思想会在首句体现出来，这就是常说的段落主题句。主题句具有鲜明的概括性，句子结构简单，段落中其他句子均用来解释、支撑或扩展主题句所表达的主题思想。主题句通常位于段首，也可位于段尾、段中。有时作者没有写出明显的主题句，要学会根据段落内容去概括主题句。

真题回顾·典例·2018新课标全国卷II·D

We've all been there: in a lift, in line at the bank or on an airplane, surrounded by people who are, like us, deeply focused on their smartphones or, worse, struggling with the uncomfortable silence.

What's the problem? It's possible that we all have compromised conversational intelligence. It's more likely that none of us start a conversation because it's awkward and challenging, or we think it's annoying and unnecessary. But the next time you find yourself among strangers, consider that small talk is worth the trouble. Experts say it's an invaluable social practice that results in big benefits.

Dismissing small talk as unimportant is easy, but we can't forget that deep relationships wouldn't even exist if it weren't for casual conversation. Small talk is the grease（润滑剂）for social communication, says Bernardo Carducci, director of the Shyness Research Institute at Indiana University Southeast. "Almost every great love story and each big business deal begins with small talk," he explains. "The key to successful small talk is learning how to connect with others, not just communicate with them."

In a 2014 study, Elizabeth Dunn, associate professor of psychology at UBC, invited people on their way into a coffee shop. One group was asked to seek out an interaction（互动）with its waiter; the other, to speak only when necessary. The results showed that those who chatted with their server reported significantly higher positive feelings and a better coffee shop experience. "It's not that talking to the waiter is better than talking to your husband," says Dunn. "But interactions with peripheral（边缘的）members of our social network matter for our well-being also."

Dunn believes that people who reach out to strangers feel a significantly greater sense of belonging, a bond with others. Carducci believes developing such a sense of belonging starts with small talk. "Small talk is the basis of good manners," he says.

32. What phenomenon is described in the first paragraph?

A. Addiction to smartphones.

B. Inappropriate behaviours in public places.

C. Absence of communication between strangers.

D. Impatience with slow service.

35. What is the best title for the text?

A. Conversation Counts. B. Ways of Making Small Talk.

C. Benefits of Small Talk. D. Uncomfortable Silence.

语篇解读：

这是一篇议论文。在当今社会，人们在公共场合或沉迷于智能手机，或与不舒服的沉默抗争，陌生人之间缺乏沟通。但人与人之间是需要适当的交谈闲聊的，闲聊是人际关系、社会交往必不可少的部分，而且也有很多好处。

答案解析：

32. C 主旨大意题。题干问的是：第一段描述了什么现象？在公共场合（比如在电梯里，在银行排队，或在飞机上）人们深深地专注于他们的智能手机，或者更糟糕的是，与不舒服的沉默抗争。由此可知，陌生人之间缺乏沟通。A项意为：沉迷于智能手机。B项意为：在公共场所不适当的行为。C项意为：陌生人之间缺乏沟通。D项意为：对缓慢的服务不耐烦。故选C项。

35. C 主旨大意题。整篇文章刚开始介绍了社会的现象（公共场合人们沉迷于智能手机，陌生人之间缺乏沟通交流），接着分析了这一问题的原因，接下来有专家对闲聊进行了研究，最后得出结论，闲聊都有什么样的好处。A项意为：谈话很重要。B项意为：闲聊的方法。C项意为：闲聊的好处。D项意为：不舒服的沉默。

故选C项。

（六）篇章结构题

篇章结构题的考查对象是整个篇章或其中的某个段落。考查同学们在理解全文的基础上对文章所描述事件的发展顺序、所说明事物的结构层次或在论述观点过程中使用的论证方法进行推测、归纳和总结的能力。在解答此类题目之前，有必要对全篇或被考查的段落进行通读以了解其大意。在高考阅读题中，这是一种较为新颖的考查方式，已经成为一种独立的题型。

篇章结构题的题干表现形式：

1. The passage is organized in order of ________.

2. Which of the following shows the structure of the passage?

3. What is most likely to be discussed in the paragraph that follows?

4. How does the passage develop?

1. 技巧方法一

考查对文章整体结构的把握，关键在于找出篇章或段落中表示层次发展的关键词，如表示时间、方位、因果关系或对比的关联词等。一般可通过仔细阅读文章，并根据其内在逻辑关系及内容来进行判断。

作者为文，有脉可循。文章绝不是互不相干的句子杂乱无章的堆砌。理清文章脉络，把握语篇实质。这就要求学生不但要理解文章的细节内容，还要把握文章的整体结构和行文脉络，即句与句、段与段之间的逻辑关系，切忌只注重词和句的理解而忽视对语篇结构的分析。

2. 技巧方法二

对于推测出作者接下来要叙述的事件或将要发表的观点题，要在正确理解篇章内容的基础上对文章的发展做出合理的推断。这些推断往往不是凭空臆断，需要重点依据篇章最后一段（特别是最后一句话）做出判断。作者总会给读者充分的证据对文章的发展进行推测：或是说明了两个对象中的一个；或是只讲了区别，没讲联系；或是只给出了理论解释，而缺少事例的证明。

合理分析，准确推断。由于题目提问方式较为单一，无非是文章或段落的发展方式，因此解题的关键在于找出文章或段落中表示层次发展的关键词如记叙文以人物为中心，以时间或空间为线索，按事件的发生、发展、结局展开故事；论述文则包含论点、论据、论证三大要素，通过解释、举例来阐述观点。可根据文章的特点，详读细节，以动词、时间、地点、事件、因果等为线索，找出关键词语，在大脑中勾画出一幅完整清晰的文章主题和细节的认知图。

真题回顾·典例·2015陕西·D

The production of coffee beans is a huge, profitable business, but, unfortunately, full-sun production is taking over the industry and bringing about a lot of damage. The change in how coffee is grown from shade-grown production to full-sun production endangers the very existence of, certain animals and birds, and even disturbs the world's ecological balance.

On a local level, the damage of the forest required by full-sun fields affects the area's birds and animals. The shade of the forest trees provides a home for birds and other species（物种）that depend on the trees' flowers and fruits. Full-sun coffee growers destroy this forest home. As a result, many species are quickly dying out.

On a more global level, the destruction of the rainforest for full-sun coffee fields also threatens（威胁）human life. Medical research often makes use of the forests' plant and animal life, and the destruction of such species could prevent researchers from finding cures for certain diseases. In addition, new coffee-growing techniques are poisoning the water locally, and eventually the world's groundwater.

Both locally and globally, the continued spread of full-sun coffee plantations（种植园）could mean the destruction of the rainforest ecology. The loss of shade trees is already causing a slight change in the world's climate, and studies show that loss of oxygen-giving trees also leads to air pollution and global warming. Moreover, the new growing techniques are contributing to acidic（酸性的）soil conditions.

It is obvious that the way much coffee is grown affects many aspects of life, from the local environment to the global ecology. But consumers do have a choice. They can purchase shade-grown coffee whenever possible, although at a higher cost. The future health of the planet and mankind is surely worth more than an inexpensive cup of coffee.

57. Which of the following shows the structure of the whole text?

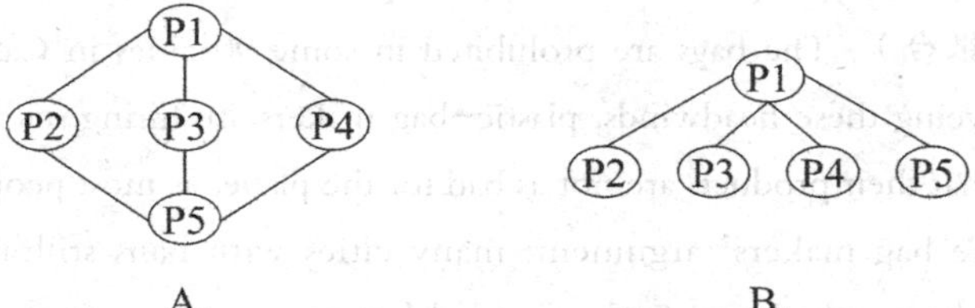

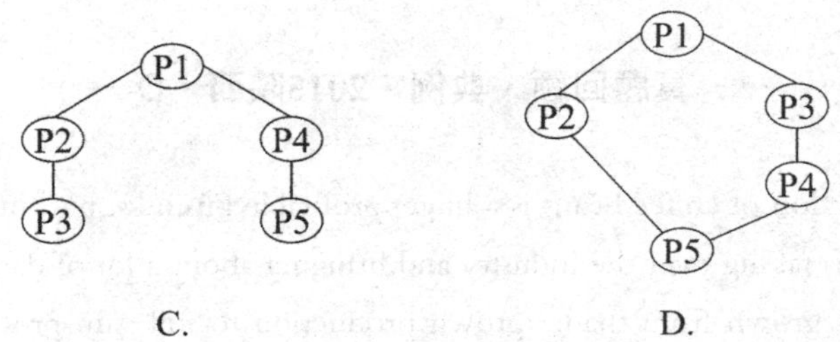

语篇解读：

文章介绍阳光充足的咖啡生产给环境和生态带来的种种危害，呼吁人们不要购买这种咖啡，而要买对环境有利的产品。

答案解析：

57. A　文章结构题。文章第一段介绍阳光充足的咖啡生产的话题，第二、三、四段介绍了阳光充足的咖啡生产带来的破坏，第五段说服人们去购买对环境有利的阴凉处种植的咖啡，所以是总分总的结构，故选A。

五、2019年阅读理解新课标主题语境篇之备考训练

（一）人与自然

人与自然，即人类与环境、动植物的关系，是高考语篇常考的主题类。

真题回顾·Passage 1·2018浙江·B

Steven Stein likes to follow garbage trucks. His strange habit makes sense when you consider that he's an environmental scientist who studies how to reduce litter, including things that fall off garbage trucks as they drive down the road. What is even more interesting is that one of Stein's jobs is defending an industry behind the plastic shopping bags.

Americans use more than 100 billion thin film plastic bags every year. So many end up in tree branches or along highways that a growing number of cities do not allow them at checkouts（收银台）. The bags are prohibited in some 90 cities in California, including Los Angeles. Eyeing these headwinds, plastic-bag makers are hiring scientists like Stein to make the case that their products are not as bad for the planet as most people assume.

Among the bag makers' argument: many cities with bans still allow shoppers to purchase paper bags, which are easily recycled but require more energy to produce and transport. And while plastic bags may be ugly to look at, they represent a small percentage of all garbage on the ground today.

The industry has also taken aim at the product that has appeared as its replacement: reusable shopping bags. The stronger a reusable bag is, the longer its life and the more plastic-bag use it cancels out. However, longer-lasting reusable bags often require more energy to make. One study found that a cotton bag must be used at least 131 times to be better for the planet than plastic.

Environmentalists don't dispute（质疑）these points. They hope paper bags will be banned someday too and want shoppers to use the same reusable bags for years.

24. What has Steven Stein been hired to do?

A. Help increase grocery sales.

B. Recycle the waste material.

C. Stop things falling off trucks.

D. Argue for the use of plastic bags.

25. What does the word "headwinds"in paragraph 2 refer to?

A. Bans on plastic bags.

B. Effects of city development.

C. Headaches caused by garbage.

D. Plastic bags hung in trees.

26. What is a disadvantage of reusable bags according to plastic-bag makers?

A. They are quite expensive.

B. Replacing them can be difficult.

C. They are less strong than plastic bags.

D. Producing them requires more energy.

27. What is the best title for the text?

A. Plastic, Paper or Neither.

B. Industry, Pollution and Environment.

C. Recycle or Throw Away.

D. Garbage Collection and Waste Control.

真题回顾 · Passage 2 · 2018浙江 · C

As cultural symbols go, the American car is quite young. The Model T Ford was built at the Piquette Plant in Michigan a century ago, with the first rolling off the assembly line（装配线）on September 27, 1908. Only eleven cars were produced the next month. But eventually Henry Ford would build fifteen million of them.

Modern America was born on the road, behind a wheel. The car shaped some of the most lasting aspects of American culture: the roadside diner, the billboard, the motel, even the hamburger. For most of the last century, the car represented what it meant to be American—going forward at high speed to find new worlds. The road novel, the road movie, these are the most typical American ideas, born of abundant petrol, cheap cars and a never-ending interstate highway system, the largest public works project in history.

In 1928 Herbert Hoover imagined an America with "a chicken in every pot and a car in every garage". Since then, this society has moved onward, never looking back, as the car transformed America from a farm-based society into an industrial power.

The cars that drove the American Dream have helped to create a global ecological disaster. In America the demand for oil has grown by 22 percent since 1990.

The problems of excessive（过度的）energy consumption, climate change and population growth have been described in a book by the American writer Thomas L. Friedman. He fears the worst, but hopes for the best.

Friedman points out that the green economy（经济）is a chance to keep American strength. "The ability to design, build and export green technologies for producing clean water, clean air and healthy and abundant food is going to be the currency of power in the new century."

28. Why is hamburger mentioned in paragraph 2?

A. To explain Americans' love for travelling by car.

B. To show the influence of cars on American culture.

C. To stress the popularity of fast food with Americans.

D. To praise the effectiveness of America's road system.

29. What has the use of cars in America led to?

A. Decline of economy.

B. Environmental problems.

C. A shortage of oil supply.

D. A farm-based society.

30. What is Friedman's attitude towards America's future?

A. Ambiguous. B. Doubtful.

C. Hopeful. D. Tolerant.

真题回顾·Passage 3·2018天津卷·A

Fire Prevention Information

The University of Adelaide employs a full-time staff of fire prevention professionals. They inspect all campus buildings and test and maintain all sprinkler（喷水灭火装置）systems, fire alarms and fire extinguishers（灭火器）. They also provide educational programs on fire safety in the residence hall. Whenever you move to a new area, you should locate the fire alarm pull stations and the two exits nearest your room.

Fire Alarms

The floors of all campus buildings are equipped with manual（手动的）fire alarm systems which include fire alarm pull stations and pipes. Most are also equipped with automatic fire alarm systems consisting of heat detectors, smoke detectors and sprinklers. For your safety, never tamper with（胡乱摆弄）these systems. False fire alarms are illegal and may lead to imprisonment.

Fire Drills

A fire drill will be conducted in your residence hall every semester. During a fire drill, please do the following

· Take your room key and ID, close and lock the door to your room.

· Exit immediately from the nearest emergency exit; do not use a lift.

· Meet outside of your residence hall and wait for further instructions.

Fire Extinguishers

Fire extinguishers are located on each floor and in each apartment. Use a fire extinguisher only if you have been trained to do so. Irresponsible use of a fire extinguisher can create a dangerous situation for other residents and could result in damage to personal property.

Misuse of a fire extinguisher will result in fines.

Smoke Detector

A smoke detector is on the ceiling in your room. Some buildings also have heat detectors on the ceilings. Do the following to ensure the safe operation of your smoke detector:

· If your smoke detector is working properly, the red light should be on. If the red light is not blinking（闪动）, contact residence hall staff immediately.

· Do not cover or block your smoke detector in any way.

· If a smoke detector sets off an alarm and there is no fire or smoke, inform your hall staff.

36. What is the main duty of the fire prevention professionals?

A. To provide part-time jobs for students.

B. To lead the students to the nearest exits.

C. To check and maintain fire prevention equipment.

D. To train teachers to be fire prevention professionals.

37. What do the automatic fire alarm systems include?

A. Pipes and smoke detectors.

B. Smoke detectors and sprinklers.

C. Fire alarm pull stations and pipes.

D. Sprinklers and fire alarm pull stations.

38. In a fire drill, the students should ________.

A. rush quickly to a lift

B. gather at the nearest exit

C. shut the door and leave at once

D. wait for instructions in the hall

39. What do we know about the use of fire extinguishers?

A. Using them wrongly results in punishment.

B. Irresponsible use of them can damage them.

C. Improper use of them can destroy the apartment.

D. Using them without a trainer present is forbidden.

40. To ensure the safe operation of the smoke detector, one should ________.

A. contact the hall staff regularly

B. cover the things that burn easily

C. start the smoke detector in a fire

D. make certain the red light is working

真题回顾 · Passage 4 · 2018天津 · D

Give yourself a test. Which way is the wind blowing? How many kinds of wildflowers can be seen from your front door? If your awareness is as sharp as it could be, you'll have no trouble answering these questions.

Most of us observed much more as children than we do as adults. A child's day is filled with fascination, newness and wonder. Curiosity gave us all a natural awareness. But distinctions that were sharp to us as children become unclear; we are numb（麻木的）to new stimulation（刺激）, new ideas. Relearning the art of seeing the world around us is quite simple, although it takes practice and requires breaking some bad habits.

The first step in awakening senses is to stop predicting what we are going to see and feel before it occurs. This blocks awareness. One chilly night when I was hiking in the Rocky Mountains with some students, I mentioned that we were going to cross a mountain stream. The students began complaining about how cold it would be. We reached the stream, and they unwillingly walked ahead. They were almost knee-deep when they realized it was a hot spring. Later they all admitted they'd felt cold water at first.

Another block to awareness is the obsession（痴迷）many of us have with naming things. I saw bird watchers who spotted a bird, immediately looked it up in field guides, and said, a "ruby-crowned kinglet" and checked it off. They no longer paid attention to the bird and never learned what it was doing.

The pressures of "time" and "destination" are further blocks to awareness. I encountered many hikers who were headed to a distant camp-ground with just enough time to get there before dark. It seldom occurred to them to wander a bit, to take a moment to see what's around them. I asked them what they'd seen. "Oh, a few birds," they said. They seemed bent on their destinations.

Nature seems to unfold to people who watch and wait. Next time you take a walk, no matter where it is, take in all the sights, sounds and sensations. Wander in this frame of mind and you will open a new dimension to your life.

51. According to Paragraph 2, compared with adults, children are more ________.

A. anxious to do wonders

B. sensitive to others' feelings

C. likely to develop unpleasant habits

D. eager to explore the world around them

52. What idea does the author convey in Paragraph 3?

A. To avoid jumping to conclusions.

B. To stop complaining all the time.

C. To follow the teacher's advice.

D. To admit mistakes honestly.

53. The bird watchers' behavior shows that they ________.

A. are very patient in their observation

B. are really fascinated by nature

C. care only about the names of birds

D. question the accuracy of the field guides

54. Why do the hikers take no notice of the surroundings during the journey?

A. The natural beauty isn't attractive to them.

B. They focus on arriving at the camp in time.

C. The forest in the dark is dangerous for them.

D. They are keen to see rare birds at the destination.

55. In the passage, the author intends to tell us we should ________.

A. fill our senses to feel the wonders of the world

B. get rid of some bad habits in our daily life

C. open our mind to new things and ideas

D. try our best to protect nature

真题回顾 · Passage 5 · 2018北京卷 · C

Plastic-Eating Worms

Humans produce more than 300 million tons of plastic every year. Almost half of that winds up in landfills（垃圾填埋场）, and up to 12 million tons pollute the oceans. So far there is no effective way to get rid of it, but a new study suggests an answer may lie in the stomachs of some hungry worms.

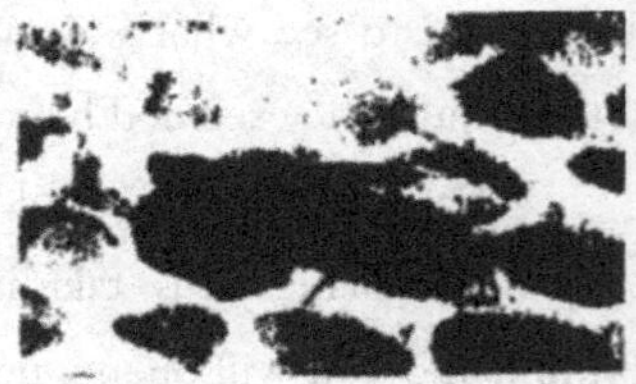

gesater wax moth

Researchers in Spain and England recently found that the worms of the greater wax moth can break down polyethylene, which accounts for 40% of plastics. The team left 100 wax worms on a commercial polyethylene shopping bag for 12 hours, and the worms consumed and broke down about 92 milligrams, or almost 3% of it. To confirm that the worms' chewing alone was not responsible for the polyethylene breakdown, the researchers made some worms into paste（糊状物）and applied it to plastic films. 14 hours later the films had lost 13% of their mass — apparently broken down by enzymes（酶）from the worms' stomachs. Their findings were published in *Current Biology* in 2017.

Federica Bertocchini, co-author of the study, says the worms' ability to break down their everyday food — beeswax — also allows them to break down plastic. "Wax is a complex mixture, but the basic bond in polyethylene, the carbon-carbon bond, is there as well," she explains, "The wax worm evolved a method or system to break this bond."

Jennifer DeBruyn, a microbiologist at the University of Tennessee, who was not involved in the study, says it is not surprising that such worms can break down polyethylene. But compared with previous studies, she finds the speed of breaking down in this one exciting. The next step, DeBruyn says, will be to identify the cause of the breakdown. Is it an enzyme produced by the worm itself or by its gut microbes (肠道微生物)?

Bertocchini agrees and hopes her team's findings might one day help employ the enzyme to break down plastics in landfills. But she expects using the chemical in some kind of industrial process — not simply "millions of worms thrown on top of the plastic".

43. What can we learn about the worms in the study?

A. They take plastics as their everyday food.

B. They are newly evolved creatures.

C. They can consume plastics.

D. They wind up in landfills.

44. According to Jennifer DeBruyn, the next step of the study is to ________.

A. identify other means of the breakdown

B. find out the source of the enzyme

C. confirm the research findings

D. increase the breakdown speed

45. It can be inferred from the last paragraph that the chemical might ________.

A. help to raise worms

B. help make plastic bags

C. be used to clean the oceans

D. be produced in factories in future

46. What is the main purpose of the passage?

A. To explain a study method on worms.

B. To introduce the diet of a special worm.

C. To present a way to break down plastics.

D. To propose new means to keep eco-balance.

真题回顾·Passage 6·山东省泰安市2018届高三第二次模拟·B

It was Groundhog Day. A winter storm had hit overnight too. I tried to open my backdoor only to find six inches of wet, heavy snow piled up against it. I knew I had quite a job of shoveling out ahead of me, so I reached over to grab my snow shovel. It looked a lot more ready to work than I did. I sighed and pulled on my boots, gloves, and heavy coat.

The wind chill was below zero and cut into my face as I slowly shoveled off my deck. After that I stayed my way over to my daughter's house shoveling the path as I walked. It took a while to get her driveway clear and I knew I still had a lot to do. Next came the paths down the hill to my own cars covered in snow. I had grabbed the broom to sweep them off as well. I winced when the breeze blew the swept snow back into my face. Then I started to shovel out my driveways. My back was aching as I worked. I wished I could be building a snowman instead of shoveling. Winter sure had seemed a lot more fun when I was a boy.

When I was done I examined my work. It didn't look half bad. I smiled and looked at the woods covered in white. They were such a special sight. I leaned on my shovel and took it all in. Then I started up the hill with the snow shovel in one hand and the broom in the other. Suddenly, an urge came over me and I dropped them both. I spread my arms, fed back into the blanket of white and happily moved my arms and legs to make an angel in the snow.

As you go through the seasons of this life take joy in your work. Take joy in your life. Remember that the course of your days rests in your own hands.

25. What's the theme of the text?

A. Enjoy winter work. B. Take things seriously.

C. Take joy in your life. D. Fight against cold.

26. Which is the correct order of what the author shoveled?

A. His deck—his daughter's driveway—his cars—his driveway.

B. His cars—his deck—his daughter's driveway—his driveway.

C. His daughter's driveway—his deck—his driveway—his cars.

D. His driveway—his daughter's driveway—his cars—his deck.

27. What can we conclude about the author from Paragraph 3?

A. He was not satisfied with his work.

B. He was absorbed in the snow sight.

C. He was fond of making snowmen.

D. He was in low spirits after work.

真题回顾·Passage 7·湖北省2018届高三5月联考·C

To eat only a vegan（素食的） diet might sound difficult, especially with many popular dishes containing meat or other animal products. Yet in 2017, veganism was described as "the fastest-growing lifestyle movement" in the UK, according to BBC news.

A study by a UK market research organization, suggests that over 542,000 Brits went vegan during the previous decade, an increase of 360%. And the main force behind this increase was those aged 15 ~ 34 years old—42% of recent vegans fall under that age range.

So why exactly has veganism become so popular among young Brits?

One reason could be that many young people want to protect the environment, as less meat consumption is known to be beneficial to the environment. Global meat manufacturing is believed to cause 18% of the world's greenhouse gas emissions（排放）, even more than that of all the world's cars, trains and planes combined. Another reason is that many of today's young people believe that it's wrong to kill animals to be used as food.

Jess Murray, 22, a student at University College London, said that he chose to become vegan after realizing that eating animals is a choice that people make, rather than something that we need to do to survive. "Becoming vegan was an ethical（道德的）decision," he told the *Guardian*.

Social media is also believed to have given rise to the increase in veganism. Platforms such as Facebook allow young vegans to connect with each other much easier, while others such as Instagram have led to the creation of "vegan celebrities（名人）", who share lips on vegan lifestyles.

Despite the rising of veganism, Laura Wyness, an expert in diet and nutrition, said that meat is very important for people's health. "A strict vegan diet makes it difficult to get some minerals and vitamins that your body needs," Wyness told BBC news.

However, the popularity of veganism doesn't seem to be fading. "It feels more like this is something that is sticking." said an expert of the Vegan Society, a UK charity that promotes veganism.

8. What can we learn about veganism, "the fastest-growing lifestyle movement" in UK?

A. It has created many popular dishes.

B. It is backed up mainly by old people.

C. It has led to further market research.

D. It has grown steeply in the past 10 years.

9. The following may account for the increase in veganism EXCEPT ________.

A. young people prefer an environment-friendly life

B. young people want to become ethical celebrities

C. meal manufacturing contributes a lot to the world's greenhouse gas

D. social media allow the vegan message to spread quickly around

10. The underlined word "sticking" in the last paragraph is equal to ________ in meaning.

A. important B. special

C. lasting D. impressive

11. Which of the following will serve as the best title of the passage?

A. Young Brits Going Vegan.

B. Veganism Comes First.

C. How to Start a Vegan Lifestyle.

D. Veganism and the Environment.

真题回顾 · Passage 8 · 湖北省2018届高三5月联考 · D

Some houses are designed to be smart. Others have smart designs. An example of the second type of house won an Award of Excellence from the American Institute of Architects.

Located on the shore of Sullivan's Island off the coast of South Carolina, the award-winning cube-shaped beach house was built to replace one smashed to pieces by Hurricane（飓风）Hugo 10 years ago. Before Hugo, many new houses built along South Carolina's shoreline were poorly constructed, and enforcement of building rules wasn't strict, according to architect Ray Huff, who created the cleverly-designed beach house. Soon after Hugo, all new shoreline houses are required to meet stricter, better-enforced rules. The new beach house on Sullivan's Island should be able to withstand a Level 3 hurricane with peak winds of 179 to 209 kilometers per hour.

At first sight, the house on Sullivan's Island looks anything but hurricane-proof. Its redwood shell makes it resemble "a large party lantern（灯笼）" at night, according to one observer. But looks can be misleading. The house's wooden frame is reinforced with long steel rods to give it extra strength.

To further protect the house from hurricane damage, Huff raised it 2.7 meters off the ground on timber pilings—long, slim wood pieces anchored deep in the sand. Pilings might appear insecure, but they are strong enough to support the weight of the house. They also raise the house above storm waves. The pilings allow the waves to run under the house instead of running into it. "These waves come ashore at terrible speeds and cause most of the damage done to beach-front buildings," said Huff.

Huff designed the timber pilings to be partially hidden by the house's ground-to-roof shell. "The shell masks the pilings so that the house doesn't look like it's standing with its pant legs（裤腿）pulled up," said Huff. In the event of a storm, the shell should break apart and let the waves rush under the house, the architect explained.

12. After the Hurricane Hugo, new houses built along South Carolina's shore line are required ________.

A. to be easily reinforced

B. to meet stricter building standards

C. to look smarter in design

D. to be designed in the shape of cubes

13. Why is the award-winning beach house strong and hurricane-proof?

A. It is in the shape of a shell.

B. It is made of redwood.

C. It is strengthened by steel rods.

D. It is built with timber and concrete.

14. What's the purpose of Huff raising the house 2.7 meters off the ground on timber pilings?

A. To anchor stronger pilings deep in the sand.

B. To prevent water from rushing into the house.

C. To withstand peak winds of about 200 km/hr.

D. To make the house look more hurricane-proof.

15. According to the last paragraph, the main function of the shell is ________.

A. to give the house a better appearance

B. to strengthen the pilings of the house

C. to protect the wooden frame of the house

D. to slow down the speed of the big waves

真题回顾·Passage 9·2018全国III·A

Welcome to Holker Hall & Gardens

Visitor Information

How to Get to Holker

By Car：Follow brown signs an A590 from JB6, M6.Approximate travel times: Windermere—20 minutes, Kendal—25 minutes, Lancaster—45 minutes, Manchester—1 hour 30 minutes.

By Rail: The nearest station is Cark-in-Cartmel with trains to Carnforth, Lancaster Preston for connections to major cities & airports.

Opening Times

Sunday—Friday (closed on Saturday)11:00 a.m.—4:00 p.m. 30 March—2nd November.

Admission Charges

	Hall & Gardens	Gardens
Adults:	£ 12.00	£ 8.00
Groups:	£ 9	£ 5.5

Special Events

Producers Market 13th April

Join us to taste a variety of fresh local food and drinks. Meet the producers and get some excellent recipe ideas.

Holker Garden Festival 30th May

The event celebrates its 22nd anniversary with a great show of the very best of gardening, making it one of the most popular events in gardening.

National Garden Day 28th August

Holker once again opens its gardens in aid of the disadvantaged. For just a small donation you can take a tour with our garden guide.

Winter Market 8th November

This is an event for all the family. Wander among a variety of shops selling gifts while enjoying a live music show and nice street entertainment.

21. How long does it probably take a tourist to drive to Holker from Manchester?

A. 20 minutes. B. 25 minutes.

C. 45 minutes. D. 90 minutes.

22. How much should a member of a tour group pay visit Hall & Gardens?

A. £ 12.00. B. £ 9.00.

C. £ 8.0 D. £ 5.50.

23. Which event will you go to if you want to see a live music show?

A. Producers' Market. B. Holker Garden Festival.

C. National Garden Day. D. Winter Market.

（二）人与自我

生活与学习、做人与做事是人与自我这类主题群语境的常考点。

真题回顾・Passage 1・2018全国Ⅱ・B

Many of us love July because it's the month when nature's berries and stone fruits are in abundance. These colourful and sweet jewels from British Columbia's fields are little powerhouses of nutritional protection.

Of the common berries, strawberries are highest in vitamin C, although, because of their seeds, raspberries contain a little more protein（蛋白质）, iron and zinc (not that fruits have much protein). Blueberries are particularly high in antioxidants（抗氧化物质）. The yellow and orange stone fruits such as peaches are high in the carotenoids we turn into vitamin A and which are antioxidants. As for cherries（樱桃）, they are so delicious who cares? However, they are rich in vitamin C.

When combined with berries of slices of other fruits, frozen bananas make an excellent base for thick, cooling fruit shakes and low fat "ice cream". For this purpose, select ripe bananas for freezing as they are much sweeter. Remove the skin and place them in plastic bags or containers and freeze. If you like, a squeeze of fresh lemon juice on the bananas will prevent them turning brown. Frozen bananas will last several weeks, depending on their ripeness and the temperature of the freezer.

If you have a juicer, you can simply feed in frozen bananas and some berries or sliced fruit. Out comes a "soft-serve" creamy dessert, to be eaten right away. This makes a fun activity for a children's party; they love feeding the fruit and frozen bananas into the top of the machine and watching the ice cream come out below.

24. What does the author seem to like about cherries?

A. They contain protein.

B. They are high in vitamin A.

C. They have a pleasant taste.

D. They are rich in antioxidants.

25. Why is fresh lemon juice used in freezing bananas?

A. To make them smell better.

B. To keep their colour.

C. To speed up their ripening.

D. To improve their nutrition.

26. What is "a juicer" in the last paragraph?

A. A dessert. B. A drink.

C. A container. D. A machine.

27. From which is the text probably taken?

A. A biology textbook. B. A health magazine.

C. A research paper. D. A travel brochure.

真题回顾 · Passage 2 · 2018天津卷 · B

When I was 17, I read a magazine article about a museum called the McNay, once the home of a watercolorist named Marian McNay. She had requested the community to turn it into a museum upon her death. On a sunny Saturday, Sally and I drove over to the museum. She asked, "Do you have the address? " "No, but I'll recognize it, there was a picture in the magazine. "

"Oh, stop. There it is!"

The museum was free. We entered, excited. A group of people sitting in the hall stopped talking and stared at us.

"May I help you?" a man asked. "No," I said. "We're fine." Tour guides got on my nerves. What if they talked a long time about a painting you weren't that interested in? Sally had gone upstairs. The people in the hall seemed very nosy（爱窥探的）, keeping their eyes on me with curiosity. What was their problem? I saw some nice sculptures in one room. Suddenly I sensed a man standing behind me. "Where do you think you are?" he asked. I turned sharply. "The McNay Art Museum!" He smiled, shaking his head. "Sorry, the McNay is on New Braunfels Street." "What's this place?" I asked, still confused. "Well, it's our home." My heart jolted（震颤）. I raced to the staircase and called out, "Sally! Come down immediately!"

"There's some really good stuff（艺术作品）up there." She stepped down, looking confused. I pushed her toward the front door, waving at the family, saying, "Sorry, please forgive us, you have a really nice place." Outside, when I told Sally what happened, she covered her mouth, laughing. She couldn't believe how long they let us look around without saying anything.

The real McNay was splendid, but we felt nervous the whole time we were there. Van Gogh, Picasso. This time, we stayed together, in case anything else unusual happened.

Thirty years later, a woman approached me in a public place. "Excuse me, did you ever enter a residence, long ago, thinking it was the McNay Museum?"

"Yes. But how do you know? We never told anyone."

"That was my home. I was a teenager sitting in the hall. Before you came over, I never realized what a beautiful place I lived in. I never felt lucky before. You thought it was a museum. My feelings about my home changed after that. I've always wanted to thank you."

41. What do we know about Marian McNay?

A. She was a painter.

B. She was a community leader.

C. She was a museum director.

D. She was a journalist.

42. Why did the author refuse the help from the man in the house?

A. She disliked people who were nosy.

B. She felt nervous when talking to strangers.

C. She knew more about art than the man.

D. She mistook him for a tour guide.

43. How did the author feel about being stared at by the people in the hall?

A. Puzzled. B. Concerned.

C. Frightened. D. Delighted.

44. Why did the author describe the real McNay museum in just a few words?

A. The real museum lacked enough artwork to interest her.

B. She was too upset to spend much time at the real museum.

C. The McNay was disappointing compared with the house.

D. The event happening in the house was more significant.

45. What could we learn from the last paragraph?

A. People should have good taste to enjoy life.

B. People should spend more time with their family.

C. People tend to be blind to the beauty around them.

D. People tend to educate teenagers at a museum.

真题回顾·Passage 3·2018北京卷·A

My First Marathon（马拉松）

A month before my first marathon, one of my ankles was injured and this meant not running for two weeks, leaving me only two weeks to train. Yet, I was determined to go ahead.

I remember back to my 7th year in school. In my first P.E. class, the teacher required us to run laps and then hit a softball. I didn't do either well. He later informed me that I was "not athletic".

The idea that I was "not athletic" stuck with me for years. When I started running in my 30s, I realized running was a battle against myself, not about competition or whether or not I was athletic. It was all about the battle against my own body and mind. A test of wills!

The night before my marathon, I dreamt that I couldn't even find the finish line. I woke up sweating and nervous, but ready to prove something to myself.

Shortly after crossing the start line, my shoe laces（鞋带）became untied. So I stopped to readjust. Not the start I wanted!

At mile 3, I passed a sign: "GO FOR IT, RUNNERS!"

By mile 17, I became out of breath and the once injured ankle hurt badly. Despite the pain, I stayed the course walking a bit and then running again.

By mile 21, I was starving!

As I approached mile 23, I could see my wife waving a sign. She is my biggest fan. She never minded the alarm clock sounding at 4 a.m. or questioned my expenses on running.

I was one of the final runners to finish. But I finished! And I got a medal. In fact, I got the same medal as the one that the guy who came in first place had.

Determined to be myself, move forward, free of shame and worldly labels（世俗标签）, I can now call myself a "marathon winner".

36. A month before the marathon, the author ________.

A. was well trained　　B. felt scared

C. made up his mind to run　　D. lost hope

37. Why did the author mention the P.E. class in his 7th year?

A. To acknowledge the support of his teacher.

B. To amuse the readers with a funny story.

C. To show he was not talented in sports.

D. To share a precious memory.

38. How was the author's first marathon?

A. He made it. B. He quit halfway.

C. He got the first prize. D. He walked to the end.

39. What does the story mainly tell us?

A. A man owes his success to his family support.

B. A winner is one with a great effort of will.

C. Failure is the mother of success.

D. One is never too old to learn.

真题回顾 · Passage 4 · 2018北京 · D

Preparing Cities for Robot Cars

The possibility of self-driving robot cars has often seemed like a futurist's dream, years away from materializing in the real world. Well, the future is apparently now. The California Department of Motor Vehicles began giving permits in April for companies to test truly self-driving cars on public roads. The state also cleared the way for companies to sell or rent out self-driving cars, and for companies to operate driverless taxi services. California, it should be noted, isn't leading the way here. Companies have been testing their vehicles in cities across the country. It's hard to predict when driverless cars will be everywhere on our roads. But however long it takes, the technology has the potential to change our transportation systems and our cities, for better or for worse, depending on how the transformation is regulated.

While much of the debate so far has been focused on the safety of driverless cars(and rightfully so), policymakers also should be talking about how self-driving vehicles can help reduce traffic jams, cut emissions (排放) and offer more convenient, affordable mobility options. The arrival of driverless vehicles is a chance to make sure that those vehicles are environmentally friendly and more shared.

Do we want to copy — or even worsen — the traffic of today with driverless cars? Imagine a future where most adults own individual self-driving vehicles. They tolerate long, slow journeys to and from work on packed highways because they can work, entertain themselves or sleep on the ride, which encourages urban spread. They take their driverless car to an appointment and set the empty vehicle to circle the building to avoid paying for parking. Instead of walking a few blocks to pick up a child or the dry cleaning, they send the self-driving minibus. The convenience even leads fewer people to take public transport — an unwelcome side effect researchers have already found in ride-hailing (叫车) services.

A study from the University of California at Davis suggested that replacing petrol-powered private cars worldwide with electric, self-driving and shared systems could reduce carbon emissions from transportation 80% and cut the cost of transportation infrastructure (基础设施) and operations 40% by 2050. Fewer emissions and cheaper travel sound pretty appealing. The first commercially available driverless cars will almost certainly be fielded by ride-hailing services, considering the cost of self-driving technology as well as liability and maintenance issues (责任与维护问题). But driverless car ownership could increase as the prices drop and more people become comfortable with the technology.

Policymakers should start thinking now about how to make sure the appearance of driverless vehicles doesn't extend the worst aspects of the car-controlled transportation system we have today. The coming technological advancement presents a chance for cities and states to develop transportation systems designed to move more people, and more affordably. The car of the future is coming. We just have to plan for it.

47. According to the author, attention should be paid to how driverless cars can ____.

A. help deal with transportation-related problems

B. provide better services to customers

C. cause damage to our environment

D. make some people lose jobs

48. As for driverless cars, what is the author's major concern?

A. Safety. B. Side effects.

C. Affordability. D. Management.

49. What does the underlined word "fielded" in Paragraph 4 probably mean?

A. Employed. B. Replaced.

C. Shared. D. Reduced.

50. What is the author's attitude to the future of self-driving cars?

A. Doubtful. B. Positive.

C. Disapproving. D. Sympathetic.

真题回顾·Passage 5·2018届北京市丰台区高三5月二模·B

Three Feet From Gold

Darby's uncle was caught by the "gold fever" in the gold-rush days, and went west to dig and grow rich. After months of labor, he was rewarded by the discovery of the shining ore（矿石）. He needed machinery to bring the ore to the surface. So, with the "strike", he returned home. And with the help of Darby, he borrowed a lot of money. After buying the machinery and having it shipped, Uncle and Darby went back to work the mine.

The first car of ore was mined. And the returns proved they had one of the richest mines in Colorado! Down went the drills! Up went the hopes of Uncle and Darby!

Then something happened! The vein（矿脉）of gold ore disappeared! They drilled on, but all in vain. Finally, they decided to quit and sold the machinery to a junk man for a few hundred dollars. The junk man called in a mining engineer to look at the mine and do a little calculating. The engineer's calculations showed that the vein would be found just three feet from where the Darbys had stopped drilling! The junk man took millions of dollars in the vein, because he knew enough to seek expert's advice before giving up.

Most of the money which went into the machinery was borrowed through the efforts of Darby, who was then a very young man. The money came from his relatives because of their faith in him. He paid back every dollar of it, although he was years in doing so.

Long afterward, Mr. Darby made another discovery that desire can be changed into gold. This discovery came after he went into the business of selling life insurance. Remembering that he lost a huge fortune, for he stopped three feet from gold, Darby profited by the experience in his chosen work, saying to himself, "I stopped three feet from gold, but I will never stop because men say 'no' when I ask them to buy insurance."

Darby sold more than a million dollars in life insurance annually. He owes his "stickability" to the lesson he learned from his "quitability" in the gold mining business.

40. Darby's uncle went back home to ________.

A. receive his reward　　B. seek financial support

C. look for more helpers　　D. consult an engineer

41. The Darbys failed in mining business because of ________.

A. quitting drilling on

B. the disappearance of the vein

C. the shortage of the machinery

D. competing against the junk man

42. From the passage, we can know Darby ________.

A. was unable to pay off the debts

B. mined his gold from the failure

C. learned a lesson from selling insurance

D. devoted himself to making new discoveries

43. The author intends to tell us that ________.

A. hopes and difficulties exist side by side

B. correct decisions stem from correct judgement

C. we should catch it when an opportunity comes

D. we won't reach our goal unless we persist

真题回顾 · Passage 6 · 2018江苏 · D

Children as young as ten are becoming dependent on social media for their sense of self-worth, a major study warned.

It found many youngsters（少年）now measure their status by how much public approval they get online, often through "like". Some change their behavior in real life to improve their image on the web.

The report into youngsters aged from 8 to 12 was carried out by Children's Commissioner（专员）Anne Longfield. She said social media firms were exposing children to major emotional risks, with some youngsters starting secondary school ill-equipped to cope with the tremendous pressure they faced online.

Some social apps were popular among the children even though they supposedly require users to be at least 13.The youngsters admitted planning trips around potential photo-opportunities and then messaging friends—and friends of friends — to demand "likes" for their online posts.

The report found that youngsters felt their friendships could be at risk if they did not respond to social media posts quickly, and around the clock.

Children aged 8 to 10 were "starting to feel happy" when others liked their posts. However, those in the 10 to 12 age group were "concerned with how many people like their posts", suggesting a "need" for social recognition that gets stronger the older they become.

Miss Longfield warned that a generation of children risked growing up worried about their appearance and image as a result of the unrealistic lifestyles they follow on platforms, and increasingly anxious about switching off due to the constant demands of social media.

She said: "Children are using social media with family and friends and to play games when they are in primary school. But what starts as fun usage of apps turns into tremendous pressure in real social media interaction at secondary school."

As their world expanded, she said, children compared themselves to others online in a way that was "hugely damaging in terms of their self-identity, in terms of their confidence, but also in terms of their ability to develop themselves".

Miss Longfield added: "Then there is this push to connect—if you go offline, will you miss something, will you miss out, will you show that you don't care about those people you are following, all of those come together in a huge way at once."

"For children it is very, very difficult to cope with emotionally." The Children's Commissioner for England's study—Life in Likes—found that children as young as 8 were using social media platforms largely for play.

However, the research—involving eight groups of 32 children aged 8 to 12—suggested that as they headed toward their teens, they became increasingly anxious online.

By the time they started secondary school—at age 11—children were already far more aware of their image online and felt under huge pressure to ensure their posts were popular, the report found.

However, they still did not know how to cope with mean-spirited jokes, or the sense of incompetence they might feel if they compared themselves to celebrities（名人）or more brilliant friends online. The report said they also faced pressure to respond to messages at all hours of the day—especially at secondary school when more youngsters have mobile phones.

The Children's Commissioner said schools and parents must now do more to prepare children for the emotional minefield（雷区）they faced online. And she said social media companies must also "take more responsibility". They should either monitor their websites better so that children do not sign up too early, or they should adjust their websites to the needs of younger users.

Javed Khan, of children's charity Bamardo's, said: "It's vital that new compulsory age-appropriate relationship and sex education lessons in England should help equip children to deal with the growing demands of social media."

"It's also hugely important for parents to know which apps their children are using."

65. Why did some secondary school students feel too much pressure?

A. They were not provided with adequate equipment.

B. They were not well prepared for emotional risks.

C. They were required to give quick responses.

D. They were prevented from using mobile phones.

66. Some social app companies were to blame because ________.

A. they didn't adequately check their users' registration

B. they organized photo trips to attract more youngsters

C. they encouraged youngsters to post more photos

D. they didn't stop youngsters from staying up late

67. Children's comparing themselves to others online may lead to ________.

A. less friendliness to each other

B. lower self-identity and confidence

C. an increase in online cheating

D. a stronger desire to stay online

68. According to Life in Likes, as children grew, they became more anxious to ____.

A. circulate their posts quickly

B. know the qualities of their posts

C. use mobile phones for play

D. get more public approval

69. What should parents do to solve the problem?

A. Communicate more with secondary schools.

B. Urge media companies to create safer apps.

C. Keep track of children's use of social media.

D. Forbid their children from visiting the web.

70. What does the passage mainly talk about?

A. The influence of social media on children.

B. The importance of social media to children.

C. The problem in building a healthy relationship.

D. The measure to reduce risks from social media.

（三）人与社会

社会服务与人际沟通、文学艺术与体育、历史社会与文化、科学与技术是人与社会类主题群语境的常考点。

真题回顾 · Passage 1 · 2018全国III · C

While famous foreign architects are invited to lead the designs of landmark buildings in China such as the new CCTV tower and the National Center for the Performing Arts, many excellent Chinese architects are making great efforts to take the center stage.

Their efforts have been proven fruitful. Wang Shu, a 49-year-old Chinese architect, won the 2012 Pritzker Architecture Prize — which is often referred to as the Nobel Prize in architecture — on February 28. He is the first Chinese citizen to win this award.

Wang serves as head of the Architecture Department at the China Academy of Art (CAA). His office is located at the Xiangshan campus（校园）of the university in Hangzhou, Zhejiang Province. Many buildings on the campus are his original creations.

The style of the campus is quite different from that of most Chinese universities. Many visitors were amazed by the complex architectural space and abundant building types. The curves（曲线）of the buildings perfectly match the rise and fall of hills, forming a unique view.

Wang collected more than 7 million abandoned bricks of different ages. He asked the workers to use traditional techniques to make the bricks into walls, roofs and corridors. This creation attracted a lot of attention thanks to its mixture of modern and traditional Chinese elements（元素）.

Wang's works show a deep understanding of modern architecture and a good knowledge of traditions. Through such a balance, he had created a new type of Chinese architecture, said Tadao Ando, the winner of the 1995 Pritzker Prize.

Wang believes traditions should not be sealed in glass boxes at museums. "That is only evidence that traditions once existed," he said.

"Many Chinese people have a misunderstanding of traditions. They think tradition means old things from the past. In fact, tradition also refers to the things that have been developing and that are still being created," he said.

"Today, many Chinese people are learning Western styles and theories rather than focusing on Chinese traditions. Many people tend to talk about traditions without knowing what they really are," said Wang.

The study of traditions should be combined with practice. Otherwise, the recreation of traditions would be artificial and empty, he said.

28. Wang's winning of the prize means that Chinese architects are ________.

A. following the latest world trend

B. getting international recognition

C. working harder than ever before

D. relying on foreign architects

29. What impressed visitors to the CAA Xiangshan campus most?

A. Its hilly environment. B. Its large size.

C. Its unique style. D. Its diverse functions.

30. What made Wang's architectural design a success?

A. The mixture of different shapes.

B. The balance of East and West.

C. The use of popular techniques.

D. The harmony of old and new.

31. What should we do about Chinese traditions according to Wang?

A. Spread them to the world.

B. Preserve them at museums.

C. Teach them in universities.

D. Recreate them in practice.

真题回顾·Passage 2·2018江苏·B

In the 1760s, Mathurin Roze opened a series of shops that boasted（享有）a special meat soup called consomme. Although the main attraction was the soup, Roze's chain shops also set a new standard for dining out, which helped to establish Roze as the inventor of the modern restaurant.

Today, scholars have generated large amounts of instructive research about restaurants. Take visual hints that influence what we eat: diners served themselves about 20 percent more pasta（意大利面食）when their plates matched their food. When a dark-colored cake was served on a black plate rather than a white one, customers recognized it as sweeter and more tasty.

Lighting matters, too. When Berlin restaurant customers ate in darkness, they couldn't tell how much they'd had: those given extra-large shares ate more than everyone else, but were <u>none the wiser</u>—they didn't feel fuller, and they were just as ready for dessert.

Time is money, but that principle means different things for different types of restaurants. Unlike fast-food places, fine dining shops prefer customers to stay longer and spend. One way to encourage customers to stay and order that extra round: put on some Mozart（莫扎特）.When classical, rather than pop music was playing, diners spent more. Fast music hurried diners out. Particular scents also have an effect: diners who got the scent of lavender（薰衣草）stayed longer and spent more than those who smelled lemon, or no scent.

Meanwhile, things that you might expect to discourage spending—"bad" tables, crowding, high prices — don't necessarily. Diners at bad tables — next to the kitchen door, say — spent nearly as much as others but soon fled. It can be concluded that restaurant keepers need not "be overly concerned about 'bad' tables", given that they're profitable. As for crowds, a Hong Kong study found that they increased a restaurant's reputation, suggesting great food at fair prices. And doubling a buffet's price led customers to say that its pizza was 11 percent tastier.

58. The underlined phrase "none the wiser" in paragraph 3 most probably implies that the customers were ________.

A. not aware of eating more than usual

B. not willing to share food with others

C. not conscious of the food quality

D. not fond of the food provided

59. How could a fine dining shop make more profit?

A. Playing classical music.

B. Introducing lemon scent.

C. Making the light brighter.

D. Using plates of larger size.

60. What does the last paragraph talk about?

A. Tips to attract more customers.

B. Problems restaurants are faced with.

C. Ways to improve restaurants' reputation.

D. Common misunderstandings about restaurants.

真题回顾 · Passage 3 · 2018江苏 · C

If you want to disturb the car industry, you'd better have a few billion dollars: Mom-and-pop carmakers are unlikely to beat the biggest car companies. But in agriculture, small farmers can get the best of the major players. By connecting directly with customers, and by responding quickly to changes in the markets as well as in the ecosystems (生态系统), small farmers can keep one step ahead of the big guys. As the co-founder of the National Young Farmers Coalition (NYFC, 美国青年农会) and a family farmer myself, I have a front-row seat to the innovations among small farmers that are transforming the industry.

For example, take the Quick Cut Greens Harvester, a tool developed just a couple of years ago by a young farmer, Jonathan Dysinger, in Tennessee, with a small loan from a local Slow Money group. It enables small-scale farmers to harvest 175 pounds of green vegetables per hour—a huge improvement over harvesting just a few dozen pounds by hand—suddenly making it possible for the little guys to compete with large farms of California. Before the tool came out, small farmers couldn't touch the price per pound offered by California farms. But now, with the combination of a better price point and a generally fresher product, they can stay in business.

The sustainable success of small farmers, though, won't happen without fundamental changes to the industry. One crucial factor is secure access to land. Competition from investors, developers, and established large farmers makes owning one's own land unattainable for many new farmers.

From 2004 to 2013, agricultural land values doubled, and they continue to rise in many regions.

Another challenge for more than a million of the most qualified farm workers and managers is a non-existent path to citizenship — the greatest barrier to building a farm of their own. With farmers over the age of 65 outnumbering (多于) farmers younger than 35 by six to one, and with two-thirds of the nation's farmland in need of a new farmer, we must clear the path for talented people willing to grow the nation's food.

There are solutions that could light a path toward a more sustainable and fair farm economy, but farmers can't clumsily put them together before us. We at the NYFC need broad support as we urge Congress to increase farmland conservation, as we push for immigration reform, and as we seek policies that will ensure the success of a diverse and ambitious next generation of farms from all backgrounds. With a new farm bill to be debated in Congress, consumers must take a stand with young farmers.

61. The author mentions car industry at the beginning of the passage to introduce ________.

A. the progress made in car industry

B. a special feature of agriculture

C. a trend of development in agriculture

D. the importance of investing in car industry

62. What does the author want to illustrate with the example in paragraph 2?

A. Loans to small local farmers are necessary.

B. Technology is vital for agricultural development.

C. Competition between small and big farms is fierce.

D. Small farmers may gain some advantages over big ones.

63. What is the difficulty for those new farmers?

A. To gain more financial aid.

B. To hire good farm managers.

C. To have farms of their own.

D. To win old farmers' support.

64. What should farmers do for a more sustainable and fair farm economy?

A. Seek support beyond NYFC.

B. Expand farmland conservation.

C. Become members of NYFC.

D. Invest more to improve technology.

真题回顾 · Passage 4 · 2018全国III · D

Adults understand what it feels like to be flooded with objects. Why do we often assume that more is more when it comes to kids and their belongings? The good news is that I can help my own kids learn earlier than I did how to live more with less.

I found the pre-holidays a good time to encourage young children to donate less-used things, and it worked. Because of our efforts, our daughter Georgia did decide to donate a large bag of toys to a little girl whose mother was unable to pay for her holiday due to illness. She chose to sell a few larger objects that were less often used when we promised to put the money into her school fund (基金) (our kindergarten daughter is serious about becoming a doctor).

For weeks, I've been thinking of bigger, deeper questions: How do we make it a habit for them? And how do we train ourselves to help them live with, need, and use less? Yesterday, I sat with my son, Shepherd, determined to test my own theory on this. I decided to play with him with only one toy for as long as it would keep his interest. I expected that one toy would keep his attention for about five minutes, ten minutes, max. I chose a red rubber ball—simple, universally available. We passed it, he tried to put it in his mouth, he tried bouncing it, rolling it, sitting on it, throwing it. It was totally, completely enough for him. Before I knew it an hour had passed and it was time to move on to lunch.

We both became absorbed in the simplicity of playing together. He had my full attention and I had his. My little experiment to find joy in a single object worked for both of us.

32. What do the words "more is more" in paragraph 1 probably mean?

A. The more, the better. B. Enough is enough.

C. More money, more worries. D. Earn more and spend more.

33. What made Georgia agree to sell some of her objects?

A. Saving up for her holiday.

B. Raising money for a poor girl.

C. Adding the money to her fund.

D. Giving the money to a sick mother.

34. Why did the author play the ball with Shepherd?

A. To try out an idea.

B. To show a parent's love.

C. To train his attention.

D. To help him start a hobby.

35. What can be a suitable title for the text?

A. Take It or Leave It. B. A Lesson from Kids.

C. Live More with Less. D. The Pleasure of Giving.

真题回顾 · Passage 5 · 2018浙江卷 · A

In 1812, the year Charles Dickens was born, there were 66 novels published in Britain. People had been writing novels for a century—most experts date the first novel to Robinson Crusoe in 1719—but nobody wanted to do it professionally. The steam-powered printing press was still in its early stages; the literacy（识字）rate in England was under 50%. Many works of fiction appeared without the names of the authors, often with something like "by a lady". Novels, for the most part, were looked upon as silly, immoral, or just plain bad.

In 1870, when Dickens died, the world mourned him as its first professional writer and publisher, famous and beloved, who had led an explosion in both the publication of novels and their readership and whose characters — from Oliver Twist to Tiny Tim— were held up as moral touchstones. Today Dickens' greatness is unchallenged. Removing him from the pantheon（名人堂）of English literature would make about as much sense as the Louvre selling off the *Mona Lisa*.

How did Dickens get to the top? For all the feelings readers attach to stories, literature is a numbers game, and the test of time is extremely difficult to pass. Some 60,000 novels were published during the Victorian age, from 1837 to1901; today a casual reader might be able to name a half-dozen of them. It's partly true that Dickens' style of writing attracted audiences from all walks of life. It's partly that his writings rode a wave of social, political and scientific progress. But it's also that he rewrote the culture of literature and put himself at the center. No one will ever know what mix of talent, ambition, energy and luck made Dickens such a singular writer. But as the 200th anniversary of his birth approaches, it is possible — and important for our own culture—to understand how he made himself a lasting one.

21. Which of the following best describes British novels in the 18th century?

A. They were difficult to understand.

B. They were popular among the rich.

C. They were seen as nearly worthless.

D. They were written mostly by women.

22. Dickens is compared with the *Mona Lisa* in the text to stress ________.

A. his reputation in France

B. his interest in modern art

C. his success in publication

D. his importance in literature

23. What is the author's purpose in writing the text?

A. To remember a great writer.

B. To introduce an English novel.

C. To encourage studies on culture.

D. To promote values of the Victorian age.

真题回顾 · Passage 6 · 2018天津卷 · C

There's a new frontier in 3D printing that's beginning to come into focus: food. Recent development has made possible machines that print, cook, and serve foods on a mass scale. And the industry isn't stopping there.

Food production

With a 3D printer, a cook can print complicated chocolate sculptures and beautiful pieces for decoration on a wedding cake. Not everybody can do that — it takes years of experience, but a printer makes it easy. A restaurant in Spain uses a Foodini to "re-create forms and pieces" of food that are "exactly the same", freeing cooks to complete other tasks. In another restaurant, all of the dishes and desserts it serves are 3D-printed, rather than farm to table.

Sustainability（可持续性）

The global population is expected to grow to 9.6 billion by 2050, and some analysts estimate that food production will need to be raised by 50 percent to maintain current levels. Sustainability is becoming a necessity. 3D food printing could probably contribute to the solution. Some experts believe printers could use hydrocolloids（水解胶体）from plentiful renewables like algae（藻类）and grass to replace the familiar ingredients（烹饪原料）. 3D printing can reduce fuel use and emissions. Grocery stores of the future might stock "food" that lasts years on end, freeing up shelf space and reducing transportation and storage requirements.

Nutrition

Future 3D food printers could make processed food healthier. Hod Lipson, a professor at Columbia University, said, "Food printing could allow consumers to print food with customized nutritional content, like vitamins. So instead of eating a piece of yesterday's bread from the supermarket, you'd eat something baked just for you on demand."

Challenges

Despite recent advancements in 3D food printing, the industry has many challenges to overcome. Currently, most ingredients must be changed to a paste(糊状物) before a printer can use them, and the printing process is quite time-consuming, because ingredients interact with each other in very complex ways. On top of that, most of the 3D food printers now are restricted to dry ingredients, because meat and milk products may easily go bad. Some experts are skeptical about 3D food printers, believing they are better suited for fast food restaurants than homes and high-end restaurants.

46. What benefit does 3D printing bring to food production?

A. It helps cooks to create new dishes.

B. It saves time and effort in cooking.

C. It improves the cooking conditions.

D. It contributes to restaurant decorations.

47. What can we learn about 3D food printing from Paragraph 3?

A. It solves food shortages easily.

B. It quickens the transportation of food.

C. It needs no space for the storage of food.

D. It uses renewable materials as sources of food.

48. According to Paragraph 4, 3D-printed food ________.

A. is more available to consumers

B. can meet individual nutritional needs

C. is more tasty than food in supermarkets

D. can keep all the nutrition in raw materials

49. What is the main factor that prevents 3D food printing from spreading widely?

A. The printing process is complicated.

B. 3D food printers are too expensive.

C. Food materials have to be dry.

D. Some experts doubt 3D food printing.

50. What could be the best title of the passage?

A. 3D Food Printing: Delicious New Technology.

B. A New Way to Improve 3D Food Printing.

C. The Challenges for 3D Food Production.

D. 3D Food Printing: From Farm to Table.

真题回顾 · Passage 7 · 北京市石景山区2018届高三上学期期末考试 · A

"Hi, Mrs. Grady," said Mark when their neighbor opened her door. "Would you like us to shovel（铲） your sidewalk and driveway?" Shoveling was Jamie's idea, a way to earn enough money for the new Ocean Kingdom video game that came out the next day.

Mrs. Grady was happy, "That would be wonderful, boys. I think the job is getting to be too much for me."

"It will cost 10 dollars," Jamie said. "If that's OK," Mark added.

"Oh dear," Mrs. Grady said disappointedly, "I haven't been able to get to the bank. I can offer homemade cookies, but I realize that's not what you had in mind."

Mark was going to say that Mrs. Grady could pay them another time, but Jamie cut him off. "We'll come back later."

Mrs. Grady doesn't look like the person who'd come to Mark's rescue last summer when Mr. Dunn's dog Goldie had just wanted to play, but Mark didn't feel comfortable around big dogs. He wanted to call for help, but his tongue seemed locked behind his teeth. Then Mrs. Grady's front door had flown open. She must have seen him from across the street. "Hold on, Mark. I'm coming!" "Goldie" she'd called. As soon as Goldie had turned her head, Mrs. Grady had slipped between Mark and the dog. She wasn't much taller than Mark, but she'd stood firm as a rock in front of him. "Goldie, go home!" Then she'd swept her broom to hurry the dog along. "Get!" Goldie had obeyed.

When Mark showed thanks to Mrs. Grady, Mrs. Grady laughed. "It was nothing. Good neighbors watch out for each other, don't they?"

And now Mrs. Grady needed Mark as much as he'd needed her last summer. He smiled and waved at Mrs. Grady, then his shovel deep into the snow.

"Hey!" Jamie shouted. "What are you doing?" Mark couldn't explain about Goldie and watching out for neighbors. "I like Mrs. Grady's cookies," he said.

36. Why did Jamie and Mark plan to clear the snow for Mrs. Grady at first?

A. To help the lady. B. To visit New Kingdom.

C. To do volunteer work. D. To earn pocket money.

37. Mrs. Grady couldn't pay them most probably because ________.

A. she didn't have enough cash B. she couldn't find the bank

C. she thought it was worthless D. she couldn't afford it

38. According to the story, which of the following words can be used to describe Mrs. Grady best?

A. Greedy. B. Hopeful.

C. Hardworking. D. Helpful.

39. Which of the following proverb can best summarize the story?

A. A penny saved is a penny earned.

B. Kindness is repaid with kindness.

C. Birds of a feather flock together.

D. Actions speak louder than words.

真题回顾·Passage 8·北京市石景山区2018届高三上学期期末考试·D

There is plenty of complaints about how social media-texting in particular—may be harming children's social and intellectual development. But a new study suggests that constant instant messaging (IM'ing) and texting among teens may also provide benefits, particularly for those who are introverted（内向的）.

British researchers studied instant messages exchanged by 231 teens, aged 14 to 18. All of the participants were "regular" or "extensive" IM'ers. In the U. S., two thirds of teens use instant messaging services regularly, with a full third messaging at least once every day.

The researchers analyzed 150 conversations in the study, and reported the results in the journal *Computers in Human Behavior*. In 100 of these chats, the study participant began IM'ing while in a negative emotional state such as sadness, distress or anger. The rest were conversations begun when the participant was feeling good or neutral. After the chat, participants reported about a 20% reduction in their distress—not enough to completely eliminate it, but enough to leave them feeling better than they had before reaching out.

"Our findings suggest that IM'ing between distressed adolescents and their peers may provide emotional relief and consequently contribute to their well-being," the authors write, noting that prior research has shown that people assigned to talk to a stranger either in real life or online improved their mood in both settings, but even more with IM. And people who talk with their real-life friends online also report feeling closer to them than those who just communicate face-to-face, implying a strengthening of their bond.

Why would digital communication do better than human contact? The reasons are complex, but may have something to do with the fact that users can control expression of sadness and other emotions via IM without exposing emotional elements like tears that some may consider as embarrassing or sources of discomfort. Studies also show that the anonymity（匿名）of writing on a device blankets the users in a sense of safety that may cause people to feel more comfortable in sharing and discussing their deepest and most authentic feelings. The research has shown that expressive writing itself can vent the stress and provide a sense of relief—and doing so, knowing that your words are reaching a sympathetic friend, may provide even more comfort and potentially be therapeutic（治愈的）. Researchers also found that introverted participants reported more relief from IM conversations when they were distressed than extroverts did. Susan Cain, author of Quiet wrote recently for ***TIME***: Introverts are often overfilled with thoughts and care deeply for their friends, family and colleagues. But even the most socially skilled introverts sometimes long for a free pass from socializing or talking on the phone. This is what the Internet offers: the chance to connect—but in measured doses and from behind a screen.

47. Which of the following statements is TRUE according to the passage?

A. Teens are more likely to send instant messages when feeling distressed.

B. Instant messaging can help completely remove teens' negative emotions.

C. Constant instant messaging can help teens control their negative emotions.

D. Chat via instant messaging services makes most participants feel good or calm.

48. The underlined word "vent" in paragraph 5 most probably means ________.

A. control B. maintain

C. reduce D. increase

49. According to the passage, what does the digital communication enable users to do?

A. Find more sympathetic friends.

B. Produce more expressive writings.

C. Share and discuss more information.

D. Avoid embarrassment and discomfort.

50. What can be concluded from the new study by British researchers?

A. Introverted teens may benefit from constant instant messaging.

B. American teens aged 14 to 18 are extensive instant messaging users.

C. Teens feeling bad often feel closer to real-life friends than to the net friends.

D. Instant messaging will prevent children's social and intellectual development.

真题回顾 · Passage 9 · 山东省菏泽市2018届高三上学期期末 · A

The advancement of human civilization is possible just because of enormous contribution made by scientists. They are one of the most influential people of today's world. With practical advantages in engineering, medicine, and technology, they have helped us to grow better understanding about the world and different working phenomenon that governs us. Their names are remembered in the sands of time for their work in the welfare of mankind with different inventions that have made our modern lives easy. Here is a list of the four great scientists we've ever seen who changed the world.

Louis Pasteur (1822—1895)

Pasteur contributed greatly towards the advancement of medical sciences developing cures for rabies, anthrax and other infectious diseases. He also invented the process of pasteurization（加热杀菌法）to make milk safer to drink. He probably saved more lives than any other person.

Otto Hahn (1879—1968)

Hahn was a German chemist who discovered nuclear fission（裂变）in 1939. He was a pioneering scientist in the field of radio-chemistry, and discovered radioactive elements in 1921. He was awarded the Nobel Prize for Chemistry in 1944.

Nikola Tesla (1856—1943)

Tesla worked on electro-magnetism and AC current. He obtained around 300 patents worldwide for his inventions from electricity to radio transmission, but many inventions developed by Tesla were not put into patent protection. He played a key role in the development of modern electricity.

James Clerk Maxwell (1831—1879)

Maxwell made great progress in understanding electro-magnetism. His research in electricity and kinetics laid the foundation for quantum（量子）physics. Einstein said of Maxwell, "The work of James Clerk Maxwell changed the world forever."

1. What contribution did Louis Pasteur make to society?

   A. The development of medicine. B. Radio-chemistry.

   C. Modern electricity. D. Quantum physics.

2. Who was thought highly of by Einstein?

   A. Louis Pasteur. B. Otto Hahn.

   C. Nikola Tesla. D. James Clerk Maxwell.

3. What can we infer about the four people?

   A. They are medical pioneers.

   B. They are Nobel Prize winners.

   C. They are great contributors to society.

   D. They are founders of modern physics.

真题回顾 · Passage 10 · 2018全国I · B

Good Morning Britain's Susanna Reid is used to grilling guests on the sofa every morning, but she is cooking up a storm in her latest role — showing families how to prepare delicious and nutritious meals on a tight budget.

In *Save Money: Good Food*, she visits a different home each week and with the help of chef Matt Tebbutt offers top tips on how to reduce food waste, while preparing recipes for under 5 per family a day. And the Good Morning Britain presenter says she's been able to put a lot of what she's leant into practice in her own home, preparing meals for sons, Sam,14, Finn,13, and Jack, 11.

"We love Mexican churros, so I buy them on my phone from my local Mexican takeaway restaurant", she explains. "I pay £5 for a portion（一份）, but Matt makes them for 26p a portion, because they are flour, water, sugar and oil. Everybody can buy takeaway food, but sometimes we're not aware how cheaply we can make this food ourselves."

The eight-part series（系列节目）, *Save Money: Good Food*, follows in the footsteps of ITV's *Save Money: Good Health*, which gave viewers advice on how to get value from the vast range of health products on the market.

With food our biggest weekly household expense, Susanna and Matt spend time with a different family each week. In tonight's Easter special they come to the aid of a family in need of some delicious inspiration on a budget. The team transforms the family's long weekend of celebration with less expensive but still tasty recipes.

24. What do we know about Susanna Reid?

A. She enjoys embarrassing her guests.

B. She has started a new programme.

C. She dislikes working early in the morning.

D. She has had a light budget for her family.

25. How does Matt Tebbutt help Susanna?

A. He buys cooking materials for her.

B. He prepares food for her kids.

C. He assists her in cooking matters.

D. He invites guest families for her.

26. What does the author intend to do in paragraph 4?

A. Summarize the previous paragraphs.

B. Provide some advice for the readers.

C. Add some background information.

D. Introduce a new topic for discussion.

27. What can be a suitable title for the text?

A. Keeping Fit by Eating Smart.

B. Balancing Our Daily Diet.

C. Making Yourself a Perfect Chef.

D. Cooking Well for Less.

参考答案

(一)人与自然

真题回顾·Passage 1·2018浙江·B

语篇解读:

文章分析了几种购物袋的使用情况，塑料袋造成了环境问题，尽管纸袋容易回收，但生产和运输需要更多的能源，希望消费者使用耐用可重复使用的袋子。

答案解析:

24. D 细节理解题。根据第一段one of Stein's jobs is defending an industry behind the plastic shopping bags和第二段plastic-bag makers are hiring scientists like Stein to make the case that their products are not as bad for the planet as most people assume，可知塑料袋生产商雇用Steven Stein是为了证明他们的产品并不像大多数人想象的那样对地球有害，是对塑料袋被禁用的解释和争论。故选D。

25. A 词义猜测题。上文介绍在美国许多大城市塑料袋被禁用，看到这种现状，塑料袋生产商雇用Steven Stein等科学家是为了证明他们的产品并不像大多数人想象的那样对地球有害。headwinds意为“逆风”，此处指塑料袋被禁用的现状，即Bans on plastic bags，故选A。

26. D 细节理解题。根据第四段However, longer-lasting reusable bags often require more energy to make.可知，塑料袋生产商认为生产耐用且能重复使用的袋子需要更多的能量，故选D。

27. A 标题归纳题。文章讲述了使用塑料袋造成的环境问题，纸袋容易回收，但生产和运输需要更多的能源，希望消费者使用耐用可重复使用的袋子。对这三种方式进行了对比，“Plastic, Paper or Neither”既能概括全文，又能吸引读者，最适合作为标题。故选A。

名师点睛:

概括主旨的方法是：先看首尾或各段开头再看全文找主题句，若无明显主题句，就通过关键词句来概括(如议论文中寻找表达作者观点态度的词句，要看懂全文的主要内容，明白了主要内容就能准确概括文章标题。第27题要求概括标题，本文讲述了使用塑料袋造成的环境问题，纸袋容易回收，但生产和运输需要更多的能源，希望消费者使用耐用可重复使用的袋子。对这三种方式进行了对比，Plastic, Paper or Neither既能概括全文，又能吸引读者，适合作为标题。

真题回顾·Passage 2·2018浙江·C

语篇解读：

文章讲述了汽车在美国经济和文化上的重要作用，也指出了汽车带来的环境问题。

答案解析：

28. B 推理判断题。根据第二段Modern America was born on the road, behind a wheel. The car shaped some of the most lasting aspects of American culture: the roadside diner, the billboard, the motel, even the hamburger.可知现代美国诞生于公路和汽车，汽车塑造了美国文化最持久的一些方面。Hamburger就是汽车塑造的美国文化的一个方面。用这个例子是说明汽车对美国文化的影响，故选B。

29. B 细节理解题。根据第四段The cars that drove the American Dream have helped to create a global ecological disaster.可知美国汽车的迅速发展，导致生态灾难。故选B。

30. C 推理判断题。根据倒数第二段中的He fears the worst, but hopes for the best. 和最后一段中的Friedman points out that the green economy（经济）is a chance to keep American strength.可知Friedman虽然对未来担心，但抱有好的希望，他指出了发展绿色经济的想法。可见Friedman对未来是充满希望的，故选C。

名师点睛：

细节理解题具体方法：①略读材料，大概了解原文，掌握中心或主旨。②按文章的体裁，作者写作的组织模式及有关的信息词，如for example、first、second等预测应该到何处寻找自己所需要的事实。③将精力放在寻找你所需要的细节上。快速通篇跳读，全文扫视，找到细节出处，待找到有细节的句子时，放慢速度，仔细核对比较内容，直至找到答案。如第28题要求分析第二段提到hamburger的作用，根据第二段Modern America was born on the road, behind a wheel. The car shaped some of the most lasting aspects of American culture: the roadside diner, the billboard, the motel, even the hamburger.可知现代美国诞生于公路和汽车，汽车塑造了美国文化最持久的一些方面。Hamburger就是汽车塑造的美国文化的一个方面。用这个例子是说明汽车对美国文化的影响。

真题回顾·Passage 3·2018天津卷·A

语篇解读：

本文是一篇说明文。文章主要从火警、消防训练、灭火器和烟雾探测器的使用等方面介绍了一些防火信息。

答案解析：

36. C　细节理解题。根据文章第一段They inspect all campus buildings and test and maintain all sprinkler（喷水灭火装置）systems, fire alarms and fire extinguishers（灭火器）.可知，专职消防人员主要职责是检查、测试和维护所有的校园建筑物防火装备。故选C。

37. B　细节理解题。根据文章Fire Alarms中的句子Most are also equipped with automatic fire alarm systems consisting of heat detectors, smoke detectors and sprinklers.可知，火灾自动报警系统由热探测器、烟雾探测器和喷头组成。故选B。

38. C　细节理解题。根据文章Fire Drills中的句子Take your room key and ID, close and lock the door to your room.和Exit immediately from the nearest emergency exit, do not use a lift.可知，在消防演习中，学生锁好门并立即从最近的紧急出口离开。故选C。

39. A　细节理解题。根据文章Fire Extinguishers中的句子Misuse of a fire extinguisher will result in fines.可知，误用灭火器会导致罚款。故选A。

40. D　细节理解题。根据文章Smoke Detector中的句子If your smoke detector is working properly, the red light should be on. If the red light is not blinking（闪动），contact residence hall staff immediately.可知，烟雾探测器是否安全运行，看红灯是否闪动。故选D。

名师点睛：文章内容较为简单，集中考查细节题，对此类题型，考生可以首先从问题中找到关键词然后以此为线索，运用略读及查阅的技巧在文中迅速寻找这一细节，找到后再把这一部分内容仔细阅读一遍，仔细比较所给选项与文中细节的细微区别。如第38题中C选择项中leave at once与文中的Exit immediately表达同一个意思；第39题中考生要理解文中fines（罚款）是A选择项中punishment（惩罚）的一种，这些都需要考生比较它们之间的细微区别。

真题回顾·Passage 4·2018天津·D

语篇解读：

本文是一篇散文。我们有多久没有仔细观察我们周围的世界了。作者通过此文告诉我们：要放慢脚步，带着我们所有的感官来感受周围世界的奇妙。

答案解析：

51. D　推理判断题。根据文章第二段Most of us observed much more as children than we do as adults.可知，与成人相比较，孩子观察得更多，从而可以推断出孩子更急于探索他们周围的世界。故选D。

52. A　推理判断题。根据文章第三段作者叙述在一个寒冷的夜晚，作者和学生徒步旅行穿过一条小溪的时候，学生们抱怨水太冷而不愿往前走，结果事实上那是一个温泉。作者举这样一个事例是为了向读者传递这样的观念：避免过早下结论。故选A。

53. C　细节理解题。根据文章第四段全段及首句Another block to awareness is the obsession（痴迷）many of us have with naming things.可知，鸟观察者发现鸟后只关心鸟的名字，并不关心它在做什么。故选C。

54. B　细节理解题。根据文章第五段I encountered many hikers who were headed to a distant camp-ground with just enough time to get there before dark. It seldom occurred to them to wander a bit, to take a moment to see what's around them.可知，徒步旅行者只关心及时到达目的地，而很少关心周围的事物。故选B。

55. A　推理判断题。文章作者想要通过此文告诉我们：大自然只展现给那些善于观察和等待的人，带着我们所有的感官来感受周围世界的奇妙。

名师点睛：

本文是一篇散文阅读。整个文章行文自由，不拘一格，对考生来说阅读有一定的难度。但我们只需要抓住贯穿全文的主线：大自然只展现给那些善于观察和等待的人，就不难理解全文大意了。文章考查细节理解题和推理判断题，考生需要根据文中事实和线索做出判断和推理。

真题回顾·Passage 5·2018北京卷·C

语篇解读：

本文是一篇科普知识类文章。从环保理念出发，文章围绕一种可以降解塑料的虫子大蜡螟展开，描述了研究进展及虫子能降解塑料的原理，即使用其胃中的酶降解塑料，为解决塑料污染问题提供了新的思路。

答案解析：

43. C　细节理解题。根据文章第二段中的“The team left 100 wax worms on a commercial polyethylene shopping bag for 12 hours, and the worms consumed and broke down about 92 milligrams, or almost 3% of it.”可知，这些虫子可以消耗聚乙烯购物袋，即塑料袋。故选C。

44. B　推理判断题。根据文章倒数第二段中的“The next step, DeBruyn says, will be to identify the cause of the breakdown. Is it an enzyme produced by the worm itself or by its gut microbes (肠道微生物)？”可知，下一步是探究酶的来源。故选B。

45. D　推理判断题。根据文章最后一段But she expects using the chemical in some kind of industrial process—not simply “millions of worms thrown on top of the plastic.”可知，研究者希望那些化学物品可以批量生产，而不是将许多虫子直接扔在垃圾堆

里。故选D。

46. C　写作意图题。全文都在围绕可以降解垃圾的虫子展开，文章的目的就是向读者呈现这种独特的降解塑料的方式。故选C。

名师点睛：

环保理念的科普类说明文历来是高考阅读理解命题的重点。文章围绕酶降解塑料，为解决塑料污染问题提供了新的思路。对一些专业词汇作了多处中文注释，降低了考生的阅读难度。最后一小题考查主旨大意，为文章选择最好的标题。考生做此题时一定要注意选择项必须要能概括整个文章的内容，不能以偏概全。如A、B、D选择项在文章中都有所涉及，但不足以概括全文，所以需要考生正确概括全文的主旨大意。

真题回顾·Passage 6·山东省泰安市2018届高三第二次模拟·B

语篇解读：

本文是一篇记叙文。本文通过讲述作者在扫雪的过程中，情不自禁欣赏雪景的经历，说明了要在生活中寻找快乐。

答案解析：

25. C　细节理解题。由最后一段As you go through the seasons of this life take joy in your work. Take joy in your life. Remember that the course of your days rests in your own hands.可知，这篇文章的主题是在你的生活中获得快乐，选C。

26. A　细节理解题。由第二段The wind chill was below zero and cut into my face as I slowly shoveled off my deck. After that I stayed my way over to my daughter's house shoveling the path as I walked. It took a while to get her driveway clear and I knew I still had a lot to do. Next came the paths down the hill to my own cars covered in snow. I had grabbed the broom to sweep them off as well. I winced when the breeze blew the swept snow back into my face. Then I started to shovel out my driveways. 可知，作者铲雪的先后顺序是：他的露天平台——女儿的车道——他自己的汽车——他的车道，故选A。

27. B　推理判断题。第三段中I smiled and looked at the woods covered in white. They were such a special sight. I leaned on my shovel and took it all in. Then I started up the hill with the snow shovel in one hand and the broom in the other. Suddenly，an urge came over me and I dropped them both. I spread my arms，fed back into the blanket of white and happily moved my arms and legs to make an angel in the snow. 描写了作者忍不住欣赏雪景，表现了内心的一种喜悦，可推知作者全神贯注欣赏雪景，选B。

名师点睛：

本文是叙事性的文章，文章有一定的趣味性，整体难度中等，主要考查细节理解和推理判断两类题型。推理判断题属于主观性较强的高层次阅读理解题，做这类题目时，同学们要严格依据作者所陈述的细节、事实以及作者的措辞、态度和语气，找出能够表露作者思想倾向和感情色彩的词句，然后利用自己已获得的相关知识进行推理判断，从而得出符合逻辑的结论。

真题回顾 · Passage 7 · 湖北省2018届高三5月联考 · C

语篇解读：

本文为夹叙夹议文章。英国市场研究组织的一项研究表明，过去的十年里素食主义在英国增长迅猛。这一增长的主要力量是那些年龄在15～34岁的年轻人。素食主义在英国的年轻人中非常流行的原因可能是由于肉类加工排放的热量大过世界上所有的汽车、火车和飞机的总和，他们认为杀死动物用作食物是不对的，年轻人想要保护环境。另外，社会媒体的参与也导致了年轻素食者的增加。

答案解析：

8. D　细节理解题。根据文章可知，素食主义主要是爱护动物、不吃动物肉的，所以A是错误的。由第二段的内容可知，素食主义者主要是15～34岁的年轻人，所以B是错误的。事件引起进一步的市场调查的原因不一定是它的增长快（the fastest-growing），故C是错误的。由第二段A study by a UK market research organization, suggests that over 542,000 Brits went vegan during the previous decade, an increase of 360%.可知，英国市场研究表明，在过去的十年里，素食主义者的人数增长了360%，增长迅猛，符合题干中的“the fastest-growing”，故选D项。

9. B　细节理解题。根据第四段的内容可知，一个原因可能是许多年轻人想要保护环境，因为少吃肉对环境有益。世界18%的温室效应被认为由全球肉类食品制造业造成的。由此可知，A不符合题意，B符合题意。根据第五段最后一句“Becoming vegan was an ethical（道德的）decision,”他们认为素食是道德上的决定，及第六段可知，社交媒体也被认为是导致素食主义增加的原因之一，因而出现了一些所谓的素食名人来分享他们的生活方式，可知素食主义者的增加不是因为他们想成为道德名人，而是分享素食主义让他们成为“名人”，这不是素食快速发展的原因，因此B符合题意。

10. C　猜测词义题。最后一段 However, the popularity of veganism doesn't seem to be fading. “It feels more like this is something that is sticking.” 前面说素食主义的流行似乎并没有消退，因此可推断出后一句意思是反而会持续下去。故sticking意为“持续”，分析选项可知，C项（lasting）意为“持久的，持续的”符合题意，故选

C项。

11. A　主旨大意题。通读全文可知，本文主要讲述过去的十年里素食主义人数在英国增长迅猛。这一增长的主要群体是那些年龄在15～34岁的年轻人。素食主义在英国年轻人中非常流行的原因可能是年轻人想要保护环境，社会媒体的参与也导致了素食者的增加。分析选项可知A项（年轻的英国人选择素食主义）符合题意，故选A项。

名师解读：

主旨大意题的解题技巧：一篇文章都是围绕着一个中心思想或一个话题展开的，因此，有的文章中最明显的特点之一是有一个反复出现的中心词，即高频词，也叫作主题词。抓住了它，便容易抓住文章的中心思想。

真题回顾·Passage 8·湖北省2018届高三5月联考·D

语篇解读：

本文为记叙文。位于南卡罗来纳州海岸的沙利文岛海滨一座玲珑的小屋以其独特的设计获得大奖。这座房子既抗风防浪，又美观坚固，实乃经典之作。

答案解析：

12. B　细节理解题。根据第二段倒数第二句Soon after Hugo, all new shoreline houses are required to meet stricter, better-enforced rules.可知，在飓风造成严重的人员伤亡和巨大的损失后，新建房屋应该符合严格的建筑规定。分析选项可知，B项（满足更严格的建筑标准）符合题意，故选B项。

13. C　细节理解题。根据第三段和第四段的内容可知，沙利文岛上的建筑获奖了。而沙利文岛上的房子乍一看不像是抗飓风的，但外表可能会误导人。房子的木制框架用长的钢棒加固，以赋予它额外的强度。为了进一步保护房屋免受飓风破坏，在地面上树起2.7米高的木头桩，深深地扎在沙子里。它们足够坚固，足以支撑房屋的重量。飓风来时波浪在房子下面，却不会冲进房子。由此可见，沙利文岛上的房子抗飓风就是由于钢棒的支撑。分析选项可知C项正确。

14. B　此题属于细节理解中的语言转述题型。这是一类间接事实细节题，答案与题目在意义上运用了词义之间的转述关系，即正确选项是原文有关词语和句子的另一种表达。根据第四段中的“The pilings allow the waves to run under the house instead of running into it.”可判断出，之所以这么做的目的是防止大水冲入房屋中。（答案定位）题干：What's the purpose of Huff raising the house 2.7 meters off the ground on timber pilings? 文章内容：allow the waves to run under the house instead of running into it. （推理关系）答案：instead of running into it对应B选项To prevent water from rushing into the house。

名师点睛:

细节理解题之语言转述型。这是一类间接事实细节题，答案与题目在意义上运用了词义之间的转述关系，即正确选项是原文有关词语和句子的另一种表达。通常这类细节题的正确选项有以下特征：（1）对原文句子中的关键词进行替换。把原文中的一些词换成意义相近的词，成为正确选项。（2）词性或者语态的变化。把原文中的一些词变换一下词性，或者改变原文句子的语态，给考生制造障碍。（3）语言简化。把原文中的复杂语言现象进行简化，使之成为正确答案。（4）正话反说。把原文中的意思反过来表达而成为正确选项（适用于寻找错误选项的题目）。本题属于把原文中的关键词进行了替换。把allows the wave to run under the house instead of running into it替换成To prevent water from rushing into the house，成为正确的选项。

15. A　细节理解题。由第四段内容可知房屋是建在木桩上的。最后一段内容为：Huff设计的木桩被房子从地面到屋顶的贝壳所隐藏，贝壳遮盖了木桩，这样房子看起来就比原来的外观好看多了，分析选项可知A项正确。

真题回顾 · Passage 9 · 2018全国III · A

语篇解读:

该文章为旅游指南。主要介绍了去Holker Hall & Gardens 旅游的相关信息，如出行方式、开放时间、旅行费用以及主要活动等。

答案解析:

21. D　细节理解题。根据第一段How to Get to Holker中By car部分Approximate travel times后面内容可知，从Manchester到Holker要用1 hour and 30 minutes，即90分钟，故选D。

22. B　细节理解题。根据Admission Charges可知，团体中的一员去Hall & Gardens 需要支付9英镑。

23. D　细节理解题。根据文章最后一段Winter Market中最后一句Wander among a variety of shops selling gifts while enjoying a live music show and nice street entertainment.可知，如果想看现场表演需要去Winter Market。故选D。

名师点睛:

文章主题和中心思想的阐述往往需要大量细节信息的支持，这些细节对于理解全文内容至关重要，同时也是归纳和概括文章中心思想的基础。命题人往往要求考生根据不同的要求阅读文章，以获得某些特定的信息，或准确地寻求所需的细节，并对细节进行直接或间接辨认和理解。文章细节的理解可以细化为：（1）一一对应型。（2）语言转述型。（3）语意理解型。（4）是非辨别型。（5）事实排序型。

此阅读理解题中的三个题目全为细节理解题。细节理解题首先要根据题干准确定位信息句，其次要对信息句进行准确的理解和判断，如第一题为转述型，1 hour and 30 minutes，即90分钟。第二题和第三题则为简单的一一对应型，只要找到信息句即可得出答案。

（二）人与自我

真题回顾 · Passage 1 · 2018全国II · B

语篇解读：

本文是一篇日常生活类说明文。文中讲述了人们热爱水果丰盛的七月，这时候各种水果营养丰富且含有对人体有益的微量元素，尤其是香蕉。我们可以利用它做一些孩子喜欢的甜点或冰激凌。

答案解析：

24. C　细节理解题。题干问的是，作者喜欢樱桃什么。根据第二段中As for cherries (樱桃), they are so delicious who cares?（至于樱桃，因为它们很好吃谁在乎呢?）可知，作者在乎的是它的美味。故选C。

25. B　细节理解题。根据第三段中的If you like, a squeeze of fresh lemon juice on the bananas will prevent them turning brown.可知，往香蕉上滴新鲜的柠檬汁是为了防止香蕉变成褐色，故新鲜的柠檬汁是被用来保持香蕉颜色的。故选B。

26. D　词义猜测题。根据最后一段中they love feeding the fruit and frozen bananas into the top of the machine and watching the ice cream come out below可知，孩子们喜欢把一些水果和冷冻的香蕉放入这台机器的上部，然后看到冰激凌从下面出来。故可以推出a juicer是一台机器。故选D。

27. B　文章出处题。文章首先指出七月是水果盛产的季节，并指出各种水果富含的营养，最后一段指出我们可以用a juicer为孩子们做一些甜点和冰激凌，故本文最可能是从健康杂志上摘取的文章。A项意为：一本生物教科书；B项意为：一本健康杂志；C项意为：一篇研究论文；D项意为：一本旅游手册。故选B。

名师点睛：

做词义猜测题时我们要注意观察划线单词的构成结构。如本文划线的单词是juicer，我们都知道“er”是单词的后缀。它既可以表示人，又可以表示物。如cleaner既可以表示清洁工，又可以表示清洁工具。根据下文的意思，可以判断出本篇阅读第三题中的a juicer表示物。

真题回顾 · Passage 2 · 2018天津卷 · B

语篇解读：

本文是一篇记叙文。文章作者和朋友原想参观McNay博物馆，在她们参观的时候，发现很多人奇怪地看着她，最后才发现自己误将一个私人住宅当成McNay博物馆。30年后，一位女士认出误撞入自己住宅的作者，指出正是因为作者的误撞入才让她意识到自己住的地方有多么美丽。

答案解析：

41. A　细节理解题。根据文章第一段When I was 17, I read a magazine article about a museum called the McNay, once the home of a watercolorist named Marian McNay.可知，Marian McNay是一名水彩画家。故选A。

42. D　细节理解题。根据文章第四段“May I help you?” a man asked. “No,” I said. “We're fine.” Tour guides got on my nerves.可知，导游令作者心烦，作者误认为屋子里的男人是位导游。故选D。

43. A　推理判断题。根据文章第四段The people in the hall seemed very nosy（爱窥探的）, keeping their eyes on me with curiosity. What was their problem?（大厅里的人看起来都非常爱窥探的，都好奇地看着我。他们有什么问题？）可以推断出，作者当时感到困惑不解。故选A。

44. D　推理判断题。根据全文可知，作者的着墨点主要在叙述参观误当成McNay博物馆的私人住宅上，这才是文章的重心，所以将真正的McNay博物馆叙述一带而过。故选D。

45. C　推理判断题。根据文章最后一段Before you came over, I never realized what a beautiful place I lived in.可知，在作者未造访她家之前，这位女士从未意识到自己住的地方有多么美丽，从而可以推断出，人们往往对周围的美视而不见。故选C。

名师点睛：

本文是叙事性的文章，文章有一定的趣味性，整体难度中等，主要考查细节理解和推理判断两类题型。推理判断题属于主观性较强的高层次阅读理解题，做这类题目时，同学们要严格依据作者所陈述的细节、事实以及作者的措辞、态度和语气，找出能够表露作者思想倾向和感情色彩的词句，然后利用自己已获得的相关知识进行推理判断，从而得出符合逻辑的结论。如第43题中考查作者被人盯着看的感受，我们需要找到文章中作者的措辞nosy、curiosity和problem，由此可以推断出作者当时非常困惑不解的心理感受。

真题回顾·Passage 3·2018北京卷·A

语篇解读：

本文是一篇故事类文章。作者讲述了没有运动天赋的他，在20多岁才开始长跑，在跑马拉松比赛前夕他踝关节受伤，但他坚持不懈，最终实现自我的故事。

36. C　细节理解题。根据文章第一段中的“Yet, I was determined to go ahead”可知，作者在马拉松前一个月下定决心要参加马拉松比赛。故选C。

37. C　写作意图题。根据文章第二段中的“He later informed me that I was ‘not athletic’”可知，作者的经历证明他在运动方面并没有天赋。故选C。

38. A　细节理解题。根据文章倒数第二段“I was one of the final runners to finish. But I finished! And I got a medal. In fact, I got the same medal as the one that the guy who came in first place had.”以及前文中作者行进经过的标志可知，虽然作者是最后到达终点的一批马拉松选手，但是他跑完了全程。故选A。

39. B　主旨大意题。根据文章最后一段“Determined to be myself, move forward, free of shame and worldly labels（世俗标签）, I can now call myself a ‘marathon winner’.”可知，作者享受到了战胜自我的快乐，认为只要努力了就算是胜利者。故选B。

名师点睛：

本文考查了细节题。在完成细节题时，要特别注意排除干扰项。干扰项的设置通常有以下几种方式：

（1）张冠李戴。命题者把文章作者的观点与他人的观点混淆起来，题干问的是作者的观点，选项中出现的却是他人的观点；或者题干问的是他人的观点，却把作者的观点放到选项中去。

（2）偷梁换柱。干扰项用了与原文相似的句型结构和大部分相似的词汇，却在不易引人注意的地方换了几个词汇，造成句意的改变。

（3）无中生有。干扰项往往是生活的基本常识和普遍接受的观点，但在原文中并无相关的信息支持点，这种选项的设置往往与问题的设问毫不相干。

（4）以偏概全。考生在做猜测文章中心思想、给文章添加标题或判断推理题时，往往会犯以偏概全的错误。产生这类错误的原因是考生受思维定势的影响或考虑不周，以局部代替整体。其具体表现为合理关联与不合理关联、准确概括与不准确概括之间的错位。不合理关联就是表层理解与深层理解相混淆。表层理解是对文章中客观事实的感知和记忆，往往是文章直接表述的结论；深层理解则是对文章中的客观事实进行逻辑推理、总结或概括后得出的结论。不准确概括是指不能准确地按题目要求概括或提取文中的表层或深层信息。

真题回顾 · Passage 4 · 2018北京 · D

语篇解读：

本文是一篇社会生活类文章。文章围绕无人驾驶汽车展开，展示了无人驾驶汽车的美好前景以及其必将到来的趋势，呼吁政府采取措施，使无人驾驶汽车为人们的生活带来更多积极的影响。

答案解析：

47. A 细节理解题。根据文章第一段中的"But however long it takes, the technology has the potential to change our transportation systems and our cities, for better or for worse, depending on how the transformation is regulated"以及后文中作者所描述的这些汽车带来的有利影响可知，作者认为我们应该注意如何让这些汽车来帮助我们解决与交通有关的问题。故选A。

48. D 细节理解题。根据文章第一段中的"But however long it takes, the technology has the potential to change our transportation systems and our cities, for better or for worse, depending on how the transformation is regulated"可知，无人驾驶汽车的普及将带领社会走向何方，取决于这段过渡期。除此之外，倒数第二段中也提到了政府对汽车降价带来的汽车数量上升的对策。而A、B、C在文中均未提到。故选D。

49. A 词义猜测题。联系上下文，"考虑到无人驾驶技术的可靠性和责任与维护问题，第一批商用无人驾驶汽车几乎会被全部投放到打车行业"。故选A。

50. B 作者态度题。由文章的最后一段以及文章很大篇幅都在讲无人驾驶汽车的优点可知，作者对无人驾驶汽车怀有积极态度。故选B。

名师点睛：

做细节理解类题型一定要关注文章中的functional words，比如，but、however、so、otherwise、therefore、besides、because等，答案往往就出现在这些功能性词汇的前后。在阅读训练中，加强对此类词汇在上下文语境中的理解，体会此类词汇的作用。

真题回顾 · Passage 5 · 2018届北京市丰台区高三5月二模 · B

语篇解读：

本文是一篇记叙文。Darby的叔叔发现了金矿，在Darby和亲戚的帮助下买到了钻探设备，但金矿脉消失了，他们只好把设备卖给了一个旧货商。旧货商找到一个采矿工程师去看矿井，发现Darby只差3英尺就能钻探到金矿。后来Darby从事销售人寿保险业务，由于有前车之鉴，他坚持不放弃，终于成功了。作者想告诉我们，除非我们坚持下去，否则我们无法实现我们的目标。

答案解析：

40. B　推理判断题。根据第一段So, with the "strike", he returned home. And with the help of Darby, he borrowed a lot of money.可知，Darby的叔叔回到家寻求资金支持。故答案为B。

41. A　推理判断题。根据第三段中They drilled on, but all in vain. Finally, they decided to quit and sold the machinery to a junk man for a few hundred dollars.可知，在采矿业务上失败了，因为他们放弃了钻探。故答案为A。

42. B　推理判断题。根据倒数第二段最后一句"I stopped three feet from gold, but I will never stop because men say 'no' when I ask them to buy insurance."和最后一段第一句Darby sold more than a million dollars in life insurance annually.可知，Darby从失败中挖掘出了他人生的金子。故答案为B。

43. D　推理判断题。根据最后一段He owes his "stickability" to the lesson he learned from his "quitability" in the gold mining business.可知，作者想告诉我们，除非我们坚持下去，否则我们无法实现我们的目标。故答案为D。

名师点睛：

推理判断题要求在理解原文文字信息的基础上，做出一定的推理判断，从而得到文章的隐含意义和深层意义。推理判断题所涉及的内容可能是文中的某一句话，也可能是某几句话，所以，推理题的答案只能根据原文文字信息推出，即对原文某一句话或某几句话所做的同义改写或综合。比如第42题，根据倒数第二段最后一句"I stopped three feet from gold, but I will never stop because men say 'no' when I ask them to buy insurance."和最后一段第一句Darby sold more than a million dollars in life insurance annually.可知，Darby从失败中挖掘出了他人生的金子，因为他从上次失败中学到了永不放弃，故答案为B。

真题回顾·Passage 6·2018江苏·D

语篇解读：

本文是一篇新闻报道，主要就"点赞中的人生"的项目研究分析了社交媒体和中学生面临的压力二者之间的关系，以及社交媒体对孩子们带来的多重影响。

65. B　细节理解题。根据第三段"...social media firms were exposing children to major emotional risks, with some youngsters starting secondary school ill-equipped to cope with the tremendous pressure they faced online." 社交媒体公司让孩子们面临重大的情感风险，一些青少年在中学时就没有能力应对他们在网上面临的巨大压力可知，中学生还没有对情感风险做好充分的准备，所以他们感到压力巨大，故选B项。

66. A　细节理解题。根据第四段"Some social apps were popular among the

children even though they supposedly require users to be at least 13”可知，尽管一些社交应用程序应该要求用户至少13岁，但是很受孩子们欢迎，一些社交应用软件公司没有严格按照年龄限制，也就是说它们没有严格检查用户注册，所以它们应该受到责备，故选A项。

67. B　细节理解题。根据第九段As their world expanded, she said, children compared themselves to others online in a way that was “hugely damaging in terms of their self-identity, in terms of their confidence, but also in terms of their ability to develop themselves”.可知，从孩子们的自我认同、自信心以及他们的发展能力方面来看，这是“极大的破坏性”，所以孩子们在网上比较自己和别人可能导致他们较低的自我认同和自信，故选B项。

68. D　推理判断题。根据第十二段和十三段的“By the time they started secondary school—at age 11—children were already far more aware of their image online and felt under huge pressure to ensure their posts were popular”可知，他们要确保他们的帖子是受欢迎的，所以他们很担心要获得更多的认可，故选D项。

69. C　细节理解题。根据第十五段“The Children's Commissioner said schools and parents must now do more to prepare children for the emotional minefield (雷区) they faced online.”以及第十七段“It's also hugely important for parents to know which apps their children are using.”可知，学校和父母现在必须做更多的准备让孩子们面对他们所面临的情感雷区，所以父母要时刻关注孩子们的社交问题，故选C项。

70. A　主旨大意题。纵观全文，文章就社交媒体给中学生带来的重大压力分析了社交媒体和中学生面临的压力二者间的关系，以及给孩子们所带来的影响，故选A项。

名师点睛：

作者态度及写作意图推断题型。每一篇文章都会包含作者的某种观点和态度，只不过有的直截了当，有的含而不露，有的通过所用词语的褒贬来体现。此类题可细分为作者态度题(表明作者的好恶)和作者观点题(表明作者对某事物的看法)。准确把握作者的情感和态度，需要注意以下几点：

（1）作者对某一事物的看法，要么支持,要么反对,带中立色彩的词最不可能是正确答案。

（2）漠不关心类词语往往不对，作者既然写文章就不会不关心。

（3）不要把自己的态度揉入其中，也要区分作者的态度和作者引用别人的态度。

（4）当作者的态度没有明确表示时，要学会根据作者使用词语的褒贬性来判断。

（5）作者的观点一般与文章的主旨相关联。

（6）绝对化或语气过于强烈的选项常常是错误的。

比如第70题，本文主要介绍了社交媒体给孩子们所带来的影响和压力，故选A。

（三）人与社会

真题回顾·Passage 1·2018全国Ⅲ·C

语篇解读：

这是一篇新闻报道。文章主要报道了中国建筑设计师王澍在其作品中融合中国传统建筑文化，获得了建筑界的诺贝尔奖——普利策奖，这让中国建筑得到了国际上的认可。

答案解析：

28. B　推理判断题。根据文章第二段的内容可知，王澍获得2012年普利策奖，而普利策奖相当于建筑界的诺贝尔奖，他是第一个获此奖的中国人，故推知中国建筑现在得到了国际上的认可。故B项正确。

29. C　细节理解题。根据文章第四段对CAA校园的描述可知，它的设计风格独特，与大多数中国大学的校园不同，许多游客对复杂的建筑空间和丰富的建筑类型感到吃惊，故C项正确。

30. D　细节理解题。根据文章第六段1995年普利策奖的获得者Tadao Ando的评语可知，王澍设计的成功之处是把中国传统元素融入现代设计，并保持两者的和谐，故D项正确。

31. D　推理判断题。根据文章最后一段和倒数第三段中In fact, tradition also refers to the things that have been developing and that are still being created可知，传统的研究要与实践相结合，在实践中进行再创造，否则就会是人工的和空洞的，故D项正确。

名师点睛：

根据事实细节，推断合理信息。推理题要求在理解原文文字信息的基础上，做出一定判断和推论，从而得到文章的隐含意义和深层意义。推理题所涉及的内容可能是文中某一句话，也可能是某几句话，但做题的指导思想都是以文字信息为依据，既不能做出在原文中找不到文字根据的推理，也不能根据表面文字信息做过多推理。也就是说，要做到判断有据，推论有理，忠实原文。切忌用自己的观点代替作者的本意，切忌片面思考，得出片面结论。

本篇阅读的第1小题和第4小题为推理判断题。第1题根据第二段第二句可知Wang Shu 获得2012年普利策奖，相当于建筑界的诺贝尔奖，再根据第三句他是第一个获此奖的中国人可知，中国建筑现在得到了国际上的认可，因得到认可才能获奖。此题的解题关键是根据原文的两个信息句进行判断，而A、C、D在原文中没有提及。

真题回顾·Passage 2·2018江苏·B

语篇解读：

本文是一篇议论文。论述了现代餐馆面临的经营困境和解决方案，通过对比快餐店和正规餐馆提出，现代餐饮业可以通过味道（比如薰衣草相比柠檬更能刺激消费者的食欲）、灯光的明暗（比如暗的灯光更能够刺激顾客食欲）等吸引顾客。

答案解析：

58. A 词义猜测题。根据该句中“...they didn't feel fuller, and they were just as ready for dessert”可知，他们没有感觉更饱，想要再吃一点甜点；据此可以判断，划线的词表示“他们没有意识到比平时吃得多”，故选A项。

59. A 细节理解题。根据第四段第三、四句“One way to encourage customers to stay and order that extra round: put on some Mozart (莫扎特). When classical, rather than pop music was playing, diners spent more.”可知，在餐馆播放古典音乐能延长顾客在餐馆的时间，从而促进餐馆赢得更多的利润，故选A项。

60. D 段意归纳题。通读尾段可知，该段第一句“Meanwhile, things that you might expect to discourage spending — 'bad' tables, crowding, high prices — don't necessarily”为该段的主题句；结合全段内容可知，该段主要论述了人们对餐馆的常见误解，故选D项。

名师点睛：

文章最后一段的首句常常是主旨大意和段落主题句所在。本文中，尤其是最后一段Meanwhile这样的关键词和破折号的提醒，很容易让学生找出答案所在。

真题回顾·Passage 3·2018江苏·C

语篇解读：

比文章主要阐述了美国小农场主所特有的优势，同时也分析了目前美国农业所面临的问题，比如美国农业目前很多人不愿意卖地，且60岁以上农民的数量远远高出年轻农民。

答案解析：

61. B 推理判断题。根据文章第一段“If you want to disturb the car industry, you'd better have a few billion dollars: Mom-and-pop carmakers are unlikely to beat the biggest car companies. But in agriculture, small farmers can get the best of the major players.”提到汽车行业，小型汽车制造商不太可能打败最大的汽车公司。然而农业就不一样了，小农场也能成为主导，由此可知，作者开篇提到汽车行业，目的是引起下文，说明了农业特色，故选B项。

62. D 推理判断题。文章第二段通过事例来证明第一段“... small farmers can

keep one step ahead of the big guys." 小农场也可能会超过大型农场可知，小农场也可能比大农场先占领先机，故选D项。

63. C 细节理解题。根据第三段"Competition from investors, developers, and established large farmers makes owning one's own land unattainable for many new farmers." 来自投资者、开发商和老牌大农场主的竞争使得许多新农民无法拥有自己的土地，可知对于新型农民来说要拥有自己的土地，即自己的农场还是困难重重的，故选C项。

64. A 细节理解题。根据最后一段"We at the NYFC need broad support as we urge Congress to increase farmland conservation, as we push for immigration reform, and as we seek policies that will ensure the success of a diverse and ambitious next generation of farmers from all backgrounds. With a new farm bill to be debated in Congress, consumers must take a stand with young farmers." 可知，除了敦促国会增加耕地，在推动移民改革的同时，寻求确保不同背景、雄心勃勃的下一代农民成功的政策，农民应该为更可持续、更公平的农业经济寻求更多的支持，故选A项。

名师点睛：

本文第61、62题属于推理判断题型。推理判断题属于主观性较强的高层次阅读理解题。做这类题时，应在理解全文的基础上，从文章本身所提供的信息出发，运用逻辑思维，同时借助一定的常识进行分析、推理、判断。一定要从整体上把握语篇内容，在语篇的表面意义与隐含意义、已知信息与未知信息之间架起桥梁，透过字里行间，去体会作者的弦外之音和言外之意。

真题回顾 · Passage 4 · 2018全国III · D

语篇解读：

这是一篇夹叙夹议的文章。文章讲述作者引导孩子主动捐献玩具，并从玩简单玩具中获得快乐的做法。

答案解析：

32. A 词义猜测题。根据文章第一段最后一句"... I can help my own kids learn earlier than I did how to live more with less" 可以推断出，人们通常认为越多越好。故选A。

33. C 细节理解题。根据文章第二段中She chose to sell a few larger objects that were less often used when we promised to put the money into her school fund(基金)可知，当我们承诺给她把卖玩具的钱放到她的教育基金里时，她同意卖玩具。故选C。

34. A 细节理解题。根据文章最后一段最后一句My little experiment to find joy in a single object worked for both of us.可知，跟Shepherd玩球是为了测试自己的一种

想法是否可行。故选A。

35. C　主旨大意题。根据文章第一段可知，作者想要教会孩子how to live more with less，而第二、三段是作者的尝试，故C适合做标题。

名师点睛：

高考中词义推断可以是一个单词的意义推断，也可以是一个短语或句子的意义推断，既可以是生词意义，也可以是熟词新意；还可以是对替代词所替代内容的判断。在阅读理解题中，所考查的词或短语的意义往往不停留在字面上，要根据短文提供的语境，通过阅读上下文，根据已知的信息或常识来推测尚不熟悉的词或词组的含义。词义猜测主要的解题策略有：语境猜词、语法猜词和常识猜词。

语境即上下文。由于上下文中的生词不是孤立存在的，其词义与句中其他词的词义或具体的语境有着密切的联系。因此在阅读过程中，许多生词的词义可以充分利用上下文中相关的单词、短语并结合具体的语境来推测。本阅读理解中第1题为词义猜测题。根据文章第一段的第三句The good news is that I can... 可以推断出，前后语义相反，后句中是live more with less，所以前句应该是“越多越好”的意思。

真题回顾 · Passage 5 · 2018浙江卷 · A

语篇解读：

本文写于Charles Dickens诞辰200周年前夕，介绍了Charles Dickens在英国小说方面的重要贡献和深远影响。

答案解析：

21. C　细节理解题。根据第一段对当时情况的描写nobody wanted to do it professionally. The steam-powered printing press was still in its early stages; the literacy（识字）rate in England was under 50%. Many works of fiction appeared without the names of the authors... Novels, for the most part, were looked upon as silly, immoral, or just plain bad.印刷技术落后，人们识字率低，作品上没有作者名字，小说被认为是愚蠢的、不道德的，毫无价值可言。故选C。

22. D　推理判断题。根据第二段Dickens' greatness is unchallenged和列举的Charles Dickens小说的影响可知，把他和*Mona Lisa*相比是为了说明Charles Dickens在英国小说方面的重要性和*Mona Lisa*在绘画方面的重要性是一样的，故选D。

23. A　写作意图题。根据文中对Charles Dickens及其作品在英国小说史上重要性的描写，和文章最后But as the 200th anniversary of his birth approaches, it is possible — and important for our own culture—to understand how he made himself a lasting one. 可知本文写于Charles Dickens诞辰200周年前夕，由此可知作者写本文是为了纪念这位伟大的作家。故选A。

名师点睛：

推理判断题要求在理解表面文字的基础上，做出判断和推论，从而得到文章隐含的意思和深层的意思，也就是通过文章中的文字信息，上下逻辑关系及事物的发展变化等已知信息，推断出作者没有直接表达的态度和观点。

本文推理判断题的考法：

（1）推测文章的观点或结论。第21题要求判断18世纪英国小说的现状，根据第一段对当时情况的描写nobody wanted to do it professionally. The steam-powered printing press was still in its early stages; the literacy rate in England was under 50%.Novels, for the most part, were looked upon as silly, immoral, or just plain bad.可知，当时印刷技术落后，人们识字率低，小说被认为是愚蠢的、不道德的，毫无价值可言。

（2）推测作者写作目的或意图。第23题判断本文的写作目的，根据文中对Charles Dickens及其作品在英国小说史上重要性的描写，和文章最后But as the 200th anniversary of his birth approaches, it is possible — and important for our own culture—to understand how he made himself a lasting one.可知，本文写于Charles Dickens诞辰200周年前夕，由此推断作者写本文是为了纪念这位伟大的作家。

真题回顾 · Passage 6 · 2018天津卷 · C

语篇解读：

本文是一篇科普类短文阅读。文章主要介绍了3D打印技术在食物上的应用取得了进展，但目前仍面临着许多方面的挑战。

答案解析：

46. B　推理判断题。根据文章Food production中叙述了没有经验的人可以用3D打印机做出复杂的巧克力雕塑和美丽的婚礼蛋糕，以及餐厅能够用3D打印出所有的菜肴和甜点，从而可以推断出3D打印的优势是节省了做饭的时间和精力。故选B。

47. D　细节理解题。根据文章第三段Some experts believe printers could use hydrocolloids (水解胶体) from plentiful renewables like algae(藻类) and grass to replace the familiar ingredients(烹饪原料).可知，3D打印机可以使用可再生材料作为食物来源。故选D。

48. B　推理判断题。根据文章第四段Food printing could allow consumers to print food with customized nutritional content, like vitamins.（食品打印可以让消费者打印定制营养的食物），从而可以推断出3D打印出来的食物可以满足个人营养需求。故选B。

49. C　细节理解题。根据文章最后一段most of the 3D food printers now are restricted to dry ingredients, because meat and milk products may easily go bad可知，阻止

3D打印食物进一步广泛使用的原因是原料必须是干的，含水多的肉和牛奶不能应用于3D打印因为很容易坏。故选C。

50. A 主旨大意题。文章主要介绍了3D打印技术在食物上的应用取得了进展，但目前仍面临着许多方面的挑战。所以适合用3D Food Printing: Delicious New Technology作为标题。故选A。

名师点睛：

科普类说明文历来是高考阅读理解命题的重点。本文内容是关于3D打印技术在食物方面的应用，文章运用了一些小标题，对一些专业词汇做了中文注释，降低了考生阅读的难度。文章逻辑性强，条理清楚，主要考查学生对语篇的整体把握和领悟能力以及对特定细节的认读和处理能力。最后一道题考查主旨大意，为文章选择恰当的标题。考生做此题时一定要注意选项必须要概括整个文章的内容，不能以偏概全。如B、C、D选项在文章中都有所涉及，但不足以概括全文，所以需要考生正确概括全文的主旨大意。

真题回顾·Passage 7·北京市石景山区2018届高三上学期期末考试·A

语篇解读：

本文通过Jamie 和 Mark为 Mrs. Grady清理雪的故事，告诉人们“善以善报答”。

答案解析：

36. D 细节理解题。根据第一段中Shoveling was Jamie's idea, a way to earn enough money for the new Ocean Kingdom video game that came out the next day.可知，Jamie 和 Mark 计划为 Mrs. Grady 清理雪是为了挣零花钱。故选D。

37. A 推理判断题。根据第四段中I haven't been able to get to the bank. I can offer homemade cookies, but I realize that's not what you had in mind. 可知，Mrs. Grady不能付给他们钱，因为她没有现金。故选A。

38. D 推理判断题。根据倒数第四段Mrs. Grady had slipped between Mark and the dog. She wasn't much taller than Mark, but she'd stood firm as a rock in front of him. "Goldie, go home!" Then she'd swept her broom to hurry the dog along. "Get!" Goldie had obeyed.可知，Mrs. Grady乐于助人。故选D。

39. B 推理判断题。根据倒数第四段Mrs. Grady had slipped between Mark and the dog. She wasn't much taller than Mark, but she'd stood firm as a rock in front of him. "Goldie, go home!" Then she'd swept her broom to hurry the dog along. "Get!" Goldie had obeyed. Mrs. Grady曾经帮助过Mark。再根据最后两段中now Mrs. Grady needed Mark as much as he'd needed her last summer. He smiled and waved at Mrs. Grady, then his shovel deep into the snow... "I like Mrs. Grady's cookies," he said. Mrs. Grady需要有

人帮助清理雪，但是手里没有现金，只有饼干，Mark愿意清理。这个故事让我们懂得“善以善报答”。故选B。

名师点睛：

本篇阅读理解中设置了三个判断推理题型，要掌握做此类题型的技巧，具体而言，我们要做到：

首先，抓住文章的主题和细节，分析文章结构，根据上下文的内在联系，挖掘文章的深层含义。在进行推理时，一定要仔细阅读，千万不可脱离原文主观臆断。

其次，对于暗含在文章中的人物的行为动机、事件的因果关系以及作者未言明的倾向等进行合乎逻辑的判断、推理、分析，抓住材料的实质。

再次，在解答推理性问题时，要清楚所要解答的问题是针对某个细节进行推断，还是针对主题思想、作者的意图进行推断。如果是针对细节的推断可迅速在阅读材料中确定推理依据的位置或范围，然后再进行推理判断。针对主题思想做推断时，其解题的主要依据是文章的主题思想，然后再分析句子之间的逻辑关系，要区分观点与例证、原因与结果、主观点与次观点。

真题回顾 · Passage 8 · 北京市石景山区2018届高三上学期期末考试 · D

语篇解读：

很多人抱怨社交媒介尤其是短信可能影响孩子社交能力的发展，但是新的研究表明，经常编辑短信可能还会对青少年尤其是性格内向的青少年有益。

答案解析：

47. A　推理判断题。根据第三段第二句In 100 of these chats, the study participant began IM’ing while in a negative emotional state such as sadness, distress or anger.可知，在所研究的150份对话中，有100份以消极的状态开头，可以推断，当心情沮丧时，青少年更愿意发短信，故选A；而根据第三段最后一句After the chat, participants reported about a 20% reduction in their distress—not enough to completely eliminate it可知，发短信只能部分消除沮丧心情，并不能完全消除，故B错误；而C、D在原文中均没有阐述。

48. C　词义猜测题。单词所在句子The research has shown that expressive writing itself can vent the stress and provide a sense of relief中，短语vent the stress and provide a sense of relief（缓解，减轻）由并列连词and连接，意思相近，由此可知vent的意思是“放出，发泄感情”，故选C。

49. D　细节理解题。根据最后一段第二句The reasons are complex, but may have something to do with the fact that users can control expression of sadness and other emotions via IM without exposing emotional elements like tears that some may consider as

embarrassing or sources of discomfort.可知，数字沟通可以避免尴尬和不安，故选D。

50. A 细节理解题。由题干中的new study定位到原文第一段第二句：But a new study suggests that constant instant messaging (IM'ing) and texting among teens may also provide benefits, particularly for those who are introverted (内向的)。本题考查英国科学家的新发现。由定位句可知，有一项新的研究表明，经常性的即时通讯和短信交流也可能有正面效应，尤其是对于那些内向的青少年而言，故答案为A。

名师点睛：

这是一篇议论文阅读，首先要弄清楚作者要证明什么观点，本文的中心句是constant instant messaging (IM'ing) and texting among teens may also provide benefits,然后用什么样的论据进行怎样的分析，最后得出了什么样的结论，理清了线索，理解文章就不是问题。看题时注意确定关键词，然后在文章中定位，找到与选项相关的内容，就可以轻松确定答案。

真题回顾·Passage 9·山东省菏泽市2018届高三上学期期末·A

语篇解读：

本文介绍了四位科学家，他们是现代物理的创始人，为社会做出了巨大贡献。

答案解析：

1. A 细节理解题。根据Louis Pasteur (1822—1895)中Pasteur contributed greatly towards the advancement of medical sciences developing cures for rabies, anthrax and other infectious diseases. He also invented the process of pasteurization（加热杀菌法）to make milk safer to drink可知，Louis Pasteur对医学的发展做出了贡献。故选A。

2. D 细节理解题。根据James Clerk Maxwell (1831—1879)中Einstein said of Maxwell, "The work of James Clerk Maxwell changed the world forever." 可知Einstein对James Clerk Maxwell高度评价。故选D。

3. C 推理判断题。通过本文对这四位科学家的介绍可知他们是现代物理的创始人。故选C。

名师点睛：

细节题的破解一般采用寻读法，即先看试题，再读文章。对有关信息进行快速定位，再将相关信息进行整合、甄别、分析、对比，有根有据地排除干扰项，选出正确答案。做此类型的题目时，还要特别注意句子的逻辑关系。英语中有许多功能词，如：表因果关系的because, since, as等；表转折关系的but, however, on the contrary, on the other hand等。第1题，根据Louis Pasteur (1822—1895)中Pasteur contributed greatly towards the advancement of medical sciences developing cures for rabies, anthrax and other infectious diseases. He also invented the process of pasteurization

（加热杀菌法）to make milk safer to drink可知，Louis Pasteur对医学的发展做出了贡献。故选A。

真题回顾 · Passage 10 · 2018全国I · B

语篇解读：

本文是一篇说明文。文章介绍了一档英国电视节目，给观众介绍如何减少食物浪费以及如何以较少的预算做出美味佳肴。

答案解析：

24. B　细节理解题。根据文章第一段Good Morning Britain's Susanna Reid is used to grilling guests on the sofa every morning, but she is cooking up a storm in her latest role可知，她开办了一个新的节目。故选B。

25. C　细节理解题。根据文章第二段中的In Save Money: Good Food, she visits a different home each week and with the help of chef Matt Tebbutt offers top tips on how to reduce food waste, while preparing recipes for under 5 per family a day.可知，Susanna在Matt Tebbutt的帮助下，提供如何减少食物浪费的建议，同时给每日生活费低于5英镑的每个家庭准备食谱。故选C。解题关键词：同义词表达with the help of和help。

26. C　写作意图题。根据文章第四段中的which gave viewers advice on how to get value from the vast range of health products on the market可知，*Save Money: Good Food*节目是*Save Money: Good Health*节目之后，给观众的一些建议：如何从众多的市场上的健康产品中获取价值。故选C。

27. D　主旨要义题。根据文章的整体内容可知，文章作者一直在讲如何用较少的钱做出好的食物。根据文章中的prepare delicious and nutritious meals on a tight budget 在资金紧张的情况下，准备可口且有营养的饭菜；how to reduce food waste, while preparing recipes for under 5 per family a day 如何减少食物浪费，同时给每日生活费低于5英镑的每个家庭准备食谱；how cheaply we can make this food ourselves 我们自己做这种食物有多便宜；less expensive but still tasty recipes 不贵但仍然可口的食谱，可以推知D正确。

名师点睛：

本篇文章学生感到比较难的是第26题，很多学生不知道作者在说什么，不明白作者的意图，感到很茫然。根据文章中的*Save Money*: *Good Food*, follows in the footsteps of ITV's *Save Money*: *Good Health*, 可知作者是为读者介绍了*Save Money*: *Good Food*这个节目是怎么来的，即背景信息。

专题三 阅读理解七选五

一、《新课标》与考纲要求

阅读理解七选五这个题型要求在一段约300词的短文中留出5个空白，要求考生从短文后的七个选项中（均为完整的句子）选出五个能填入文章空处的最佳选项，其中两项为多余的迷惑选项，主要考查考生对文章的整体内容和结构以及上下文逻辑意义的理解和掌握。其命题形式深受英语四六级和考研阅读多项选择题的影响，体现了《新课标》中“用英语获取、处理和运用信息的能力；逐步获取用英语思维的能力”的阅读学习和教学理念。该题型命题形式仍然具有客观题的特点，又与完形填空具有异曲同工之妙，只是选项少，以句子的形式出现，考查目的和侧重点不完全相同而已。

从《考试说明》对该题型命题目的的表述“主要考查考生对文章的整体内容和结构以及上下文逻辑意义的理解和掌握”，可以得出以下结论：该题备选项可分为主旨概括句（文章整体内容）、过渡性句子（文章结构）和注释性句子（上下文逻辑意义）三类。其多余的两个干扰项也往往从这三方面进行设置，例如主旨概括句或过于宽泛或以偏概全或偏离主题、过渡性句子不能反映文章的行文结构、注释性句子与上文脱节等。

文章体裁以说明文为主，语篇模式较为固定：提出问题、提供解决方案。文章题材较为固定，与学生的日常生活、学习紧密相关。

二、试题分析

近三年新课标全国卷高考七选五实况分析

年份	卷别	体裁	词数	题材	话题
2018	全国卷I	说明文	259	家庭生活	室内设计中颜色的选择问题
	全国卷II	说明文	223	社会生活	列举了早晨锻炼对人身体的四个好处
	全国卷III	说明文	195	社会生活	介绍了跳舞的好处
2017	全国卷I	记叙文	225	个人生活	作者对野营活动由抵触到喜欢的转变过程
	全国卷II	说明文	196	工作	如何避免工作时被打断
	全国卷III	说明文	244	个人生活	如何做计划、建立好生物钟，保持早睡早起的好习惯

续 表

年份	卷别	体裁	词数	题材	话题
2016	全国卷I	说明文	195	文化科技	密码的设置方法和破解方法
	全国卷II	说明文	262	家庭生活	自己建设花园的具体建议
	全国卷III	说明文	201	家庭生活	买鱼和烧鱼的常识

三、题型解读

分析篇章结构，把握全篇文脉是阅读填空题解题的关键。英语的语篇（discourse）通常是由句子和语段（sentence group）构成的。语段是句子和语篇之间的中间层次，句子虽然能够单独地表达相对完整的思想，但是它不能表达多方面的、比较复杂的思想，只有把几个句子结合为较大的言语片段，才能表达一个相对独立的层意。所谓的“积句而成章，积章而成篇”，就是这个道理。

分析文章的层次包含两种形式：一种是分析整篇文章的层次，也就是段落；另一种是分析每一个段落内部的层次，也就是语篇层次。

语篇与段落是有区别的：语段是篇章结构的中间层次，是由句子到篇的一种过渡形式；段落（paragraph）是在某些语体（如记叙文、议论文）中比语段更大的意义单位，较小的段落可以只包括一个语段或一个句子，一般来说，一个段落通常由几个语段构成。构成语段的方式有两种，一是靠句际间意义的结合，二是靠句际间的关联词、逻辑性插入语来连接。在分析语段层次时，可以借助句际间的连接词语做出判断，但最主要的还是要真正体会句际间的意义关系，把握作者的思路，从语序上去发现断续点，理清层次，好的文章的层次非常清晰，只有层层入手，才能真正理解文章。

四、高考英语七选五阅读解题步骤与技巧

七选五的考查形式是给考生呈现一篇缺了五句话的英语文章，并要求考生根据文章的结构、逻辑、上下文的内容选出相应的五句话填入空白处，将文章补充完整。具体的解题步骤有以下几点。

1. 步骤一

快速浏览一遍七个备选选项，先确定哪个选项适合放在文章的什么位置。通常有四个位置：标题、句首、句中、句尾。不同位置的句子有不同的特征。有时有的答案表述上就是错误的，可以直接从备选项中清除，以降低难度。

2. 步骤二

快速浏览文章，确定文章体裁，抓住文章结构。一般说来，记叙文的语言是按

时间发展顺序或因果关系排列的，常用的连接词有：then, later, after that, soon, after a while, in the end, so, as a result, because of that等。说明文常采用总—分—总的结构形式，第一段说明要说明的主题，下面几段多是从不同的角度来说明问题，最后总结，所以各段之间多是平行关系，经常出现举例说明的现象。议论文先抛出议题，然后从正反两个方面进行讨论，最后得出结论。新闻体裁的应用文首句为主题句，下面展开细节性的报道。

3. 步骤三

分析篇章结构，找出各段的主题句或主旨大意。分析文章的层次包含两种形式：一种是分析整篇文章的层次，也就是段落，说明文和议论文这样体裁的文章，每段的第一句多是主题句。找到主题句有助于帮助确定选择的范围，即所选句子必须和该段主题一致。另一种是分析每一个段落内部的层次，也就是语篇层次。要真正体会句子间的意义关系，把握作者的思路，从语序上去发现断续点，理清层次。

4. 步骤四

注意各选项中出现的句子衔接手段，寻找句中的衔接标志词。文章的衔接手段有：重复使用某一词语或子范畴的词语，使用同义语表达，用总称指代具体事物或用具体事物指代整体，使用代词避免重复等。上述方法有助于段落的平稳过渡，使文章的每个段落、每个句子甚至每个短语连贯、融为一体。段落一致与句子衔接是文章连贯的两个必要因素。

5. 步骤五

区分相似项，阅读理解七选五备选答案中有两个多余的选项，会对文章中两个空的选择构成干扰，这时要特别细致地比对相似选项，方法和做阅读理解题时区分相似项一样。

6. 步骤六

用代入法，检查答案是否合理。将所有选择的答案放回空白处，通读全文，检查文章内容是否语义连贯合理、紧扣主题，语篇结构是否通顺连贯、具有一致性、合乎逻辑，写作思路是否清晰明了，格式以及用语是否恰当贴切，从而判断选择的答案是否正确。

五、解题技巧

1. 从细节逻辑上判断——因果关系

在做题时最重要的是要读懂空白前后的句子，明白这几句话的确切意思，然后根据意思的连贯性或逻辑性从选项中选取正确答案。在读懂意思的基础上，判断它们之间的关系来进一步确认答案。

因果关系主要指前后的句子有着原因和结果之间的关系，这种关系往往说明了前因后果或者前果后因等情况。表示因果关系的连词有as a result结果，thus/therefore因此，so (such)...如此……以至于，等等。

2. 从细节逻辑上判断——转折关系

转折关系主要指英语行文中后句对前句构成逆转逻辑关系。如果空格前后两句话之间是逻辑上的逆转，则空格处很有可能是个转折逻辑的句子。

表示转折关系的连接词有：however然而，nevertheless仍然、然而、不过，nonetheless尽管如此、依然、然而, still还、然而, though可是、不过、然而, yet然而, in spite of不顾、不管, at any rate无论如何、至少, in any case无论如何、不管怎样，whoever无论是谁, whatever无论什么，on the contrary正相反, in contrast与此相反, 相比之下, by contrast相反、相比之下, in comparison比较起来、比较地, by comparison相比之下, conversely相反(地), otherwise否则、除此以外，not... but不是……而是，as well也，等等。

3. 从细节逻辑上判断——例证关系

前后句的某句是为了证明另一句而举的例子。例证的形式多样，但就其本质而言无非是思维上的形象（例子、类比等）和抽象（观点）的辩证关系，用到的思维过程无非就是基本的归纳（从例子到观点）和推理（从观点到例子）。

4. 从细节逻辑上判断——递进关系

递进关系主要指英语行文中后句对前句是一种顺承逻辑关系。如果空格前后两句话之间是逻辑上的层进关系，则空格处很有可能是个递进的句子。

表示递进关系的连词有：also也、而且, further另外（的）, furthermore而且、此外，likewise同样地，照样地；也，又，similarly相似地、类似地，moreover而且、再者、此外，in addition另外、加之，what's more更重要的是, too也、还, either也, neither两者都不, not only... but also不但……而且，等等。

5. 从细节逻辑上判断——平列关系

表示列举关系的有：first首先、第一，second第二，third第三；firstly第一、首先，secondly第二(点)、其次，thirdly第三；first第一，next其次，then那么、然后……；in the first place第一、首先，in the second place第二、其次，for one thing首先、一则，for another thing其次，to begin with首先、第一，to conclude最后，等等。

6. 从词汇线索上判断——代词

英语表达中的代词出现的频率极高，代词的作用是指代前面提及的名词或形容词概念，巧妙利用这样的指代关系和根据代词的单复数差异可以准确而快速地解题。

7. 从词汇线索上判断——同义词/近义词

英语前言后语之间往往有同义词、近义词、近义表达语甚至相同词汇的重复使用，这是我们解题的一个很好的判断线索。其实就其本质而言，上文讲的代词和下文将涉及的上下义词和同一范畴词都是特殊的同义/近义词。

8. 从词汇线索上判断——上下义词/同一范畴词

上下义词和同一范畴词就是前者包含了后者，或可以说后者是前者的一个子集。利用前后句中这样的特殊的同义关系常常可以很轻松地解题。

9. 从试题位置上判断——问题在段首

假如问题出现在段首，它通常是段落的主题句。认真阅读后文内容，根据段落一致性原则，查找同义词或其他相关的词，推断出主题句。

另外，着重阅读后文一两句，锁定线索信号词，然后在选项中查找相关特征词。通常正确答案的最后一句与空白后的第一句在意思上是紧密衔接的，因此这两句间会有某种的衔接手段，尤其当选项是几句话时。

10. 从试题位置上判断——问题在段尾

所选答案是引出下一段的内容。如果在选项中找不出与前文之间的关联，此时可考虑与下一段开头是否有一定的衔接。认真阅读下一段开头几句，看是否与选项的最后一句紧密连接起来。

分析与前文是转折或是对比关系。此时要注意在选项中查找表示转折、对比的关联词，同时注意选项中所讲内容是否与前文在同一主题上形成对立、对比关系。

如果第一段的段尾是空格，要认真阅读，看此处是细节还是主题。通常文章第一段要提出文章的主题，如果在段尾提出主题，会用一些信号词如转折词引出来，正确答案中应有这样的特征词。

段尾通常是结论、概括性语句。注意在选项中查找表示结果、结论、总结等的信号词，如therefore、as a result、thus、hence、in short、to sum up、to conclude、in a word等词语，选项中也可发现前文的同义词句。

六、题型考点解题策略

认真研读2016—2018年全国新课标卷的七选五部分，总结了关于此题型的4个考点，分别为文章标题类、段落主题句类、段意过渡句、细节类。在下面的篇幅中，针对这4个考点逐一进行深入分析，帮助学生更好地理解和掌握此类题型。

（一）文章标题类

真题回顾·典例1·2018新课标全国卷Ⅰ

Color is fundamental in home design—something you'll always have in every room. A grasp of how to manage color in your spaces is one of the first steps to creating rooms you'll love to live in.Do you want a room that's full of life? Professional? Or are you just looking for a place to relax after a long day? __B__ , color is the key to making a room feel the way you want it to feel.

A. While all of them are useful

B. Whatever you' re looking for

C. If you' re experimenting with a color

真题回顾 · 典例2 · 2017新课标全国卷II

Interruptions are one of the worst things to deal with while you're trying to get work done. __B__ , there are several ways to handle things.Let's take a look at them now.

A. If you' re busy, don' t feel bad about saying no

B. When you want to avoid interruptions at work

C. Set boundaries for yourself as your time goes

F. It might seem unkind to cut people shirt when they interrupt you

真题回顾 · 典例3 · 2017新课标全国卷III

Lots of people find it hard to get up in the morning, and put the blame on the alarm clock.In fact, the key to easy morning wake-up lies in resetting your body clock. __C__ Here's how to make one.

A. Get a sleep specialist.

B. Find the right motivation.

C. A better plan for sleep can help.

D. And consider setting a second alarm.

解题策略：解答此类题，可以通过快速浏览，从整体上把握文章的体裁、语篇结构和脉络，从而把握文章的主旨大意。

（二）段落主题句类

真题回顾 · 典例1 · 2018新课标全国卷I

__D__ . They're the little spots of color like throw pillows, mirrors and baskets that most of us use to add visual interest to our rooms. Less tiring than painting your walls and less expensive than buying a colorful sofa, small color choices bring with them the significant benefit of being easily changeable.

A. Whatever you're looking for

B. If you're experimenting with a color

C. Small color choices are the ones we're most familiar with

D. Color choices in this range are a step up from the small ones in two major ways

真题回顾·典例2·2018新课标全国卷II

__B__ Studies found that people who woke up early for exercise slept better than those who exercised in the evening.Exercise energizes you, so it is more difficult to relax and have a peaceful sleep when you are very excited.

A. You will stick to your diet.

B. Your quality of sleep improves.

C. You prefer healthy food to fast food.

真题回顾·典例3 ·2018新课标全国卷II

__A__ If you work out bright and early in the morning, you will be more likely to stick to healthy food choices throughout the day.Who would want to ruin their good workout by eating junk food? You will want to continue to focus on positive choices.

A. You will stick to your diet.

B. Your quality of sleep improves.

C. You prefer healthy food to fast food.

真题回顾·典例4·2018新课标全国卷III

__B__ We dance from Florida to Alaska, from north to south and sea to sea.We dance at weddings, birthdays, office parties and just to fill the time.

A. So why do we dance?

B. Dance in the U.S. is everywhere.

F. Dancing seems to change their feeling completely.

G. They stayed up all night long singing and dancing.

真题回顾·典例5·2018新课标全国卷Ⅲ

__A__ "I can tell you about one young couple," says Bridges. "They're learning to do traditional dances.They arrive at the class in low spirits and they leave with a smile.

A. So why do we dance?

B. Dance in the U.S. is everywhere.

G. They stayed up all night long singing and dancing.

真题回顾·典例6·2018新课标全国卷Ⅲ

__F__ We have done a lot of it since.Recently, we bought a twenty-eight-foot travel trailer complete with a bathroom and a built-in TV set.There is a separate bedroom, a modern kitchen with a refrigerator.The trailer even has matching carpet and curtains.

D. I was to learn a lot about camping since then, however.

E. I must say that I have certainly come to enjoy camping.

F. After the trip, my family became quite interested in camping.

（三）段意过渡句

真题回顾·典例1·2018新课标全国卷Ⅰ

Over the years, there have been a number of different techniques to help designers approach this important point. __A__, they can get a little complex.But good news is that there're really only three kinds of decisions you need to make about color in your home: the small ones, the medium ones, and the large ones.

A. While all of them are useful

B. Whatever you're looking for

E. It's not really a good idea to use too many small color pieces

真题回顾·典例2·2018新课标全国卷Ⅰ

Medium color choices are generally furniture pieces such as sofas, dinner tables or bookshelves. __G__ . They require a bigger commitment than smaller ones, and they have a more powerful effect on the feeling of a space.

D. Small color choices are the ones we're most familiar with

E. It's not really a good idea to use too many small color pieces

G. Color choices in this range are a step up from the small ones in two major ways

真题回顾·典例3·2018新课标全国卷III

If you are already making the time to exercise, it is good indeed! With such busy lives, it can be hard to try and find the time to work out. <u>G</u> Working out in the morning provides additional benefits beyond being physically fit.

E. You can keep your head clear for 4 ~ 10 hours after exercise.

F. After you exercise, you continue to burn calories throughout the day.

G. If you are planning to do exercise regularly, or you're doing it now, then listen up!

真题回顾·典例4·2018新课标全国卷II

Your metabolism（新陈代谢）gets a head start. <u>F</u> If you work out in the mornings, then you will be getting the calorie（卡路里）burning benefits for the whole day, not in your sleep.

E. You can keep your head clear for 4 ~ 10 hours after exercise.

F. After you exercise, you continue to burn calories throughout the day.

G. If you are planning to do exercise regularly, or you're doing it now, then listen up!

真题回顾·典例5·2018新课标全国卷III

"I adore dancing," says Lester Bridges, the owner of a dance studio in Iowa. "I can't imagine doing anything else with my life." Bridges runs dance classes for all ages. "Teaching dance is wonderful. <u>D</u> It's great to watch them.For many of them, it's a way of meeting people and having a social life."

C. If you like dancing outdoors, come to America.

D. My older students say it makes them feel young.

E. I keep practicing even when I'm extremely tired.

真题回顾·典例6·2018新课标全国卷III

So, do we dance in order to make ourselves feel better, calmer, healthier? Andrea Hillier says, "Dance, like the pattern of a beating heart, is life.Even after all these years, I want to get better and better. E I find it hard to stop! Dancing reminds me I'm alive."

E. I keep practicing even when I'm extremely tired.

F. Dancing seems to change their feeling completely.

G. They stayed up all night long singing and dancing.

（四）细节类

真题回顾·典例1·2018新课标全国卷I

The large color decisions in your rooms concern the walls, ceilings, and floors. Whether you're looking at wallpaper or paint, the time, effort and relative expense put into it are significant. F .

B. Whatever you're looking for

C. If you're experimenting with a color

F. So it pays to be sure, because you want to get it right the first time

真题回顾·典例2·2018新课标全国卷II

Your productivity is improved.Exercising makes you more awake and ready to handle whatever is ahead of you for the day. E

C. You prefer healthy food to fast food.

D. There is no reason you should exercise in the morning.

E. You can keep your head clear for 4 ~ 10 hours after exercise.

真题回顾·典例3·2018新课标全国卷III

"I can tell you about one young couple," says Bridges. "They're learning to do traditional dances.They arrive at the class in low spirits and they leave with a smile. F ."

C. If you like dancing outdoors, come to America

E. I keep practicing even when I'm extremely tired

F. Dancing seems to change their feeling completely

七、2019年阅读七选五新课标主题语境篇之备考训练

真题回顾·Passage 1·2018新课标全国卷I

根据短文内容，从短文后的选项中选出能填入空白处的最佳选项。选项中有两项为多余选项。

Color is fundamental in home design—something you'll always have in every room. A grasp of how to manage color in your spaces is one of the first steps to creating rooms you'll love to live in. Do you want a room that's full of life? Professional? Or are you just looking for a place to relax after a long day? __36__, color is the key to making a room feel the way you want it to feel.

Over the years, there have been a number of different techniques to help designers approach this important point. __37__, they can get a little complex.But good news is that there're really only three kinds of decisions you need to make about color in your home: the small ones, the medium ones, and the large ones.

__38__. They're the little spots of color like throw pillows, mirrors and baskets that most of us use to add visual interest to our rooms.Less tiring than painting your walls and less expensive than buying a colorful sofa, small color choices bring with them the significant benefit of being easily changeable.

Medium color choices are generally furniture pieces such as sofas, dinner tables or bookshelves. __39__. They require a bigger commitment than smaller ones, and they have a more powerful effect on the feeling of a space.

The large color decisions in your rooms concern the walls, ceilings, and floors. Whether you're looking at wallpaper or paint, the time, effort and relative expense put into it are significant. __40__.

A. While all of them are useful

B. Whatever you're looking for

C. If you're experimenting with a color

D. Small color choices are the ones we're most familiar with

E. It's not really a good idea to use too many small color pieces

F. So it pays to be sure, because you want to get it right the first time

G. Color choices in this range are a step up from the small ones in two major ways

真题回顾·Passage 2·北京市城六区2018届高三一模

If you are reading this article in print, chances are that you will only get through half of what I have written.And if you are reading this online, you may not even finish a fifth. __51__. They suggest that many of us no longer have the concentration to read articles through to their conclusion.

So are we getting stupider? Actually, our online habits are damaging the mental power we need to process and understand textual information.Round-the-clock news makes us read from one article to the next without necessarily engaging fully with any of the content.Our reading is frequently interrupted by the noise of the latest e-mail and we are now absorbing short bursts of words on Twitter and Facebook more regularly than longer texts. __52__. But we are gradually forgetting how to sit back, think carefully, and relate all the facts to each other.

__53__. A desperate bunch of academics want us to take our time while reading, and re-reading.They ask us to switch off our computers every so often and rediscover both the joy of personal engagement with printed texts, and the ability to process them fully.What's to be done then? Most slow readers realize that total rejection of the web is extremely unrealistic.They feel that getaway from technology for a while is the answer. __54__.

Personally, I'm not sure whether I could ever go offline for long.Even while writing this article, I am switching constantly between sites, skimming too often, absorbing too little.Internet reading has become too rooted in my daily life for me to change.I read essays and articles not in hard copy but as PDFs.I suspect that many readers are in a similar position. __55__. You can download a computer application called Freedom, which allows you to read in peace by cutting off your Internet connection.Or if you want to avoid being disturbed by the Internet, you could always download offline reader Instapaper for your iPhone.If you're still reading my article, that is slow reading.

A. The Internet is probably part of the problem

B. Now some campaigns are advocating slow reading

C. These are the two findings from the recent research projects

D. But if you just occasionally want to read more slowly, help is at hand

E. Some of them have suggested turning their computers off for one day a week

F. Slow reading can help connect a reader to neighborhood and become popular

G. Because of the Internet, we have become very good at collecting information

真题回顾·Passage 3·2018浙江卷

Secret codes（密码）keep messages private.Banks, companies, and government agencies use secret codes in doing business, especially when information is sent by computer.

People have used secret codes for thousands of years. __1__ Code breaking never lags（落后）far behind code making.The science of creating and reading coded messages is called cryptography.

There are three main types of cryptography. __2__ For example, the first letters of "My elephant eats too many eels" spell out the hidden message "Meet me".

__3__ You might represent each letter with a number, for example.Let's number the letters of the alphabet, in order, from 1 to 26.If we substitute a number for each letter, the message "Meet me" would read "1 3 5 5 2 0 13 5".

A code uses symbols to replace words, phrases, or sentences.To read the message of a real code, you must have a code book. __4__ For example, "bridge" might stand for "meet" and "out" might stand for "me". The message "Bridge out" would actually mean "Meet me". __5__ However, it is also hard to keep a code book secret for long. So codes must be changed frequently.

A. It is very hard to break a code without the code book.

B. In any language, some letters are used more than others.

C. Only people who know the keyword can read the message.

D. As long as there have been codes, people have tried to break them.

E. You can hide a message by having the first letters of each word spell it out.

F. With a code book, you might write down words that would stand for other words.

G. Another way to hide a message is to use symbols to stand for specific letters of the alphabet.

参考答案

真题回顾·Passage 1·2018新课标全国卷I

语篇解读：

本文是一篇说明文。文章讲述了室内设计中颜色的选择问题。

答案解析：

36. B　36题后面是逗号，接下来另起一个简单句，可以从句子结构角度排除

D、E、F、G项。根据前文的三个问句可知，此处是从中选择一种。故选B（不管你寻找哪一种）。

37. A 前文：在过去的许多年里，有许多技术帮助设计者实现这一要点；下文：它们有点复杂。所以A（尽管它们都很有用）承上启下，符合题意。

38. D 本空是一个主题句，总说选择小颜色是我们很熟悉的方法。后文说小颜色的具体用途。故选D。

39. G 前文"中型颜色选择通常是指一些例如沙发、餐桌或者书架等家具的颜色选择"，接着表明这种范围的颜色选择是对小型颜色选择在两种方式上的进一步提示，故选G。

40. F 前文the time, effort and relative expense put into it are significant你所付出的时间、精力和相关的费用是巨大的。后文"那肯定是值得的，因为你想第一次把它弄好"。故选F。

真题回顾·Passage 2·北京市城六区2018届高三一模

语篇解读：

本文讲述的是"慢读的艺术"。研究表明我们中的许多人不再专注于阅读文章，实际上，我们的网络习惯正在破坏我们处理和理解文本信息所需要的精神力量。大多数慢读者意识到，完全拒绝网络是非常不现实的，他们觉得暂时摆脱科技是解决问题的办法。

答案解析：

51. C 根据下文：他们认为，我们中的许多人不再专注于阅读文章。此处的they应该是指代前文出现的事物，也就是C项中的the two findings，"最近的研究项目有两个发现"，故选C。

52. G 根据上句：我们的阅读经常被最新电子邮件的噪音所打断，我们现在在Twitter和Facebook上吸收简短的一连串的单词比长篇大论更有规律。可知因为有了互联网，我们变得非常善于收集信息。故选G。

53. B 根据下文：一群学者极其希望我们在阅读或重读的时候要放慢速度。可知现在一些活动提倡缓慢阅读。故选B。

54. E 根据上文：大多数慢读者意识到，完全拒绝网络是非常不现实的。他们觉得暂时摆脱科技是解决问题的办法。由此推知，E项Some of them have suggested turning their computers off for one day a week.（他们中的一些人建议每周把电脑关掉一天。）与上文匹配。

55. D 根据空格下句：你可以下载一个叫作Freedom的电脑程序，这样你就可以通过切断你的网络连接来阅读。由此可知此处的意思是：如果你只是偶尔想要读得慢一些，那么帮助就在手边。故选D。

名师点睛：

做七选五时“尤其代词不可放”，意思是：在填空处的前后语境中出现的一些代词不可忽视。有这样一道题：“They can be rich resources to improve your knowledge.”，该选项中凭空多出一个代词they，这说明什么问题？代词是起替代作用的，一定是前文出现的事物被they替代了，找到被替代的名词就可以了。从文中一找，前面的语境是“Volunteering brings together all kinds of people.” 所以they替代的就是前文的all kinds of people。这样的现象在阅读理解七选五中很多，能帮助大家解决不少难题。本题第1空，根据下文：他们认为，我们中的许多人不再专注于阅读文章。此处的they应该是指代前文出现的事物，也就是C项中的the two findings，“最近的研究项目有两个发现”，故选C。

真题回顾·Passage 3·2018浙江卷

语篇解读：

本文是一篇说明文，主要介绍了密码的设置和破解的方法。比如利用该字母在字母表中排序的数字来代表该字母，或者利用一些单词的首字母来组成一个密码等。

答案解析：

1. D　根据后面一句“Code breaking never lags（落后）far behind code making”可知，此空选D（只要有密码的存在，人们就会试图去破解它们）。

2. E　根据后面一句“For example, the first letters of ‘My elephant eats too many eels’ spell out the hidden message ‘Meet me’.”可知，此空选E（你可以拼写每个单词的第一个字母来隐藏信息）。

3. G　上一段介绍了第一种密码类型，本段介绍的是第二种类型，再根据空后的内容可知，空处选G（另外一种隐藏信息的方式是用符号来代表字母表中的特定字母）。

4. F　由前一句的“a code book”和空后的“‘bridge’might stand for...‘me.’”可知，此空选F（有了密码书，你就可以写下代表其他单词的单词）。

5. A　本段介绍的是密码书，根据空后的转折可知，此处选A(没有密码书是很难破解密码的)。

专题四 完形填空

一、《新课标》与考纲要求

高考英语完形填空是测试学生语言综合能力的填空补缺式障碍性阅读。它以语篇信息为基础，以中心脉络信息为主线，多层面反复式信息暗示，纵横向立体式信息照应，给考生提供足够的解题信息。

1. 测试特点

作为选拔性考试，高考必须具有较高信度、效度和必要的区分度以及一定的难度。完形填空正好满足了这一需求，它集中了短文的任意设空和单项填空两种题型的优点，综合考查考生的英语基础知识和语言运用能力，包括词汇辨析能力、阅读理解能力、分析判断能力、逻辑推理能力和跨文化交际能力，因而是高考试题中要求最高、难度最大的一种题型。

2. 选材特点

（1）文章材料多以叙述为主，叙议结合。近几年高考中，故事性记叙文体仍占主要地位，但夹叙夹议的文体在逐年递增，且有占主导地位的趋势。此外，也有说明文体和议论文体的不断呈现，使得完形填空的选材枝繁叶茂、缤纷多彩。

（2）文章长度基本上保持在250～280个单词，文章难度与中学英语教材相当，但也会因整个试卷的难易度进行适当的调整。总体上，完形填空的选材在向长句、难句、原汁原味的地道英语发展，有向难的趋势。

（3）挖空密度相对稳定，平均词距在10～12个单词，填空分布力求均衡，以不影响文章的“跳读”理解为限度。

3. 设题特点

高考完形填空按句组层次和语篇层次设空题居多，这种设题方式体现了“突出语篇”的命题思路。设题主要以考查实词为主，同时辅以虚词考查。所谓实词即指有实际信息意义的词类，如动词、名词、形容词、副词等，其中动词、名词是考查重点。所谓虚词就是不能单独充当句法成分的词，有连接或附着各类实词的语法意义，如连词、介词、冠词等。而连词则是虚词的考查重点，因为它可以测试考生上下文的衔接、逻辑等综合能力。

具体设空考点是：名词词义辨析5～6个；名词词组辨析或搭配1个；动词词义辨析6～8个；动词词组辨析或搭配1～2个；形容词词义辨析2～3个；副词词义辨析

1～2个；代词/连词/介词1个；可设一个固定短语之类的。设空考点请尽量按上述要求进行编写，不要出现只主考名词或只主考动词的现象。

第一句话不能设空，空与空间隔词数为10个左右，不能太多或太少。

选项必须是考纲词且为同类。正确项唯一，错项具有干扰性。

试题难度以中档为主，兼顾少量的容易题和较难题。

二、试题分析

2016—2018年新课标卷高考英语完形填空试题分析

年份	试卷类型	体裁	词数	话题	考点分布
2018年	新课标卷I	夹叙夹议文	271	讲述了“我”在大二学的免费课程下棋及对“我”生活的指导意义	动词9　名词7 形容词3　副词1
	新课标卷II	记叙文	277	讲述了作者13年后和儿子见面的情景	动词9　名词3 形容词5　副词2 介词1
	新课标卷III	记叙文	271	讲述Dennis Williams认真对待陌生人发来的手机短信，使陌生人倍受感动的故事	动词10　名词6 形容词4
2017年	新课标卷I	记叙文	251	学习美式手语的经历和感受	名词5　动词10 形容词4　副词1
	新课标卷II	记叙文	266	介绍作者的学生Feddy的性格特征及多年后的生活、工作状况	名词8　动词9 形容词3
	新课标卷III	记叙文	271	讲述了一个加拿大青年在和女朋友分手后，希望免费赠送自己为女朋友购买的环球航空旅行机票的故事，体现了年轻人无私的精神	名词7　动词9 形容词4
2016年	新课标卷I	记叙文	253	讲述了司机Larry在路上遇到着火的汽车，积极救人的故事	动词7　名词 4 形容词3　副词1 连词2　代词1 介词短语2
	新课标卷II	夹叙夹议文	262	作者通过自身的经历总结出，电话中的感受有时与现实生活中的感受不一致，因为像微笑这样无声的信号无法通过电话传播	动词6　名词 4 形容词5　副词3 介词短语2
	新课标卷III	记叙文	276	作者通过刻苦训练，最终实现了成为足球队明星球员的目标	动词8　名词4 形容词5　副词 1 连词1　代词1

三、题型解读策略与技巧

（一）完形填空之记叙文

记叙文一直受高考完形填空命题者的青睐，在高考完形填空题材中占有相当大的比重。这是因为其有人物、情节发展等线索可循，内容情节深刻，常涉及人物心理活动的细致描写，篇章与语句的结构变化丰富多彩。这种类型的试题，更能考查考生根据文章的整体内容选择符合文章情节的答案，可以充分体现考生对事物的应变能力。

仔细研读近几年高考完形填空我们不难发现，记叙文是出现频率最高的一类文体，多以记人和叙事为主。具体地说，它是借助叙述、描写等手段记叙社会中的人物和事件的发展过程，用以表现作者的态度和观点。记叙文多以人的思想和行为为中心，以时间或空间的变化为线索，按事件的发生、发展和结束来展开叙述。研读记叙型完形填空，可看出以下趋势：

1. 首句完整，线索清楚

一般作者在第一句话就交代了人物的姓名、身份、业绩或事件发生的时间、地点，然后再介绍事件的发生、发展，最后得出结果。

从历年的试题可以看出，完形填空首句一般不设题。这为我们理解文章的内在联系提供了一个“窗口”，它的句意往往为全文提供中心信息。所以应充分重视首句的指示作用，利用它为解题找到一个突破口，据此拓展思维，争取开局胜利。

2. 叙述灵活，侧重语境

文章以叙述为主，人物间对话较少，绝大部分篇章是作者在描述事件，较少加入作者的观点或评论。因此，常会出现态度与观点的跳跃变换，或语气上的差异。这增加了情景的迷惑性和干扰性，从而突出了对语境的依赖，实现了在理解上下文的基础上，通过语境，辨析词语，做出选择。

高考完形填空题逐渐摒弃语法分析，朝深层化和语境化的方面挖掘，因此考生只有借助上下文乃至全文语境启示或限定，揣摩作者的心情，以及他对各个角色、各个事件的态度。在答题过程中，除了对关联用语的把握外，还要把握语气、动作等的描写。

3. 实词为主，虚词为辅

高考记叙型完形填空，篇章不长，一般在200～280个词，始终紧扣话题中心，形成一个主题连续体。选项一般为同一词类或同一范畴。重点集中于动词、名词、形容词或副词等实词上，介词、连词、冠词等虚词的考查相对较少。实词为主，虚词为辅，更能体现在语境中考查英语运用能力这一思路。

4. 瞻前顾后

在完形填空的解题过程中，从空格前面的相关语句中寻找解题依据的方法通常被称为“瞻前法”；所谓“顾后”，是指在做完形填空时参考空后的有关信息来解题。

5. 理清线索，把握方向

记叙文一般按事件发展的顺序叙述，有时用倒叙。答题时，通过理清人物间的关系，把握人物各自所做的事情，从而把握细节，找准作者的记叙方向，正确理解文章。

真题回顾·典例·2018新课标全国卷Ⅲ

When most of us get a text message on our cell phone from an unknown person, we usually say “sorry, __41__ number!” and move on. But when Dennis Williams __42__ a text that clearly wasn’t intended for him, he did something __43__.

On March 19, Dennis got a group text __44__ him that a couple he didn’t know were at the hospital, waiting for the __45__ of a baby.

“Congratulations! But I think someone was mistaken,” Dennis __46__. The baby was born and update texts were __47__ quickly from the overjoyed grandmother, Teresa.In her __48__, she didn’t seem to realize that she was __49__ the baby’s photos with a complete stranger. “Well, I don’t __50__ you all but I will get there to take pictures with the baby,” replied Dennis before asking which room the new __51__ were in.

Much to the family’s surprise, Dennis stuck to his __52__! He turned up at the hospital __53__ gifts for the new mother Lindsey and her baby boy. Lindsey’s husband was totally __54__ by the unexpected visit. “I don’t think we would have randomly invited him over but we __55__ it and the gifts.”

Teresa __56__ a photo of the chance meeting on a social networking website __57__ by the touching words: “What a __58__ this young man was to our family! He was so __59__ and kind to do this.” The post has since gained the __60__ of social media users all over the world, receiving more than 184,000 shares and 61,500 likes in just three days.

41. A. unlucky B. secret C. new D. wrong
42. A. received B. translated C. copied D. printed
43. A. reasonable B. special C. necessary D. practical
44. A. convincing B. reminding C. informing D. warning
45. A. wake-up B. recovery C. growth D. arrival

46. A. responded	B. interrupted	C. predicted	D. repeated
47. A. coming in	B. setting out	C. passing down	D. moving around
48. A. opinion	B. anxiety	C. excitement	D. effort
49. A. comparing	B. exchanging	C. discussing	D. sharing
50. A. accept	B. know	C. believe	D. bother
51. A. parents	B. doctors	C. patients	D. visitors
52. A. dream	B. promise	C. agenda	D. principle
53. A. bearing	B. collecting	C. opening	D. making
54. A. discouraged	B. relaxed	C. astonished	D. defeated
55. A. admit	B. need	C. appreciate	D. expect
56. A. found	B. selected	C. developed	D. posted
57. A. confirmed	B. simplified	C. clarified	D. accompanied
58. A. pity	B. blessing	C. relief	D. problem
59. A. smart	B. calm	C. sweet	D. fair
60. A. sympathy	B. attention	C. control	D. trust

语篇解读：

本文为记叙文。文章主要讲述了Dennis Williams认真对待陌生人发来的手机短信，使陌生人倍受感动的故事。

答案解析：

41. D　考查形容词。根据后文But when Dennis Williams __42__ a text that clearly wasn't intended for him, he did something __43__ 以及后文他所做的事情可以得知，大部分人会回应拨错号了。A. unlucky不幸的；B. secret秘密的；C. new新的；D. wrong错误的。故选D。

42. A　考查动词。根据文章第一句When most of us get a text message on our cell phone from an unknown person可以推知，他收到了手机短信。A. received收到；B.translated翻译；C. copied复制；D. printed印刷。故选A。

43. B　考查形容词。根据后文内容可知，他做了与众不同的事情，所以用special合适。A. reasonable合理的；B. special特别的；C. necessary必要的；D. practical现实可行的。

44. C　考查动词。根据后句a couple he didn't know were at the hospital, waiting for the __45__ of a baby可知，这对陌生夫妇是在告诉他这个消息。A. convincing让人信服的；B. reminding提醒；C. informing通知；D. warning警告。故选C。

45. D　考查名词。根据下文The baby was born可知，他们在等候新生儿的到来。A. wake-up醒来；B. recovery恢复；C. growth成长；D. arrival到来。故选D。

46. A　考查动词。根据前句内容可知，这是Dennis的回复。A. responded回复；B.interrupted打断；C. predicted预料；D. repeated重复。故选A。

47. A　考查动词短语。根据本句The baby was born and update texts were __47__ quickly from the overjoyed grandmother, Teresa.可知，消息很快再次进来。A. coming in进来；B. setting out着手；C. passing down使流传；D. moving around走来走去。故选A。

48. C　考查名词。根据本句In her __48__, she didn't seem to realize that she was __49__ the baby's photos with a complete stranger.可知，这位妈妈太兴奋，没有意识到把照片分享给了陌生人。A. opinion观点；B. anxiety焦虑；C. excitement兴奋；D. effort努力。故选C。

49. D　考查动词。根据后文... I will get there to take pictures with the baby," replied Dennis before asking which room the new __51__ were in可知，Dennis 收到了Teresa发来的照片，所以是她跟陌生人分享了照片。A. comparing比较；B. exchanging交换；C. discussing讨论；D. sharing分享。故选D。

50. B　考查动词。根据前文Dennis got a group text __44__ him that a couple he didn't know可知，Dennis不认识他们。A. accept接受；B. know认识，了解；C. believe相信；D. bother打扰，麻烦。故选B。

51. A　考查名词。根据前文可以推知，这对夫妇为新父母。A. parents父母；B. doctors医生；C. patients病人；D. visitors游客。故选A。

52. B　考查名词。根据后文He turned up at the hospital __53__ gifts for the new mother Lindsey and her baby boy. 可知，他坚守了自己对于新妈妈Lindsey和她的孩子礼物的承诺。A. dream梦想；B. promise承诺；C. agenda会议议程；D. principle原则。故选B。

53. A　考查动词。根据语境可知，他是拿着礼物来的。A. bearing携带，拿；B. collecting收集；C. opening打开；D. making制造。故选A。

54. C　考查形容词。根据unexpected可知，她丈夫是十分惊讶。A. discouraged沮丧的；B. relaxed放松的；C. astonished吃惊的；D. defeated打败的。故选C。

55. C　考查动词。根据语境以及后文往网上发帖可知，Teresa夫妇十分感激Dennis的到来以及带来的礼物。A. admit承认；B. need需要；C. appreciate感激；D. expect期望。故选C。

56. D　考查动词。根据后文The post has since gained the __60__ of social media users all over the world, receiving more than 184,000 shares and 61, 500 likes in just three days.可知，她把照片传到了网上。A. found发现；B. selected选择；C. developed发展；D. posted发帖。故选D。

57. D 考查动词。根据语境可知，照片后面附着一段感人的文字。A. confirmed确定；B. simplified简化；C. clarified分类；D. accompanied伴随着。故选D。

58. B 考查名词。根据语境可推知，这位母亲认为这位年轻的陌生人来看望宝宝是上帝的祝福。A. pity同情，怜悯；B. blessing祝福；C. relief放松，如释重负；D. problem问题。故选B。

59. C 考查形容词。根据语境He was so __59__ and kind to do this.可知，与kind并列，所以用sweet，表示甜美善良。A. smart聪明的；B. calm冷静的；C. sweet甜美的；D. fair公平的。故选C。

60. B 考查名词。根据文章最后一句The post has since gained the __60__ of social media users all over the world, receiving more than 184,000 shares and 61, 500 likes in just three days.可知，三天里有184000人分享，61500个点赞，所以引起了极大的关注。A. sympathy同情；B. attention关注；C. control控制；D. trust信任。故选B。

（二）完形填空之夹叙夹议文

1. 命题规律

夹叙夹议的文章是高考完形填空中最有难度的，也是最热门的一类体裁。所选文章语言地道、寓意深刻、可读性强。文章常常在平淡的叙述中蕴含着深刻的人生哲理。此类选材倾向于注重短文本身的教育意义。作者首先叙述一件事，在叙述过程中或结束后发表自己的看法或由此事引出一个深刻的社会问题。文章的显著特点是首句可能在传达一个事件信息或透视一种社会现象，而后对此进行深度评价，或由此引发一种深层次的思考，具有记叙与议论的双重性，文情并茂，发人深思。解题时，应借助上下文乃至全文的语境揣摩作者的心境，及其对各个角色、各个事件的态度。

（1）命题规律一

事例—观点：先叙述作者自己的某一个生活经历或见闻，然后针对这一事件发表自己对生活的看法，或揭示生活的真理。

（2）命题规律二

观点—事例：作者先提出一种观点或看法，然后围绕这一观点或看法用具体的事例加以说明，一般是一个事例，有时也可能是用几个事例从不同的侧面来说明。

（3）命题规律三

观点—事例—观点：提出一种观点或见解，然后用某一事例来阐述这一观点，最后再进一步地总结和升华。

2. 应试技巧

（1）关注首句，领会大意

通过首句可以明确文章话题，了解篇章结构，预测全文内容。尾句往往是作者的点睛之笔，通过尾句一般可以更加真实、确切地体会到作者的写作意图、对待事件的真实态度等核心内容。

例：

From my second grade on，there was one event I feared every year：the piano recital（独奏会）和尾句的With his first recital，my father taught me more about courage and determination than all the words he used those 30 plus years ago.表明了文章的主旨：作者本来很反感弹钢琴，但是父亲的行为感动了自己。作者认为他的实际行动比30多年以前说的话更有感染力。

（2）注重语境，理清行文逻辑

夹叙夹议文以叙述为主，绝大部分篇幅是在描述事件，而作者的观点及态度往往隐含在叙述中，这就要求考生增强语篇意识，抓住文章的叙事线索，弄清文章的内在逻辑关系，根据上下文内容做出选择，适当进行逻辑推理是解题的关键。

（3）找准标志词，弄清故事的发展模式

夹叙夹议文通常使用对比、强调、让步、举例、结论、顺序和对照等手法。考生应注意观察文章的结构特点，根据表达这些手法的衔接词来正确理解故事情节。

常见的标志词有：①并列关系：and，not only...but also，that is to say等；②因果关系：because，for，so that，in order that，due to，thanks to，thus，therefore，so等；③对比关系：while，whereas，as，rather than，instead of等；④转折关系：although，though，even if，nevertheless，despite，but，yet，however，on the contrary等；⑤递进关系：also，then，besides，in addition，furthermore，what's more等；⑥顺序关系：first，then，on one hand等；⑦转变话题：by the way，what I really mean...等。

真题回顾·典例·2018新课标全国卷Ⅰ

During my second year at the city college, I was told that the education department was offering a "free" course, called Thinking Chess, for three credits.I __41__ the idea of taking the class because, after all, who doesn't want to __42__ a few dollars? More than that, I'd always wanted to learn chess.And, even if I weren't __43__ enough about free credits, news about our __44__ was appealing enough to me.He was an international grandmaster, which __45__ I would be learning from one of the game's __46__. I could hardly wait to __47__ him.

Maurice Ashley was kind and smart, a former graduate returning to teach, and this __48__ was no game for him; he meant business.In his introduction, he made it __49__ that our credits would be hard-earned.In order to __50__ the class, among other criteria, we had to write a paper on how we plan to __51__ what we would learn in class to our future professions and, __52__, to our lives.I managed to get an A in that __53__ and learned life lessons that have served me well beyond the __54__.

Ten years after my chess class with Ashley, I'm still putting to use what he __55__ me: "The absolute most important __56__ that you learn when you play chess is how to make good __57__. On every single move you have to __58__ a situation, process what your opponent（对手）is doing and __59__ the best move from among all your options." These words still ring true today in my __60__ as a journalist.

41. A. put forward　B. jumped at　C. tried out　D. turned down
42. A. waste　B. earn　C. save　D. pay
43. A. excited　B. worried　C. moved　D. tired
44. A. title　B. competitor　C. textbook　D. instructor
45. A. urged　B. demanded　C. held　D. meant
46. A. fastest　B. easiest　C. best　D. rarest
47. A. interview　B. meet　C. challenge　D. beat
48. A. chance　B. qualification　C. honor　D. job
49. A. real　B. perfect　C. clear　D. possible
50. A. attend　B. pass　C. skip　D. observe
51. A. add　B. expose　C. apply　D. compare
52. A. eventually　B. naturally　C. directly　D. normally
53. A. game　B. presentation　C. course　D. experiment
54. A. criterion　B. classroom　C. department　D. situation
55. A. taught　B. wrote　C. questioned　D. promised
56. A. fact　B. step　C. manner　D. skill
57. A. grades　B. decisions　C. impressions　D. comments
58. A. analyze　B. describe　C. rebuild　D. control
59. A. announce　B. signal　C. block　D. evaluate
60. A. role　B. desire　C. concern　D. behavior

语篇解读：

本文是一篇夹叙夹议的文章。文章讲述了“我”在大二学的免费课程——下棋及它对“我”生活的指导意义。

答案解析：

41. B　考查动词短语辨析。“我在大二时，学校教育处提供一种名叫思维象棋的免费课程，这个课程3个学分。我急于上这门课程，是因为我想节省点钱。”put forward提出；jumped at急于接受；tried out尝试；turned down拒绝。故选B。

42. C　考查动词辨析。“我在大二时，学校教育处提供一种名叫思维象棋的免费课程，这个课程3个学分。我急于接受这个课程，是因为我想节省点钱。”waste浪费；earn赚钱；save节省；pay付钱。故选C。

43. A　考查形容词辨析。“我总是想学象棋，即便是我对免费的学分不激动，单是我们导师的信息就足以吸引我。”excited激动的；兴奋的；worried担心的；moved感动的；tired劳累的。故选A。

44. D　考查名词辨析。“我总是想学象棋，即便是我对免费的学分不激动，单是我们导师的消息就足以吸引我。”title头衔；题目；competitor竞赛者；textbook教科书；instructor导师。故选D。

45. D　考查动词辨析。这意味着“我”将师从这个游戏最好的大师之一。urged督促；demanded要求；held握住；meant意味着。故选D。

46. C　考查形容词词义辨析。这意味着“我”将师从这个游戏最好的大师之一。fastest最快的；easiest最容易的；best最好的；rarest最稀少的。故选C。

47.B 考查动词词义辨析。“我迫不及待地想见到他。”interview面试；meet见面；challenge挑战；beat击败。故选B。

48. D　考查名词词义辨析。一位先前的毕业生回校教书，这项工作对他来说根本不是游戏。chance机会；qualification合格；honor荣誉；job工作。故选D。

49. C　考查形容词辨析。在他的介绍中，他明确指出这些学分不容易得到。real真实的；perfect完美的；clear清楚的；possible可能的。故选C。

50. B　考查动词词义辨析。为了通过考试，我们必须写一篇关于把我们在课堂里学到的东西应用于未来职业中的文章。attend参加；pass通过；skip跳跃；observe遵守。故选B。

51. C　考查动词词义辨析。我们必须写一篇关于把我们在课堂里学到的知识应用于未来职业中的文章。apply把……运用于……

52. A　考查副词词义辨析。最终，把我们在课堂里学的知识应用到我们的生活中。eventually最终；naturally自然地；directly直接地；normally正常地。故选A。

53. C　考查名词辨析。“我”设法在这个课程中获得了个A。game游戏；presentation介绍；陈述；course课程；experiment实验。故选C。

54. B　考查名词辨析。“我”还学习了课堂之外对“我”很有用的生活课程。criterion标准；classroom教室；department部门；系；situation情况。故选B。

55. A　考查动词词义辨析。和Ashley学了象棋课程之后10年里，“我”仍在应用他教“我”的东西。taught教；wrote写；questioned提问；promised承诺。故选A。

56. D　考查名词词义辨析。你在学下棋的时候，学到的绝对重要的技能是如何做出好的决定。fact事实；step步；manner方式；skill技能。故选D。

57. B　考查名词词义辨析。你在学下棋的时候，学到的绝对重要的技能是如何做出好的决定。grades等级；decisions决定；impressions印象；comments评论。故选B。

58. A　考查动词词义辨析。每一步你都必须分析形势，审视对手要做什么。analyze分析；describe描述；rebuild重建；control控制。故选A。

59. D　考查动词词义辨析。从你所有的选择中，评估出最好的一步。announce宣布；signal发信号；block阻塞；evaluate评估。故选D。

60. A　考查名词词义辨析。现在这些话对“我”作为一名新闻记者的角色来说仍然是正确的 。

（三）完形填空之说明文

1. 命题特点

说明文往往围绕一个问题从不同的侧面来加以说明，通常结构严谨，句子结构复杂，因此也是高考完形填空题中较难理解的一种文体。其主要特点为：

（1）开头点题

在说明文类的完形填空中，作者一般在文章的首句直接提出说明的对象，这是掌握说明细节的前提。

（2）结构清晰

说明文一般按一定的顺序展开。理清文章的说明顺序，对于正确把握文意和上下文的逻辑关系，选择正确答案具有重要意义。

（3）难度较大

说明文往往采用比较正式的文体，表述准确严谨，生词、术语较多，句子较长，结构较为复杂。

（4）遣词用字简练

说明文一般采用简练的语言，按一定的方法介绍事物的类别、性质、特点、构造、成因、关系或事物的运动变化、发展的过程及其规律。

（5）条理清晰

说明文十分讲究条理性，一般采取时间顺序、空间顺序、逻辑顺序或认知顺序来说明事物或事理。

2. 应试策略

（1）快速弄清语篇解读

对于此类文章我们结合选项，进行粗读或略读，对文章的大意要先有一个大体的了解。说明文往往生词较多，而题材又比较广泛，所以阅读时，首先要掌握文章的大意。

（2）弄清楚说明的顺序

把握了说明顺序，就能准确把握文章的脉络，加强对整篇文章的理解。

（3）把握文章的组织结构，理清事实细节

把握语篇特征对理解文意与答题极为有利。说明性的文章一般都是一篇完整的、意思表达清楚的、逻辑比较严密的短文。在阅读这类文章时，我们一定要仔细研读文章的开头和结尾，从主题句着手，找出支持句，然后寻找文章的结论。我们要特别注意，不要被表面的一些细节所迷惑，我们在理解细节的基础上，还要斟酌文字的内涵意义，从而对文章进行深层次的理解。

应逐句精读短文，逐题分析选项，对特定的语境做深入的理解，克服思维定势。

（4）注重上下文语境

按照词不离句、句不离文的原则逐项填空。

（5）熟练做题方法，遵循四个原则

① 上下一致。分析每个选项必须从全文出发，从大处着手，避免孤立地分析每个空格，造成误选。

② 语法正确。从语法的角度去考虑动词的时态、语态以及词类用法。

③ 逻辑合理。在完形填空题中，逻辑推理非常重要，有时每个选择项从语法上讲正确，但是有的是不合语境逻辑的。

④ 符合搭配。英语中固定搭配很多，要熟练掌握，才能做好此类题目。

真题回顾 · 典例 · 做人与做事 · 2018浙江卷

We have all heard how time is more valuable than money, but is it __36__ to have too much?

I __37__ back in high school I spent most of my day at school since I also __38__ a team sport.By the time I got home, I only had a few hours to do my homework, and I had to do it __39__.

When I got into college, things __40__ I suddenly found myself out of class before noon time.Because of all this __41__ there was no sense of __42__ to do my school work immediately. I was performing this action of waiting until it later became __43__. Once that happened, I just kept __44__ my studying further and further back in my day.Then I got to the point where I was __45__ really late at night to get my work alone.

One day I __46__ a former classmate of mine who was __47__ a lot of money running a sideline（副业）. Since his regular job was __48__, I asked him why he just didn't do his sideline full-time.He said without the job, he would __49__ have too much time and would just do what I did back in __50__. He said that if he __51__ the job, he would lose his __52__ to work and succeed.

So, try __53__ your time with other work. This is why there is a __54__ that if you want something done, ask a __55__ person to do it.

36. A. true B. fair C. strange D. possible
37. A. remember B. admit C. understand D. expect
38. A. watched B. loved C. coached D. played
39. A. at last B. right away C. of course D. mattered
40. A. happened B. repeated C. changed D. mattered
41. A. extra B. difficult C. valuable D. limited
42. A. duty B. achievement C. urgency D. direction
43. A. burden B. relief C. risk D. habit
44. A. pushing B. taking C. setting D. calling
45. A. hanging out B. staying up C. jogging round D. showing off
46. A. met B. helped C. treated D. hired
47. A. raising B. wasting C. demanding D. making
48. A. safe B. important C. boring D. rewarding
49. A. luckily B. hardly C. hopefully D. simply
50. A. childhood B. college C. town D. business
51. A. quit B. found C. accepted D. kept
52. A. heart B. chance C. drive D. way
53. A. saving B. filling up C. giving up D. trading
54. A. message B. story C. saying D. fact
55. A. careful B. busy C. reliable D. kind

语篇解读：

本文通过作者亲身经历告诉我们：拥有太多时间就会拖延做事情，时间紧迫反而能合理安排时间把事情做好。

答案解析：

36. D 考查形容词。A. true真实的；B. fair公平的；C. strange奇怪的；D. possible可能的。句意：我们都听说过时间比金钱更有价值，但是拥有的时间太多可能会把事情做好吗？表示“可能的”，表示作者的疑问，故选D。

37. A 考查动词。A. remember记得；B. admit承认；C. understand理解；D. expect期望。此处表示回忆起高中时自己的生活，表示“回忆起”是remember back，故选A。

38. D　考查动词。A. watched观察；B. loved热爱；C. coached训练；D. played玩。此处指自从"我"进行团体体育锻炼后多数时间在学校，表示"进行体育锻炼"是play sport，故选D。

39. B　考查固定短语。A. at last最后；B. right away立刻，马上；C. of course当然；D. mattered要紧，重要。因为在校时间多，在家做作业的时间就少了，所以在家时必须马上写作业。下文do my school work immediately给了提示，故选B。

40. C　考查动词。A. happened发生；B. repeated重复；C. changed改变；D. mattered要紧。大学生活和高中生活不一样，所以说发生了改变。根据常识选C。

41. A　考查形容词。A. extra额外的；B. difficult. 困难的；C. valuable有价值的；D. limited有限的。此处指大学里有许多额外的时间，故选A。

42. C　考查名词。A. duty责任；B. achievement成就；C. urgency紧急；D. direction方向。大学里没有马上做作业的紧迫感，与高中时抓紧时间做作业形成对比，故选C。

43. D　考查名词。A. burden负担；B. relief救济；C. risk冒险；D. habit习惯。由于不急着写作业，所以后来就形成了等的习惯。故选D。

44. A　考查动词。A. pushing推；B. taking拿；C. setting放置；D. calling呼唤。与上文的waiting呼应，指形成等的习惯后，"我"就不断地把学习往后推，越推越远。根据常识也可知答案，故选A。

45. B　考查动词短语。A. hanging out挂出，常去某处；B. staying up熬夜；C. jogging round慢跑；D. showing off炫耀。根据late at night可知是熬夜，此处指作业等到最后熬夜完成，故选B。

46. A　考查动词。A. met遇见；B. helped帮助；C. treated治疗；D. hired雇用。此处指遇到了以前的同学，根据句意选A。

47. D　考查动词。A. raising举起；B. wasting浪费；C. demanding要求；D. making获得。此处指经营副业挣了许多钱，"挣钱"是make money,故选D。

48. C　考查形容词。A. safe安全的；B. important重要的；C. boring无聊的；D. rewarding有益的。因为他的常规工作是无聊的，所以作者建议他把副业作为全职工作。故选C。

49. D　考查副词。A. luckily幸运地；B. hardly几乎不；C. hopefully有希望地；D. simply简单地。朋友说如果没有这个工作，很简单他就会有太多无聊的时间。根据句意可知选D。

50. B　考查名词。A. childhood童年时期；B. college大学；C. town城镇；D. business商业。他就会像"我"大学时一样因为有太多的时间而不忙着做事，与上文内容呼应，故选B。

51. A　考查动词。A. quit放弃；B. found发现；C. accepted接受；D. kept保持。如果他放弃工作，就会失去工作和成功的动力。与作者的建议呼应，故选A。

52. C　考查名词。A. heart心脏；B. chance机会；C. drive驱动力；D. way方法。此处指如果他放弃工作，就失去了紧迫感，就会失去工作和成功的动力。表示“动力”，故选C。

53. B　考查动词。A. saving节约；B. filling up装满；C. giving up放弃；D. trading交易。句意：试着用其他工作装满你的时间，使自己忙起来。故选B。

54. C　考查名词。A. message消息；B. story故事；C. saying谚语；D. fact事实。此处指if you want something done, ask a __55__ person to do it.这句谚语，故选C。

55. B　考查形容词。A. careful小心的；B. busy忙碌的；C. reliable可靠的；D. kind善良的。此处指如果你想做某事，请忙碌的人去做。忙碌的人会抓紧时间完成，不忙的人只会拖延时间。故选B。

（四）完形填空之议论文

1. 命题规律

议论文是一种剖析事物、论述事理、发表见解或提出主张的说理性文章。议论文的目的不仅是客观地解释事物，还力图说服读者相信并接受某一观点。英语议论文不完全等同于汉语的议论文，它涉及的范围要小得多。有人把英语中的议论文理解为论证文、推理文或辩论文，还有人直接将议论文归入到了说明文当中。但笔者认为就写作目的与写作手法而言，英语议论文与英语说明文还是有一定的区别的。首先，英语说明文主要是对提出的主题进行“说明”和“阐述”，并不进行正反评判和推理，也不强迫读者接受作者的观点；而英语议论文主要是就某一主题，在摆出正反两方面观点的基础上，通过论证、推理、辩论等手段，试图让读者最终接受作者对这一主题的某种观点。尽管有时也不一定非常明确地交待正反观点，但力图通过推理让读者赞同自己的观点始终是英语议论文的主要目的。

不管是在汉语中，还是在英语中，议论文都是由论点（作者的观点，也就是被证明的对象）、论据（用来证明论点的依据，是说明论点的理由和材料）和论证（运用论据证明论点的过程与方法），这三个要素构成的，这也是一个提出问题——分析问题——解决问题的过程。因此，典型的议论文一般由序论（提出问题，即what）、本论（分析问题，即why）和结论（解决问题，即how）三个部分构成，其具体的结构模式有以下三种：

（1）模式一

引言段（提出观点）——正方论点一（支持作者观点的较弱论点）、正方论点二（支持作者观点的较强论点）、正方论点三（支持作者观点的最强论点）——结论段（总结+解决方法，论断或建议）。

在这种模式中，文章主体段（中间部分）的每一个部分论述一个论点，这些论点以其重要性按序排列，最有力、最重要的论点在最后面，以示强调。

（2）模式二

引言段（提出观点）——反面意见（反方观点+作者的反驳）、正方论点一（支持作者观点的较弱论点）、正方论点二（支持作者观点的较强论点）、正方论点三（支持作者观点的最强论点）——结论段（总结+解决方法，论断或建议）。

在这种模式中，文章主体段的一开始就提出对立方的反面意见及作者对这种意见的反驳，以后各部分仍分别陈述作者的不同论点。

（3）模式三

引言段（提出观点）——反方观点一+进行反驳的正方论点、反方观点二+进行反驳的正方论点、反方观点三+进行反驳的正方论点——结论段（总结+解决方法，论断或建议）。

在这种模式中，作者在文章主体段的每一部分都先提出一个反面观点，然后再进行反驳。

议论文有自己的语言个性，它不同于记叙文的生动形象，也不同于说明文的简明易懂。议论是对具体事物、事理做出的理论上的分析与阐述，因此，它的语言是自然客观的、抽象的、概括的。同时，它的语言也很准确，合乎逻辑。文中会较多地使用，诸如since（既然），now that（既然），therefore（因而），in that case（在那种情况下），so（所以），It follows that...（因而……），If... we may conclude that...（如果……我们可以这样下结论……），should it be the case（如果是这样的话……），I don’t want to... but...（我并不想……但是……），It is true that... but...（诚然……但是……），even if...（即使……）等有辩论和推理含义的连接和过渡词语与结构，以增强语言的准确性和逻辑性。此外，作者的写作态度一般也较诚恳，在文章中通常使用的是与读者平等交流的语气，不会给人以居高临下、以势逼人的感觉，在遣词造句方面多使用虚拟语气、让步状语从句和can、may、might、could、would、should等情态动词。

2. 应试策略

（1）通览

把握作者的观点和态度。议论文往往体现作者对某一事物的观点，而作者的观点就是文章的论点。考生要把握作者的观点，把握作者对某一事物是褒还是贬，是赞成还是反对，而通常把握了作者的观点也就找准了文章的论点。

把握文章的开头，总结文章的结尾。议论文的篇首或结尾出现话题中心，通过首段或末段把握文章的主题。

（2）试填

注意段与段之间的逻辑。议论文往往围绕某一个论点用不同的论据加以佐证，往往每一段就是一个论据，而论据和论据之间又相互联系、互为补充，每一段往往就是其中一个角度或侧面。

（3）复核

通读全文，检验每条论据是否都合情合理，都能强而有力地支撑论点。

真题回顾·典例·2018北京卷

The Homeless Hero

For many, finding an unattended wallet filled with ￡400 in cash would be a source（来源）of temptation（诱惑）. But the __16__ would no doubt be greater if you were living on the streets with little food and money.All of this makes the actions of the homeless Tom Smith __17__ more remarkable.

After spotting a __18__ on the front seat inside a parked car with its window down, he stood guard in the rain for about two hours waiting for the __19__ to return.

After hours in the cold and wet, he __20__ inside and pulled the wallet out hoping to find some ID so he could contact（联系）the driver, only to __21__ it contained 400 in notes, with another 50 in spare change beside it.

He then took the wallet to a nearby police station after __22__ a note behind to let the owner know it was safe.When the car's owner John Anderson and his colleague Carol Lawrence returned to the car—which was itself worth 35, 000—in Glasgow city centre, they were __23__ to find two policemen standing next to it.The policemen told them what Mr.Smith did and that the wallet was __24__.

The pair were later able to thank Mr.Smith for his __25__.

Mr.Anderson said: "I couldn't believe that the guy never took a penny.To think he is sleeping on the streets tonight __26__ he could have stolen the money and paid for a place to stay in.This guy has nothing and __27__ he didn't take the wallet for himself; he thought about others __28__. It's unbelievable.It just proves there are __29__ guys out there."

Mr.Smith's act __30__ much of the public's attention.He also won praise from social media users after Mr.Anderson __31__ about the act of kindness on Facebook.

Now Mr.Anderson has set up an online campaign to __32__ money for Mr.Smith and other homeless people in the area, which by yesterday had received ￡8,000."I think the faith that everyone has shown __33__ him has touched him.People have been approaching him in the street; he's had job __34__ and all sorts," Mr.Anderson commented.

For Mr.Smith, this is a possible life-changing __35__. The story once again tells us that one good turn deserves another.

16. A. hope	B. aim	C. urge	D. effort
17. A. still	B. even	C. ever	D. once
18. A. wallet	B. bag	C. box	D. parcel
19. A. partner	B. colleague	C. owner	D. policeman
20. A. turned	B. hid	C. stepped	D. reached
21. A. discover	B. collect	C. check	D. believe
22. A. taking	B. leaving	C. reading	D. writing
23. A. satisfied	B. excited	C. amused	D. shocked
24. A. safe	B. missing	C. found	D. seen
25. A. service	B. support	C. kindness	D. encouragement
26. A. when	B. if	C. where	D. because
27. A. rather	B. yet	C. already	D. just
28. A. too	B. though	C. again	D. instead
29. A. honest	B. polite	C. rich	D. generous
30. A. gave	B. paid	C. cast	D. drew
31. A. learned	B. posted	C. cared	D. heard
32. A. borrow	B. raise	C. save	D. earn
33. A. of	B. at	C. for	D. in
34. A. details	B. changes	C. offers	D. applications
35. A. lesson	B. adventure	C. chance	D. challenge

语篇解读：

这是一篇夹叙夹议类文章。文章讲述了流浪汉Tom发现一辆车窗开着的汽车前座上有一个钱包。Tom冒雨等了数个小时，在查找不到车主身份的情况下将钱包交到了警察局。钱包的主人Mr.Anderson在得知这一切后，将Tom的善举发布到了Facebook上。Tom的行为引发了人们的好评和帮助。这件事印证了一句俗语：善有善报。

答案解析：

16. C　考查名词词义辨析。A. hope希望；B. aim目标；C. urge强烈的欲望，冲动；D. effort努力。上一句提到，对很多人来说，一个装有400英镑无人看管的钱包是一种诱惑（它诱惑着人们将其据为己有）。结合该句中的比较级greater可知，对于一个无家可归的人来说，这样的一个钱包是一个更大的诱惑，将其据为己有的欲望会更大。该空对应上一句中的“a source（来源）of temptation（诱惑）”，C选项正确。

17. B　考查副词词义辨析。A. still仍然；B. even更加，愈发，甚至；C. ever曾经；D. once曾经，一度。所有这一切使得流浪汉Tom Smith的行为更加不同寻常。even在该句中修饰比较级more remarkable。B选项正确。

18. A　考查名词词义辨析。A. wallet钱包；B. bag包；C. box盒子，箱子；D. parcel包裹，包袱。由第三段中的After hours in the cold and wet, he __20__ inside and pulled the wallet out hoping to find some ID可知，Tom Smith发现一辆汽车的前排座上有一个钱包。当时这辆车停在那儿，窗户摇了下来。A选项正确。

19. C　考查名词词义辨析。A.partner同伴，伙伴；B.colleague同事；C.owner主人；D.policeman警察。Tom冒雨等待车主回来。C选项正确。

20. D　考查动词词义辨析。A. turned转动；B. hid藏，隐藏；C. stepped迈步，举步；D. reached伸手去拿，到达。由后面的pulled the wallet out可知，在雨里等了数个小时后，Tom将手伸进车窗，将钱包拿了出来。D选项正确。

21. A　考查动词词义辨析。A. discover发现；B. collect搜集；C. check核对，检查；D. believe相信。Tom将钱包拿出来企图找到一些身份证明，这样他就能联系司机了，结果他却发现钱包里装着400的纸币和50的零钱。A选项正确。

22. B　考查动词词义辨析。A. taking带走；B. leaving留下，落下，离开；C. reading读；D. writing写。他拿着钱包去了附近的警察局，在车上留下了一张便条，其目的是让车主知道他的钱包是安全的。B选项正确。

23. D　考查形容词词义辨析。A. satisfied满意的；B. excited兴奋的；C. amused被逗乐的；D. shocked震惊的。当车主返回时，发现自己的车边有警察，应该感到很惊讶。故D选项正确。

24. A　考查形容词/动词词义辨析。A. safe安全的；B. missing不见的，丢失的；C. found发现，找到；D. seen看见。由该段开头可知，Tom将钱包带去了警察局，因此该处警察告诉Mr. Anderson他的钱包是安全的。A选项正确。

25. C　考查名词词义辨析。A. service服务；B. support支持；C. kindness善意，善良；D. encouragement鼓励。Tom将钱包交给警察，没有据为己有，这是一种善举。故C选项正确。

26. A　考查状语从句引导词。A. when在……情况下，既然；B. if如果；C. where表地点；D. because因为。在Tom本来可以偷了钱去支付一个可以睡觉的地方的情况下，他仍然选择了露宿街头（没有偷钱）。所以Mr.Anderson对Tom的行为感到很惊讶。A选项正确。

27. B　考查副词词义辨析。A. rather相当；B. yet但是；C. already已经；D. just

仅仅。Tom什么都没有，但是他没有拿走钱包。前后两句话之间是转折关系，故B选项正确。

28. D 考查副词词义辨析。A. too也；B. though但是；C. again再，又；D. instead代替。Tom没有拿走钱包，他考虑的是别人，没有考虑自己。D选项正确。

29. A 考查形容词词义辨析。A. honest诚实的；B. polite礼貌的；C. rich富有的；D. generous慷慨的。Tom没有拿走钱包，而是把它交到了警察局，这是一种诚实的行为。A选项正确。

30. D 考查动词词义辨析。A. gave给；B. paid支付；C. cast投掷，投射；D. drew吸引。Tom的行为引起了公众的关注。D选项正确。

31. B 考查动词词义辨析。A. learned学习，学会；B. posted发布，张贴；C. cared关心，在意；D. heard听到。由后面的Facebook（一个社交网站）可知，在Mr.Anderson将Tom的善举发布到Facebook上之后，Tom赢得了社交媒体使用者的赞扬。B选项正确。

32. B 考查动词词义辨析。A. borrow借；B. raise筹集；C. save挽救，节省；D. earn挣（钱）。Mr.Anderson在网上发起一个运动来为Tom和其他无家可归的人筹钱。B选项正确。

33. D 考查介词。大家向Tom表示出的信任触动了Tom。faith意为“信任，相信”，常和介词in搭配，意为“对……的信任，相信……”，故D选项正确。

34. C 考查名词词义辨析。A. details细节；B. changes改变；C. offers提供（物），给予（物），提议；D. applications应用，申请。该句指Tom得到了人们的帮助，人们为他提供工作和其他的东西。C选项正确。

35. C 考查名词词义辨析。A. lesson课；B. adventure冒险；C. chance机会；D. challenge挑战。这件事对于流浪汉Tom来说是一个可以改变终生的机会。C选项正确。

四、2019年完形填空新课标主题分析篇之备考训练

（一）人与自然

真题回顾 · Passage 1 · 绵阳南山中学2018届高三热身考试

Have you ever been tempted to cut a corner or to take the easiest route, though you know it may not __21__ be the best one? Or have you ever made a __22__ because it was quick and simple, knowing that it might come back to bite you later?

I appreciate a parable（寓言）Danish philosopher Soren Kierkegard told about the __23__ of taking the easy route.It is story about a __24__ duck.Though life was difficult __25__, the beautiful creature __26__ the boundless heavens and the endless stretches of wilderness.Soaring about treetops and towns, the duck was a symbol of freedom to its tame counterparts（相对物）, who could not __27__.

One evening during fall migration, he __28__ to enter a barnyard where a farmer was __29__ his ducks. The beautiful creature ate the __30__ the farmer sprinkled（撒）about and liked it so much that he stayed the night in a bed of __31__ straw. He ate the duck's corn again the next day. And the next. And the next...

When __32__ came, he heard his old companions flying overhead and an almost forgotten longing deep __33__ him awoke.The duck had reduced his instinct for freedom over the __34__ winter. Now he longed to __35__ his comrades in the sky, but he had grown fat and unable to fly.The wild duck had become a tame duck.

The easy way through our problems, though __36__, may not be the best way.Always remember.The only place you will find success before __37__ is in the dictionary! It's always easier to borrow than to save; easier to jump in now than to do the hard work of planning; easier to cut corners than to do it right; easier to __38__ the same than to make changes.

__39__ you want to fly, you may have to pay a price.But __40__ is worth it—at any cost! Are you ready to soar?

21. A. likely B. necessarily C. gradually D. obviously
22. A. bet B. difference C. decision D. suggestion
23. A. results B. conditions C. benefits D. dangers
24. A. wild B. fat C. clever D. brave
25. A. at one time B. at times C. at once D. at night
26. A. ignored B. admired C. hated D. disliked
27. A. think B. dream C. fly D. run
28. A. attempted B. intended C. happened D. decided
29. A. watching B. feeding C. washing D. gathering
30. A. bread B. wheat C. grain D. corn
31. A. warm B. thin C. hard D. damp
32. A. winter B. fall C. spring D. summer
33. A. within B. beyond C. to D. for
34. A. bitter B. cold C. comfortable D. tough
35. A. join B. visit C. welcome D. greet

36. A. interesting B. surprising C. instructive D. attractive
37. A. pay B. effort C. reward D. prize
38. A. go B. get C. become D. remain
39. A. If B. Before C. Although D. Since
40. A. adventure B. experience C. justice D. freedom

真题回顾·Passage 2·湖南师大附中2018届高三高考模拟卷一

One morning in early fall, I found a pair of wild geese on our pond.The beautiful sight caught me by __21__, because we'd never seen geese there before.I __22__ they would soon be on their way, so I enjoyed the __23__ to be close to them.I wondered where they came from and why they'd __24__ our pond.

The next morning, the geese were __25__ our guests, so I watched them at a distance to show them I meant no __26__. Still, I couldn't __27__ getting a closer look.I stopped by some trees near the water's edge and quietly looked at them through the __28__. I was surprised to see that they were __29__ me.

As the days passed, I continued to see them every day.They craned their necks and raised their heads __30__ but seemed to realize I was a friend.Later, my __31__ about why they were staying at the pond so long changed to concern.It wouldn't be long before the __32__ winter came and the pond froze over.

One day, as they were feeding in the grass, I discovered the reason for their __33__ — the male had a broken left __34__. He was unable to fly, and his mate would not leave him behind.I asked a wildlife biologist friend what I should do.He explained that sometimes a broken wing will __35__ by itself and suggested that I let nature take its course.

On the first day of November, I __36__ sight of the geese running toward the pond, beating their wings with great effort.Both __37__ climbed higher and flew over the pond. Then they turned back toward me, flying no more than 50 feet over my head as if to say goodbye.Then they were __38__.

The season's first snow fell the every next day.The birds must have __39__ that winter was coming and that it was time to go.I miss them very much now and I'll never forget their __40__ to each other.We can all learn a lesson or two from this pair.

21. A. anger B. surprise C. terror D. sorrow
22. A. denied B. imagined C. realized D. assumed
23. A. opinion B. opportunity C. feeling D. message

24. A.decided B. ordered C. chosen D. forgotten
25. A.also B. still C. even D. seldom
26. A.violence B. pain C. harm D. punishment
27. A.bear B. stop C. risk D. resist
28. A.windows B. forests C. villages D. branches
29. A.laughing at B. shouting at C. staring at D. waving at
30. A.cautiously B. positively C. skeptically D. clearly
31. A.worry B. hesitation C. claim D. curiosity
32. A.short B. cruel C. mild D. early
33. A.love B. plan C. journey D. visit
34. A.wing B. foot C. leg D. eye
35. A.test B. appear C. drop D. heal
36. A.fixed B. caught C. met D. remembered
37. A.hopefully B. curiously C. recently D. gradually
38. A.out of sight B. out of question C. out of place D. out of reach
39. A.sensed B. planned C. found D. smelt
40. A.advice B. respect C. devotion D. attention

（二）人与自我

真题回顾 · Passage 1 · 认识自我 · 2018天津卷

No one is born a winner.People make themselves into winners by their own __16__.

I learned this lesson from a(n) __17__ many years ago.I took the head __18__ job at a school in Baxley, Georgia.It was a small school with a weak football program.

It was a tradition for the school's old team to play against the __19__ team at the end of spring practice.The old team had no coach, and they didn't even practice to __20__ the game.Being the coach of the new team, I was excited because I knew we were going to win, but to my disappointment we were defeated.I couldn't __21__ I had got into such a situation. Thinking hard about it, I came to __22__ that my team might not be the number one team in Georgia, but they were __23__ me.I had to change my __24__ about their ability and potential.

I started doing anything I could to help them build a little __25__. Most important, I began to treat them like __26__. That summer, when the other teams enjoyed their __27__, we met every day and __28__ passing and kicking the football.

Six months after suffering our __29__ on the spring practice field, we won our first game and our second, and continued to __30__. Finally, we faced the number one team in the state. I felt that it would be a __31__ for us even if we lost the game.But that wasn't what happened.My boys beat the best team in Georgia, giving me one of the greatest __32__ of my life!

From the experience I learnt a lot about how the attitude of the leader can __33__ the members of a team. Instead of seeing my boys as losers, I pushed and __34__ them.I helped them to see themselves __35__, and they built themselves into winners.

Winners are made, but born.

16. A. luck	B. tests	C. efforts	D. nature
17. A. experiment	B. experience	C. visit	D. show
18. A. operating	B. editing	C. consulting	D. coaching
19. A. successful	B. excellent	C. strong	D. new
20. A. cheer for	B. prepare for	C. help with	D. finish with
21. A. believe	B. agree	C. describe	D. regret
22. A. realize	B. claim	C. permit	D. demand
23. A. reacting to	B. looking for	C. depending on	D. caring about
24. A. decision	B. attitude	C. conclusion	D. intention
25. A. pride	B. culture	C. fortune	D. relationship
26. A. leaders	B. partners	C. winners	D. learners
27. A. rewards	B. vacations	C. health	D. honor
28. A. risked	B. missed	C. considered	D. practiced
29. A. defeat	B. decline	C. accident	D. mistake
30. A. relax	B. improve	C. expand	D. defend
31. A. shame	B. burden	C. victory	D. favor
32. A. chances	B. thrills	C. concerns	D. offers
33. A. surprise	B. serve	C. interest	D. affect
34. A. encouraged	B. observed	C. protected	D. impressed
35. A. honestly	B. individually	C. calmly	D. differently

真题回顾 · Passage 2 · 湖南长沙雅礼中学、河南实验中学2018届高三联考

How can I forget the day? On 14 July 1974 I travelled in an overcrowded bus to an unheard town called Shendurni.The next day, I was to join the faculty of a junior college there. __21__ about my new job, but anxious and fearful too, I was out of my __22__ zone. Around 7 p.m.it started pouring with rain.Wondering about my new career in an unknown land, I had __23__ in my seat.I woke up with a(n) __24__ to the sound of the conductor announcing the name of my bus stop.I looked out.It was pitch-dark.Ah, a power cut. __25__ unusual during heavy rains. "Conductor Sahab, can I get a __26__ for myself here? I'm new to the place," I heard myself ask __27__. "Arrebhai, get off my bus and let us go.We __28__ to reach the next station on time.Where will you get a place to stay in this goddamned town?" He shouted back.Amid mounting panic, I felt a __29__ tap on my shoulder.As I looked back, a warm smile __30__ me. "I'm Sawant, from the next town.The bus __31__ there for the night and returns tomorrow morning.Why don't you buy a ticket for the next stop? You can spend the night at my place, and join work tomorrow." I thanked him from my heart and accepted his __32__. By the time the bus reached the final stop, it was 8:30 p.m.The kind soul led me to his house.He and his wife took great __33__ to make my stay comfortable.I was __34__ with warm water for a bath, followed by a hot __35__ and a comfortable bed.All this took place in semi-darkness.No lights yet.I was up early the next morning and my benefactor（恩人）came to __36__ me off.I could not see his face clearly, as it was __37__ dark.I made it __38__ the college in time and taught there for almost 11 years. All this while I __39__ him, even asking my new friends and students to help find the kind soul.But Mr. Sawant remained __40__. Perhaps I had got his name wrong. My only regret: I could not thank him again.

21. A. Excited　　B. Interested　　C. Worried　　D. Annoyed
22. A. home　　B. school　　C. comfort　　D. dilemma
23. A. knocked off　　B. dropped off　　C. turned off　　D. nodded off
24. A. start　　B. jump　　C. ear　　D. eye
25. A. Something　　B. Anything　　C. Everything　　D. Nothing
26. A. seat　　B. room　　C. ticket　　D. map
27. A. sadly　　B. quickly　　C. nervously　　D. surprisingly
28. A. come　　B. get　　C. need　　D. ask
29. A. sudden　　B. soft　　C. real　　D. warm
30. A. waved　　B. welcomed　　C. greeted　　D. shook
31. A. stops　　B. arrives　　C. leaves　　D. drives
32. A. family　　B. solution　　C. invitation　　D. request
33. A. pleasure　　B. energy　　C. minds　　D. pains
34. A. provided　　B. armed　　C. impressed　　D. blessed

35. A. chat B. discussion C. meal D. tea
36. A. allow B. keep C. show D. see
37. A. yet B. still C. already D. also
38. A. to B. in C. from D. for
39. A. sent for B. searched for C. cared for D. waited for
40. A. silent B. strange C. unbelievable D. untraceable

真题回顾 · Passage 3 · 河北省石家庄市第二中学2018届高三仿真模拟一

When Mrs.Green told her pupils to draw a picture of something for which they were thankful, she thought how little these children in a(an) __21__ neighborhood, had to be __22__ for. Most of the __23__ would draw pictures of turkeys（火鸡）or of Thanksgiving tables full of everything __24__ to eat.That was what they believed was __25__ them.

What made Mrs.Green __26__ was David's picture. David was so disappointed and likely to be __27__ close in his shadow as they went outside for breaks.David's drawing was __28__ this:

A hand, whose hand? The class was strongly attracted by his image. "I think it must be the __29__ of God __30__ us food," said one student.

"A __31__," said another, "because they __32__ the turkeys."

"It looks more like a policeman, and they __33__ us." "I think," Lucy said __34__, "that it is __35__ to be all the hands that help us, but David could only draw one of them."

Mrs.Green had almost forgotten David in her __36__ at finding the class so responsive（共鸣的）. Having the others working on another project, she bent over his __37__ and asked whose hand it was.

David whispered, "It's yours, Teacher."

Then Mrs.Green __38__ she had taken David by the hand from time to time; she often did that with the children. But that it should have __39__ so much to David ...

Perhaps, she thought this was her Thanksgiving, and everybody's Thanksgiving—not the things given to us, but the small __40__ that we give something to others.

21. A. bettering B. developing C. interesting D. worsening
22. A. eager B. thankful C. ready D. greedy
23. A. class B. school C. group D. boys
24. A. rare B. delicious C. expensive D. fit
25. A. convinced of B. informed of C. warned of D. expected of

26. A. satisfied B. touched C. amazed D. encouraged
27. A. found B. shut C. hidden D. stuck
28. A. only B. simply C. clearly D. exactly
29. A. head B. arm C. hand D. foot
30. A. fetching B. earning C. sending D. bringing
31. A. worker B. carpenter C. farmer D. banker
32. A. raise B. milk C. have D. grow
33. A. bring B. protect C. watch D. guard
34. A. seriously B. rudely C. naughtily D. noisily
35. A. proved B. known C. said D. supposed
36. A. surprise B. pride C. pleasure D. wonder
37. A. picture B. book C. schoolbag D. desk
38. A. realized B. wished C. remembered D. believed
39. A. sensed B. meant C. accounted D. affected
40. A. ways B. chances C. abilities D. hopes

（三）人与社会

真题回顾 · Passage 1 · 湖北省襄阳四中2018届高三5月四模

One fall in the mid-1950s, I took some time off and got a train ticket to visit relatives in Cleveland.I was __41__ out of school and had begun working as an office clerk.On my return trip, I noticed a couple across the aisle（通道）— a(n) __42__ and a young woman — having a conversation.

__43__, I realized the two of them weren't traveling together after all, but had just met on the train.The woman finally got off at Rochester, New York, leaving the soldier __44__. I couldn't help noticing his good looks out of the corner of my __45__.

He asked __46__ he could look at the train timetable I was holding, and then if he could __47__ next to me so we could chat. He's a fast mover, I thought.I'll have to __48__ for this one.I invited him to __49__ the too-large lunch my aunt had __50__ for my trip, and we __51__ all the way to my stop in Oneida, and we __52__ addresses and he said he would be in __53__.

After a week, I still hadn't heard from him and had begun to think he'd forgotten about me.Then, on Saturday, the phone rang and a __54__ voice asked if I would like to see a movie with him that evening. He'd come to Oneida, and we __55__ seeing *On the*

Waterfront at the Kallet Theatre.

We had a few more __56__ during his Army leave, and then he was __57__ overseas. For the next few years, we __58__ and he visited me on other holidays.Today we've been together more than 55 years, raising three daughters who now have daughters of their own.

Before taking my trip to Cleveland all those years ago, I was warned never to speak to __59__ on a train.I'm certainly __60__ I didn't listen.

41. A. absent B. fresh C. expert D. anxious
42. A. armyman B. businessman C. policeman D. salesman
43. A. Immediately B. Eventually C. Hurriedly D. Imaginarily
44. A. aside B. annoyed C. amazed D. alone
45. A. eye B. ear C. shoulder D. seat
46. A. when B. where C. if D. how
47. A. sit B. wait C. lean D. bend
48. A. set out B. make out C. hang out D. watch out
49. A. prepare B. share C. deliver D. order
50. A. carried B. packed C. allocated D. stored
51. A. argued B. wept C. talked D. ate
52. A. found B. announced C. exchanged D. described
53. A. need B. despair C. pain D. touch
54. A. familiar B. mature C. strange D. particular
55. A. gave up B. added up C. ended up D. got up
56. A. discussions B. dates C. lessons D. deals
57. A. injured B. attracted C. assigned D. employed
58. A. separated B. settled C. practiced D. corresponded
59. A. strangers B. officers C. conductors D. writers
60. A. curious B. glad C. aware D. sorry

真题回顾·Passage 2·郑州2018届三模

Fifteen years ago, I took a summer vacation in Lecce in Italy.After climbing up a hill for a full view of the blue sea, I paused to catch my __21__ and then positioned myself to take a photo.

Unfortunately, just as I took out my camera, a woman approached from behind and __22__ herself right in front of my __23__.Like me, she was here to stop, sigh and appreciate the scenery.

__24__ as I was, after about 15 minutes, my camera scanning the sun and reviewing the shot I would __25__ take, I was upset.Should I ask her to __26__ so that I could take just one picture of the landscape? Sure, I could have asked her, but something __27__ me doing so.She seemed so __28__ in her observation.I didn't want to mess with that.

Another 15 minutes passed and I grew more __29__. The woman was still there.I decided to take the photo __30__. And now when I look at it, I think her __31__ in the photo is what makes the image __32__. The landscape, beautiful on its own, somehow comes to life and breathes __33__ this woman is engaging with it.This photo, with the __34__ beauty that unfolded before me and the woman who __35__ it, now hangs on the wall in my bedroom. What would she think if she knew that her figure is captured（捕捉）and __36__ on a stranger's bedroom wall? A bedroom, after all, is a very private space, in which a woman I don't even know has been kept forever. In some ways, she has been __37__ in my house.

Perhaps we all live in each other's space.Perhaps this is what photos are for: to __38__ us that we all appreciate beauty, and that we all share a common __39__ for pleasure and connection.

This photo is a reminder, a captured moment, an unspoken __40__ between two women, separated only by a thin square of glass.

21. A. sight　B. breath　C. way　D. attention
22. A. planted　B. found　C. lost　D. enjoyed
23. A. concern　B. photo　C. view　D. direction
24. A. Cautious　B. Curious　C. Casual　D. Patient
25. A. eventually　B. randomly　C. extremely　D. hurriedly
26. A. back away　B. go over　C. move along　D. stay out
27. A. caught　B. sent　C. got　D. prevented
28. A. anxious　B. content　C. quiet　D. confident
29. A. excited　B. annoyed　C. worried　D. confused
30. A. anyway　B. somehow　C. instead　D. indeed
31. A. beauty　B. behavior　C. determination　D. presence
32. A. puzzling　B. disappointing　C. interesting　D. boring
33. A. unless　B. because　C. although　D. until
34. A. strange　B. regrettable　C. distant　D. unique
35. A. ruined　B. created　C. missed　D. discovered
36. A. protected　B. observed　C. frozen　D. drawn

37. A. hanging	B. living	C. shining	D. wandering
38. A. promise	B. tell	C. convince	D. remind
39. A. respect	B. plan	C. desire	D. sense
40. A. conversation	B. result	C. trust	D. love

参考答案

（一）人与自然

真题回顾・Passage 1・绵阳南山中学2018届高三热身考试

语篇解读：

这是一篇故事类阅读。通过野鸭的故事说明了自由值得一切代价。

答案解析：

21. B　考查副词。句意：尽管你知道这可能不是最好的路线。A. likely很可能，或许；B. necessarily必要地，必定地；C. gradually逐步地；D. obviously明显地。故选B。

22. C　考查名词。句意：或者你曾经做过一个决定。A. bet打赌；B. difference差异，不同；C. decision决定，决心；D. suggestion建议。故选C。

23. D　考查名词。句意：我很欣赏一个寓言，丹麦哲学家Soren Kierkegard告知的采取简单路线的危险。A. results结果；B. conditions条件；C. benefits福利；D. dangers危险。故选D。

24. A　考查形容词。句意：这是关于一只野鸭的故事。A. wild野生的；B. fat肥胖的；C. clever聪明的；D. brave勇敢的。故选A。

25. B　考查介词短语。句意：虽然生命有时是困难的，但美丽的生物却欣赏着无边无际的天空和无尽的荒野。A. at one time曾经，一度；B. at times偶尔，有时；C. at once马上，立刻；D. at night在夜里。故选B。

26. B　考查动词。句意：虽然生命有时是困难的，但美丽的生物却欣赏着无边无际的天空和无尽的荒野。A. ignored忽略；B. admired欣赏；C. hated憎恨；D. disliked不喜欢。故选B。

27. C　考查动词。句意：这只鸭子对于它温顺的同伴们来说是自由的象征，它们不能飞。A. think想；B. dream梦想；C. fly飞；D. run跑。故选C。

28. C　考查动词。句意：它碰巧进入了一个农家院子，在那里一个农正在喂养他的鸭子。A. attempted企图；B. intended打算，准备；C. happened发生；D. decided决定。故选C。

29. B　考查动词。句意：在那里一个农民正在喂养他的鸭子。A. watching观看；B. feeding喂养；C. washing洗涤；D. gathering聚集。故选B。

30. D　考查名词。根据后文He ate the duck's corn again the next day（第二天，它又吃了鸭子的玉米），可知它吃了鸭子的玉米。A. bread面包；B. wheat小麦；C. grain粮食；D. corn玉米。故选D。

31. A　考查形容词。句意：晚上，它睡在铺着温暖稻草的床上。A. warm温暖的；B. thin薄的；C. hard努力的；D. damp潮湿的。故选A。

32. C　考查名词。句意：春天来了，它听见它的老伙伴们从头顶上飞过。A. winter冬天；B. fall秋天；C. spring春天；D. summer夏天。故选C。

33. A　考查介词。句意：在它的内心深处，一种几乎被遗忘的渴望被唤醒。A. within在……里面；B. beyond超过，越过；C. to到，向；D. for为了。故选A。

34. C　考查形容词。句意：这只鸭子在舒适的冬天里减少了它的自由本能。A. bitter苦的，痛苦的；B. cold寒冷的；C. comfortable舒适的；D. tough艰苦的。故选C。

35. A　考查动词。句意：现在它渴望和它的战友们一起在天上飞。A. join加入；B. visit参观；C. welcome欢迎；D. greet欢迎。故选A。

36. D　考查形容词。句意：不过，我们的问题很简单。吸引力可能不是最好的方法。A. interesting有趣的；B. surprising令人吃惊的；C. instructive有益的；D. attractive有吸引力的。故选D。

37. B　考查名词。句意：永远记住。在努力之前，你唯一能找到成功的地方就是字典！A. pay工资，薪水；B. effort努力，成就；C. reward报酬，报答；D. prize奖品。故选B。

38. D　考查动词。句意：保持不变比做出改变更容易。A. go走；B. get使得；C. become成为；D. remain保持。故选D。

39. A　考查连词。句意：如果你想飞，你可能要付出代价。A. If如果；B. Before在……之前；C. Although虽然；D. Since因为。故选A。

40. D　考查名词。句意：但是自由是值得的，不惜任何代价！A. adventure冒险；B. experience经历；C. justice公平；D. freedom自由。故选D。

真题回顾·Passage 2·湖南师大附中2018届高三高考模拟卷一

语篇解读：

这篇文章主要讲述了作者家旁边的池塘里来了两只大雁，原来是一只大雁受伤了，它的伴侣留下来陪它，作者被它们的精神所感动。

答案解析：

21. B　考查名词。根据because we'd never seen geese there before可知这美丽的景象令人非常惊奇。anger 生气，surprise 惊奇，terror恐怖，sorrow悲伤，所以选B。

22. D　考查动词。句意：我设想它们很快会上路，所以我享受接近它们的机会。denied拒绝，imagined想象，realized实现，assumed设想。

23. B　考查名词。句意：我设想它们很快会上路，所以我享受接近它们的机会。opinion观点，opportunity机会，feeling 感觉，message消息。

24. C　考查动词。句意：我想知道它们从哪里来，并且为什么会选择我们这里的池塘。decided决定，ordered命令，chosen选择，forgotten忘记。

25. B　考查副词。句意：第二天早晨，大雁依旧是我们的客人，所以我站在远处看着它们，表明我没有伤害它们的意思。also也，still仍然，even甚至，seldom很少。

26. C　考查名词。句意：第二天早晨，大雁依旧是我们的客人，所以我站在远处看着它们，表明我没有伤害它们的意思。violence暴力，pain疼痛，harm伤害，punishment惩罚。

27. D　考查动词。句意：随着时间的流逝，我忍不住靠近它们看一看。bear承受，stop停止，risk冒险，resist抵抗。

28. D　考查名词。由I stopped by some trees near the water's edge可知“我”透过树枝安静地看着它们。windows窗户，forests森林，villages村庄，branches树枝。

29. C　考查动词短语。句意：我吃惊地看到它们正盯着我看。laughing at嘲笑， shouting at 对……大喊，staring at盯住，waving at朝……挥手。

30. A　考查副词。句意：它们伸长脖子，小心地抬起头。cautiously 慎重地，positively 肯定地，skeptically怀疑地，clearly清楚地。

31. D　考查名词。由about why they were staying at the pond so long判断出这是一种好奇心。worry担心，hesitation犹豫，claim声称， curiosity好奇心。

32. B　考查形容词。由and the pond froze over可知，不会太久严酷的冬天将会来临。short短的， cruel严酷的，mild温和的，early早期的。

33. D　考查名词。句意：一天，它们在吃草，我发现了它们到访的原因。love爱，plan计划，journey旅行，visit参观。

34. A　考查名词。由He was unable to fly，可知雄雁左翅膀受伤了。wing翅膀，foot脚，leg腿，eye眼睛。

35. D　考查动词。由and suggested that I let nature take its course可知他解释说，有时候受伤的翅膀可以自己治愈。test检验，appear出现，drop滴，heal治愈。

36. B　考查固定短语。句意：我看到大雁绕着池塘跑。catch sight of看到；瞥见，是固定短语。

37. D　考查副词。句意：两只大雁逐步地向上攀升，飞过池塘。hopefully有希望地， curiously 好奇地，recently 最近，gradually逐步地。

38. A　考查固定短语。句意：然后我就看不见它们了。out of sight是固定用法，意思是“看不见”。

39. A　考查动词。句意：鸟儿一定感觉冬天来临了。sensed感觉，planned计划，found发现，smelt感觉。

40. C　考查名词。句意：我现在非常想念它们，我永远不会忘记它们彼此间的奉献。advice建议，respect尊敬，devotion奉献，attention注意。

（二）人与自我

真题回顾·Passage 1·认识自我·2018天津卷

语篇解读：

本文是一篇记叙文。多年前作者担任过一个学校足球队的教练，在一次比赛中输给了学校的新队。作者开始反思，不停地训练和鼓励队员，最终不可思议地赢得州里最强的对手。从这次经历中，作者感悟到：没有人天生就是赢家，只有依靠自己的努力才能成为赢家。

答案解析：

16. C　考查名词以及对语境的理解。A. luck幸运；B. tests测试；C. efforts努力；D. nature自然。根据前一句No one is born a winner（没有人天生就是赢家），根据常识可知，只有依靠自己的努力才能成为赢家。故选C。

17. B　考查名词以及对语境的理解。A. experiment实验；B. experience经历；C. visit参观；D. show展示。根据下文可知，作者是从一次经历中得出这样的教训的。故选B。

18. D　考查动词以及对语境的理解。A. operating操作；B. editing编辑；C. consulting咨询；D. coaching指导。根据后文Being the coach of the new team, I was excited because I knew we were going to win, but to my disappointment we were defeated.可知，作者在一所学校担任总教练工作。故选D。

19. D　考查形容词以及对语境的理解。A. successful成功的；B. excellent杰出的；C. strong强壮的；D. new新的。根据前半句It was a tradition for the school's old team中的old team提示可知，春季训练结束时，学校新老队伍对抗是一个传统。故选D。

20. B　考查动词短语以及对语境的理解。A. cheer for为……欢呼；B. prepare for为……准备；C. help with帮助某人做……；D. finish with结束于；和……断绝关系。老队没有教练，他们甚至不练习来准备比赛。故选B。

21. A　考查动词以及对语境的理解。A. believe相信；B. agree同意；C. describe描述；D. regret后悔。根据前句but to my disappointment we were defeated可知，作者不能相信会遇到这样的情况。故选A。

22. A　考查动词以及对语境的理解。A.realize意识到；B.claim宣称；C.permit允许；D.demand要求。短语come to realize开始意识到。句意：我开始意识到我的队也许不是佐治亚州头号队伍。故选A。

23. C　考查动词短语以及对语境的理解。A. reacting to对……起反应；B. looking for寻找；C. depending on依靠；D. caring about关心。句意：但他们都在依靠我。故选C。

24. B　考查名词以及对语境的理解。A. decision决定；B. attitude态度；C. conclusion结论；D. intention意图。句意：我不得不改变我对他们能力和潜力的态度。故选B。

25. A　考查名词以及对语境的理解。A. pride自豪，自尊心；B. culture文化；C. fortune幸运；D. relationship关系。句意：我开始做任何我能做的事情来帮助他们建立一点自尊心。故选A。

26. C　考查名词以及对语境的理解。A. leaders领导；B. partners伙伴；C. winners获胜者；D. learners学习者。根据后文Instead of seeing my boys as losers, I pushed and __34__ them. 以及文中最后一句可知，作者开始像对待获胜者一样对待他们。故选C。

27. B　考查名词以及对语境的理解。A. rewards报酬；B. vacations假期；C. health健康；D. honor荣誉。根据That summer可知，当其他队队员享受着他们假期的时候。故选B。

28. D　考查动词以及对语境的理解。A. risked冒险；B. missed错过；C. considered考虑；D. practiced练习。根据上文The old team had no coach, and they didn't even practice to __20__ the game.提示可得出答案。这里指练习传球和踢球。故选D。

29. A　考查名词以及对语境的理解。A. defeat打败；B. decline跌落；C. accident事故；D. mistake错误。根据上文but to my disappointment we were defeated提示可得出答案。在春季训练赛场遭受失败之后。故选A。

30. B　考查动词以及对语境的理解。A. relax放松；B. improve提高，改善；C. expand扩大；D. defend防御。根据前句we won our first game and our second可知，我们继续在提高。故选B。

31. C　考查名词以及对语境的理解。A. shame羞愧；B. burden负担；C. victory胜利；D. favor赞成。句意：即使我们输掉比赛，我们感觉它是一场胜利。故选C。

32. B　考查名词以及对语境的理解。A. chances机会；B. thrills激动；C. concerns关心；D. offers提供。根据前句My boys beat the best team in Georgia可知，是作者一生中最激动人心的一次！故选B。

33. D　考查动词以及对语境的理解。A. surprise惊讶；B. serve服务；C. interest兴趣；D. affect影响。句意：从这次经历，我意识到领袖的态度如何能够影响队里的每个成员。故选D。

34. A　考查动词以及对语境的理解。A. encouraged鼓励；B. observed观察；C. protected保护；D. impressed影响。根据I pushed可知，作者在推动和鼓励他们。故选A。

35. D　考查副词以及对语境的理解。A. honestly诚实地；B. individually个别地；C. calmly镇静地；D. differently不同地。根据后句and they built themselves into winners可知，作者帮助他们以不同的方式看待自己。故选D。

名师点睛：

本文是一篇记叙类的完形填空，难度中等偏易。考生需认真阅读短文，仔细审题，主要是要理解全文的中心思想：没有人天生就是赢家，只有依靠自己的努力才能成为赢家。考生做题时，首先抓住文章开头的中心句，然后要注意抓住故事情节，理解文章脉络，领会作者的写作意图，注重语境的理解，前后句之间的联系，在语境中斟酌所选的答案。

真题回顾·Passage 2·湖南长沙雅礼中学、河南实验中学2018届高三联考

语篇解读：

本文是一篇记叙文。作者在去任教的路上遇到大雨，在一位好心人的帮助下，在他家度过了一晚，第二天顺利到达了学院，在那里一教就是11年。但是作者唯一遗憾的是没有找到那位好心人，再次感谢他。

答案解析：

21. A　考查形容词。A. Excited兴奋的；B. Interested感兴趣的；C. Worried担忧的；D. Annoyed烦恼的。句意：我对我的新工作感到兴奋，但也感到焦虑和恐惧，我走出了自己的舒适区。根据后面的but可知，与后文的anxious and fearful相反，故选A项。

22. C　考查名词。A. home家；B. school学校；C. comfort舒适；D. dilemma困境。句意：我对我的新工作感到兴奋，但也感到焦虑和恐惧，我走出了自己的舒适区。故选C项。

23. D　考查动词词组。A. knocked off击倒，中断；B. dropped off减弱，下降；C. turned off关掉；D. nodded off犯困。句意：我在一个陌生的地方对我的新职业感到疑惑，我在座位上打盹。根据下句中的woke up可推知，是"在打盹"，故选D项。

24. A　考查名词。A. start开始；B. jump跳跃；C. ear耳朵；D. eye眼睛。句意为：我一觉醒来，听到列车员宣布我的公共汽车站的名字。故A项切题。

25. D　考查不定代词。A. Something某事；B. Anything任何事情；C. Everything每件事情；D. Nothing无事，无物。句意：在大雨中没有什么特别的。故D项切题。

26. B　考查名词。A. seat座位；B. room房间；C. ticket票；D. map地图。句意：

我可以在这里为自己找个房间吗？我是新来的。根据下文可知，是找房间，不是找座位、票和地图。故选B项。

27. C　考查副词。A. sadly伤心地；B. quickly迅速地；C. nervously紧张不安地；D. surprisingly令人惊奇地。句意：我听到自己紧张不安地询问。故C项切题。

28. C　考查动词。A. come来；B. get得到；C. need需要；D. ask问。句意：我们需要准时到达下一个车站。故选C项。

29. B　考查形容词。A. sudden突然的；B. soft松软的；C. real真的；D. warm温暖的。句意：在越来越多的恐慌中，我感到肩膀被轻轻一拍。故选B项。

30. C　考查动词。A. waved挥动；B. welcomed欢迎；C. greeted问候；D. shook摇动。句意：当我回头看时，一个温暖的微笑在迎接我。故选C项。

31. A　考查动词。A. stops停止；B. arrives到达；C. leaves离开；D. drives驾驶。句意：公共汽车在那里停留过夜，明天早上返回。故选A项。

32. C　考查名词。A. family家庭；B. solution解决方案；C. invitation邀请；D. request请求。句意：我衷心地感谢他，并接受了他的邀请。根据下文可知，是接受邀请。故选C项。

33. D　考查名词。A. pleasure快乐；B. energy精力；C. minds思想；D. pains疼痛。句意：他和他的妻子煞费苦心地让我过得舒适。take great pains to do sth.煞费苦心做某事，故选D项。

34. A　考查动词。A. provided提供；B. armed武装；C. impressed留下印象；D.blessed祝福。句意：我被提供热水澡，接着是热餐和舒适的床。故选A项。

35. C　考查名词。A. chat聊天；B. discussion讨论；C. meal餐饭；D. tea茶。句意：我被提供热水澡，接着是热餐和舒适的床。故选C项。

36. D　考查动词。A. allow允许；B. keep保持；C. show显示；D. see看见。句意：第二天一早我就起床了，我的恩人来为我送行。see sb.off为某人送行，故选D项。

37. B　考查副词。A. yet然而；B. still仍然；C. already已经；D. also也。句意：我看不清他的脸，因为天还黑。根据上文的No lights yet，故选B项。

38. A　考查介词。句意：我及时赶到了学院，在那里教了将近11年学。to表示“向，朝着”，这里表示去了学院，故选A项。

39. B　考查动词词组。A. sent for派人去叫；B. searched for寻找；C. cared for关心，喜爱；D. waited for等待。句意：在我寻找他的时候，我甚至要求我的新朋友和学生帮助找到这个善良的灵魂。故选B项。

40. D　考查形容词。A. silent沉默的；B. strange奇怪的；C. unbelievable难以置信的；D. untraceable难以寻找的。根据下一句Perhaps I had got his name wrong可知，“我”没找到Mr. Sawant。故选D项。

真题回顾 · Passage 3 · 河北省石家庄市第二中学2018届高三仿真模拟一

语篇解读：

本文是一篇记叙文。在贫困地区任教的格林老师在感恩节上课时，让同学们画出自己最感激的东西，使格林老师感到惊讶的是大卫画了一只手；那么他画的是谁的手呢？孩子们给出了不同的答案。大卫说：画的是格林老师的手。此时老师记起经常手牵手地呵护大卫和孩子们。这对于大卫来说十分重要。由此老师感悟到：感恩并非只是回馈的实物，而是给予启迪的感恩方式。

答案解析：

21. D　考查形容词词义辨析。A. bettering更好的；B. developing发展中的；C. interesting有趣的；D. worsening逐渐变坏的。根据该句中的how little these children... had to be thankful for（几乎没有可感激的）可知，该地区是逐渐变坏的。故选D。

22. B　考查形容词词义辨析。A. eager 热切的；B. thankful感激的；C. ready准备好的；D. greedy贪婪的。根据第一句中的When Mrs.Green told her pupils to draw a picture of something for which they were thankful提示可知，此处填thankful与之相呼应。故选B。

23. A　考查名词词义辨析。A. class班级；B. school学校；C. group团体；D. boys男孩。根据下文出现的class提示可知。这里指班级里大多数同学都画的是火鸡。故选A。

24. B　考查形容词词义辨析。A. rare少有；B. delicious美味的；C. expensive贵的；D. fit合适的。根据孩子们的心理和上文的turkey可知，这里指关于感恩节餐桌上好吃的东西。故选B。

25. D　考查动词短语词义辨析。A. convinced of信服；B. informed of告诉；C. warned of警告；D. expected of期盼。"they believed"在此处是插入语，可忽略。这里指他们坚信那是老师对他们所期待的。故选D。

26. C　考查形容词词义辨析。A. satisfied满意的；B. touched感动的；C. amazed惊讶的；D. encouraged鼓励的。根据上下文可知，老师以为学生会画火鸡等美味，使她感到惊讶的是大卫与众不同画了一只手。故选C。

27. A　考查动词词义辨析。A. found发现；B. shut关闭；C. hidden隐藏；D. stuck坚持。根据上下文可知，下课后，人们发现大卫处于自己的世界里（在他人看来大卫由于失望而变得自闭）。故选A。

28. B　考查副词词义辨析。A. only仅有；B. simply简单；C. clearly清晰地；D. exactly确切地；simply常用来引出解释，用在此处符合语境(大卫画的仅仅是这样)。故选B。

29. C　考查名词词义辨析。A. head头；B. arm膀臂；C. hand手；D. foot脚。根据上文多次提到hand可以得出答案。它一定是上帝之手。故选C。

30. D　考查动词词义辨析。A. fetching去取；B. earning获得；C. sending送；D. bringing带来。God（上帝）不用“挣得、去取、送达”，而是顺便“带来bring”。故选D。

31. C　考查名词词义辨析。A. worker工人；B. carpenter木匠；C. farmer农场主；D. banker银行家。农场养火鸡，因此应该是农场主farmer。故选C。

32. A　考查动词词义辨析。A. raise提高；B. milk给……喂牛奶；C. have有；D. grow生长。raise在这里指“饲养”之意。根据语境可知这里指饲养火鸡。故选A。

33. B　考查动词词义辨析。A. bring带来；B. protect保护；C. watch观看；D. guard看守。警察的职责是保护(protect)民众的。故选B。

34. A　考查副词词义辨析。A. seriously认真地；B. rudely粗鲁地；C. naughtily调皮地；D. noisily吵闹地。根据it is supposed to be all the hands that help us, but David could only draw one of them（画的应该是所有给予我们帮助的手，但大卫可能只画了其中一只）可知，Lucy做出了严谨的答案，因此使用A 项“严肃认真地seriously”符合语境。故选A。

35. D　考查动词词义辨析。A. proved证明；B. known知道；C. said说；D. supposed假设。此处是表达推断的语境，D项“is supposed to be 应该是”表达了说话人推断的意思。故选D。

36. C　考查名词词义辨析。A. surprise惊讶；B. pride自豪；C. pleasure快乐；D. wonder惊奇。该句的意思是：老师沉浸于该话题引起孩子们共鸣的喜悦中而几乎忘记了大卫。pride 不与at 连用而与of 连用。故选C。

37. D　考查名词词义辨析。A. picture图画；B. book书；C. schoolbag书包；D. desk课桌。这里指课堂上，老师俯身于书桌前询问大卫，而不可能俯身于图画、书或者书包。故选D。

38. C　考查动词词义辨析。A. realized意识到；B. wished希望；C. remembered记得；D. believed相信。根据该空后的时态和句意可知，听到大卫的回答“我画的是您的手”后，格林老师想起/记起……其他三个选项“意识到、但愿、坚信”不能表达“格林老师曾手牵手呵护学生”的事实。故选C。

39. B　考查动词词义辨析。A. sensed感觉；B. meant意义；C. accounted解释；D. affected影响。格林老师对所有学生都手牵手呵护，但这对大卫来说意义重大(mean much to him)，因为他比较自闭、孤僻。故选B。

40. A　考查名词词义辨析。A. ways方式；B. chances机会；C. abilities能力；

D. hopes希望。最后格林老师感悟到：感恩时，重要的不是回馈的实物，而是给予启迪的感恩方式(ways)。其他选项不符合此处语境。故选A。

名师点睛：

解答完形填空的技巧如下。

（1）找出词语之间的习惯搭配，或固定搭配；如第32题考查动词raise的用法，为“饲养、抚养”之意。如 raise cattle（饲养牲口）和raise children（抚养孩子）。如果学生对此固定搭配不了解就很难选择出正确的答案。

（2）结合生活，结合生活常识，善于观察生活，积累生活常识，就能够利用常识去做恰当的选择。如第31题就是根据常识可知，火鸡一般在农场养，因此应该是农场主farmer。其他选择项都与常识不相符合。

（3）上下文对照，做完形填空题时，单独看一句话是找不到正确答案的，需要读下句或者若干句才能明白。所谓上下对照，即在上文和下文中找到与正确答案相关的关键词。因此，做题时要有边读边在大脑中储存上下文信息的能力，捕捉关键词。

（4）词语或词义复现。词汇复现往往会使语篇中的句子相互衔接得更紧密，词语的复现，对解题也很有帮助。

（三）人与社会

真题回顾·Passage 1·湖北省襄阳四中2018届高三5月四模

语篇解读：

本文是一篇记叙文。作者在车上遇到了一位回家探亲的军人，后来他们开始约会、通信。作者曾被告诉“在火车上不要和陌生人说话”，她庆幸没有听别人的话。

答案解析：

41. B　考查形容词。A. absent缺席的；B. fresh新鲜的；C. expert熟练的；D. anxious焦虑的。句意：我刚从学校毕业，开始做办公室文员一职。故B项切题。

42. A　考查名词。A. armyman军人；B. businessman商人；C. policeman警察；D. salesman推销员。句意：在我回来的路上，我注意到有一对夫妇在过道里——一个军人和一个年轻的女士正在交谈。根据下文的leaving the soldier可知A项切题。

43. B　考查副词。A. Immediately立刻；B. Eventually最后；C. Hurriedly匆忙地；D. Imaginarily想象中的。句意：最后，我意识到他们俩不是一起旅行，而是在火车上相遇了。故B项切题。

44. D　考查副词。A. aside在旁边；B. annoyed烦恼的；C. amazed吃惊的；D. alone独自地。句意：这名女子最终在纽约的罗切斯特下车，把这名士兵单独留下。leave sb.alone把某人单独留下，故D项切题。

45. A　考查名词。A. eye眼睛；B. ear耳朵；C. shoulder肩膀；D. seat座位。句意：我情不自禁地从我眼角的余光注意到他较好的外表。故A项切题。

46. C　考查状语从句。A. when当……时候；B. where在哪里；C. if是否；D. how怎样。句意：他问是否能看一下我拿着的火车时刻表，是否他能坐在我旁边，这样我们就可以聊天了。此处是if引导的宾语从句，故C项切题。

47. A　考查动词。A. sit坐；B. wait等待；C. lean倾斜；D. bend弯曲。句意：他问是否能看一下我拿着的火车时刻表，是否他能坐在我旁边，这样我们就可以聊天了。故A项切题。

48. D　考查动词词组。A. set out出发；B. make out理解，辨认出；C. hang out挂出，闲逛；D. watch out小心，提防。他动作很快，“我”必须要小心提防他。watch out for留意，密切注意，故D项切题。

49. B　考查动词。A. prepare准备；B. share分享；C. deliver递送；D. order命令。句意：我邀请他来分享我阿姨为我的旅行打包的非常丰盛的午餐，故B项切题。

50. B　考查动词。A. carried搬运，携带；B. packed包装；C. allocated分派；D. stored储存。句意：我邀请他来分享我阿姨为我的旅行打包的非常丰盛的午餐，故B项切题。

51. C　考查动词。A. argued争论；B. wept哭泣；C. talked交谈；D. ate吃。句意：我们一路聊到我下车，我们交换了地址，他说他会和我联系。故C项切题。

52. C　考查动词。A. found发现；B. announced宣布；C. exchanged交换；D. described描述。句意：我们一路聊到我下车，我们交换了地址，他说他会和我联系。故C项切题。

53. D　考查名词。A. need需要；B. despair绝望；C. pain疼痛；D. touch接触。句意：我们一路聊到我下车，我们交换了地址，他说他会和我联系。根据addresses可知D项切题。

54. A　考查形容词。A. familiar熟悉的；B. mature成熟的；C. strange奇怪的；D. particular特别的。句意：在星期六，电话铃响了，一个熟悉的声音问我是否愿意在那天晚上和他一起去看电影。故A项切题。

55. C　考查动词词组。A. gave up放弃；B. added up合计；C. ended up结束；D. got up起床。句意：我们在the Kallet Theatre 看了*On the Waterfront*。固定词组：end up doing sth.以做某事而结束，故C项切题。

56. B　考查名词。A. discussions讨论；B. dates日期，约会；C. lessons功课，教训；D. deals交易。句意：在他的军队休假期间，我们又多了几次约会，然后他被派往海外。故B项切题。

57. C　考查动词。A. injured使受伤；B. attracted吸引；C. assigned分配；D. employed雇佣。句意：在他的军队休假期间，我们又多了几次约会，然后他被派往海外。故C项切题。

58. D　考查动词。A. separated分离；B. settled解决，定居；C. practiced练习；D. corresponded符合，协调。句意：在接下来的几年里，我们通信了，他在其他的假日里来看望我。故D项切题。

59. A　考查名词。A. strangers陌生人；B. officers军官；C. conductors指挥；D. writers作者。句意：在我多年前去克利斯兰旅行之前，我被警告不要在火车上和陌生人说话。故A项切题。

60. B　考查形容词。A. curious好奇的；B. glad高兴的；C. aware意识到的；D. sorry难过的。句意：我很高兴我没有听。故B项切题。

名师点睛：

完形填空的解题技巧之一就是要根据上下文来学会“推理”出最佳选项。同学们要遵循“上下求索”的原则来查找信息。有的暗示可能设在空格附近。比如本完形填空中第42小题，根据下文的leaving the soldier才能知道刚才是一个军人和一个年轻的女士在交谈。故A项正确。

真题回顾·Passage 2·郑州2018届三模

语篇解读：

本文是一篇记叙文。文章主要向我们描述了作者无奈之下拍摄的一张被女人干扰的照片却显得尤为生动，由此道出了对人生的感悟。

答案解析：

21. B　考查名词辨析。A. sight视野；B. breath呼吸；C. way方法；D. attention注意力。catch one’s breath停下来缓缓气。本句意思是爬山过程中停下来缓缓气。故选B项。

22. A　考查固定搭配。plant oneself为固定搭配，意为“站立不动，处于固定位置”。句意：不幸的是，正当我拿出相机的时候，一个女人从后面走过，站在我面前，挡住我的视野。故选A项。

23. C　考查名词辨析。A. concern关注；B. photo照片；C. view视野；D. direction方向。根据上一句，可知是有个女人挡住了我的视野，故选C项。

24. D　考查形容词辨析。A. Cautious小心的，谨慎的；B. Curious好奇的；C. Casual随便的；D. Patient耐心的。根据后面的内容，“我等了约15分钟”，可知“我”是耐心的。故选D项。

25. A　考查副词辨析。A. eventually最后，最终；B. randomly随便地；C. extremely

非常；D. hurriedly匆忙地。句意为：回顾我将最后拍摄的镜头，我很沮丧。A项符合题意。

26. C 考查动词短语辨析。A. back away为了让出地方而后退，不愿考虑；B. go over复习；C. move along往前走，走开；D. stay out留在户外。根据下一句“so that I could take just one picture of the landscape”可知，意思是：“我是不是应该让她走开（move along），让我拍一张风景照呢？”故选C项。

27. D 考查动词辨析。A. caught赶上，看见；B. sent送；C. got得到；D. prevented阻止。根据前面“I could have asked her, but”（我本来可以请她走开的）及转折连词but可知，“我”没有这样做，分析选项可知，prevent sb. to do sth.为“阻止某人做某事”符合题意（但有些事阻止了“我”这样做），故选D项。

28. B 考查形容词辨析。A. anxious焦急的，渴望的；B. content满足的，满意的；C. quiet安静的；D. confident自信的。根据下一句“I didn't want to mess with that.”（她在欣赏风景，我不想打断她。），be content to to愿意做某事，乐于做某事。因此B项符合题意。

29. B 考查形容词辨析。A. excited激动的；B. annoyed生气的；C. worried焦急的；D. confused迷惑的。根据上下文可知，这个女人在“我”前面站过了15分钟，还在那儿一动不动。那么久，所以“我”生气（annoyed）了。故选B项。

30. A 考查副词辨析。A. anyway无论如何；B. somehow不知怎么的；C. instead相反地；D. indeed真正地。“我决定无论如何（anyway）也要拍照。”故选A项。

31. D 考查名词辨析。A. beauty美人，美好；B. behavior行为；C. determination决心，决定；D. presence存在，出席。“由于那个女人站在我面前，所以我拍的照片有她的（存在）。”故选D项。

32. C 考查形容词辨析。A. puzzling令人为难的，费解的；B. disappointing令人失望的；C. interesting有趣的；D. boring无趣的，令人厌烦的。根据后面的内容可知，后来“我”看这个照片时，因为这个女人的出现而使照片变得有趣了。故选C项。

33. B 考查连词辨析。A. unless除非；B. because因为；C. although尽管；D. until直到。“因为这个女人的参与，风景便更美了。”两句之间是因果关系，故选B项。

34. D 考查形容词辨析。A. strange奇怪的；B. regrettable遗憾的，后悔的；C. distant遥远的，冷漠的；D. unique独特的。“这张照片，展现给我的是独特美。”故选D项。

35. A 考查动词辨析。A. ruined破坏；B. created创造；C. missed错过；D. discovered发现。因为这个女人站在“我”的面前，把“我”拍的风景挡住了，所以说是她破坏了“我”拍的照片。故选A项。

36. C　考查动词辨析。根据前面的内容，作者把这个女人抓拍在照片里，也就是说她定格在作者拍的照片里了。分析选项（protecte保护；observe观察，庆祝；freeze结冰，使定格；draw绘画，拉），只有C项（frozen）符合题意。现在这个女人的身影定格在陌生人的照片里。故选C项。

37. B　考查动词辨析。A. hanging逗留；悬挂；B. living生活，住；C. shining发光；D. wandering漫游。根据前面这个女人被定格在“我”的照片里，而照片是挂在“我”家，也就是说在某些方面，她一直住在（living）“我”的房子里。故选B项。

38. D　考查动词辨析。A. promise许诺；B. tell告诉；C. convince使相信；D. remind提醒。在最后有提示“This photo is a reminder”，也许这就是拍照片的目的：提醒（remind）我们。故选D项。

39. C　考查名词辨析。A. respect尊敬；B. plan计划；C. desire渴望；D. sense感觉。句意：也许这就是照片的目的：提醒我们都欣赏美，我们都有快乐和联系的愿望。故选C项。

40. A　考查名词辨析。A. conversation谈话，会话，交流；B. result结果；C. trust信任；D. love爱。这张照片是一个提醒，一个被捕捉的时刻，两个女人之间的一次无声的交流（conversation）。因为“我”把她拍在照片里，“我”欣赏着照片，就是一种无声的交流。故选A项。

专题五 语法填空

一、《新课标》与考纲要求

高考中的语法填空题型主要是最新课标学科素养中的语言知识的考查。理清语言知识的细目，以语篇为依托，对语法和词汇知识进行全面复习，做到心中有数。

英语语法知识包括词法知识和句法知识：词法关注词的形态变化，如名词的数、格，动词的时、态（体）等；句法关注句子结构，如句子的成分、语序、种类等。词法和句法之间的关系非常紧密。在语言使用中，语法知识是“形式—意义—使用”的统一体，与语音、词汇、语篇和语用知识紧密相连，直接影响语言理解和表达的准确性和得体性。

新课标全国卷语法填空题，是2014年开始实施的，到2018年，已经连续考了五年。根据《2018年高考英语科全国卷考纲说明》，对语法填空题型约定了命题素材为短文形式。要求如下：在一篇200词左右的语言材料中留出10个空格，部分空格的后面给出单词的基本形式，要求考生，阅读下面材料，在空格处填入1个适当的单词或括号内单词的正确形式。

二、试题分析

2016—2018年新课标卷高考英语语法填空试题分析

年份	试卷类型	体裁	词数	话题	考点分布
2018年	新课标卷I	说明文	196	跑步的好处，它可以帮助人们延年益寿	提示词7个 61. 副词的级 62. 不定式 63. 动名词 64. 时态 65. 比较句型 66. 定语从句 67. 名词数 68. 词形变化 69. 词形变化 70. 代词或名词
	新课标卷II	说明文	208	中国为保护环境在农作物种植上有了一些变化，并得到了世界上知名人士的认可	提示词7个 61. 时态 62. 冠词 63. 副词 64. 非谓语动词 65.连词 66. 词性转换 67.词性转换 68. 时态 69. 定语从句 70. 省略句

续表

年份	试卷类型	体裁	词数	话题	考点分布
2018年	新课标卷III	记叙文	193	在中非偶遇大猩猩，彼此惊恐的经历	61. 宾语从句 62. 冠词 63. 最高级 64.动词 65. 非谓语 66. 名词 67. 动词短语 68. 代词 69. 时态 70.非谓语
2017年	新课标卷I	说明文	223	低脂肪、低盐的饮食趋势及其对人们健康的影响	61. 介词 62. 名词的数 63. 非谓语动词 64.谓语动词 65. 冠词 66.比较级 67. 主谓一致 68.非谓语动词 69. 形容词 70. 定语从句
	新课标卷II	说明文	201	世界第一个地铁的形成和发展	61. 名词的数 62. 介词 63. 非谓语动词 64. 冠词 65. 被动语态 66. 副词 67. 代词 68. 时态 69. 名词 70. 形容词
	新课标卷III	说明文	215	Sarah Thomas在学业和诱人的职业面前所做出的选择	61. 非谓语动词 62. 冠词 63. 时态和语态 64. 定语从句 65. 非谓语动词 66. 名词 67. 名词的数 68. 介词 69. 动词时态 70. 副词
2016年	新课标卷I	记叙文	197	作者的成都之旅及其与大熊猫之间的故事	61. 名词 62. 时态和语态 63. 副词 64. 介词 65. 定语从句 66. 非谓语 67. 非谓语 68. 代词 69. 复数 70. 冠词
	新课标卷II	说明文	192	缓解工作中的压力的一些方法	61. 形容词的比较级 62. 词性转换 63. 主谓一致和时态 64. 介词 65. 连词 66. 名词复数 67. 词性转换 68. 冠词 69. 非谓语动词 70. 祈使句
	新课标卷III	说明文	196	筷子的材质和中国使用筷子的历史及文化内涵	61. and 连词 62. 时态和语态 63. 非谓语动词 64. 非谓语动词 65. 状语从句 66. 副词 67. 定语从句 68. 名词 69. 时态和主谓一致 70. 介词

三、题型解读

作为高考新题型的语法填空试题，近年高考英语该题型具有如下特点：文章以记叙文和说明文为主，文章长度控制在190~220词，10道题中，有6~7道试题给出提示词，考查的要点分为词法和语法两部分，词法部分包括：①词类的转换，结合语境考查给出的提示词的名词、形容词或副词变化；②介词的固定搭配，名词的复数形式及运用；语法部分包括：时态和语态的综合运用，非谓语动词，各种从句等。

从近年课标卷的语法填空试题看，给出提示词的考点主要包括：词类的转换（名词与动词的转换，形容词与副词的转换）；形容词比较级与最高级的变化；名词单复数的变化；动词的时态语态、情态动词和虚拟语气、谓语动词与非谓语动词的变化等。给出提示词考点多为实词，所填写的词汇根据语境和短文或对话内容可以是1~3个单词。挖空分布均匀，考点的安排注重多样化。不给提示词的考点主要包括：连词（并列连词和从属连词）、介词（动词与介词的搭配、介词与名词的搭配）、代词和冠词等。

四、应试技巧

（一）有提示词题目的解题技巧

有提示词题目一般考查谓语动词、非谓语动词、形容词、副词、名词等。

有提示词题目是指“使用括号中词语的正确形式填空”这类题，近年来的高考题只考查谓语动词的时态和被动语态、非谓语动词、形容词和副词的比较级、词类转化等四种情况。

1. 谓语动词

当句子缺少谓语动词时， 括号中的动词就是谓语动词。此时，要根据语境确定用哪种时态，根据主语与该动词的主动或被动关系确定用主动语态还是用被动语态。具体解题技巧如下：

第一步：确定句中是否缺谓语或并列谓语，如缺谓语动词，则填谓语动词。

第二步：若为谓语动词，就要看主语与谓语之间是主动关系还是被动关系，以确定用主动语态还是被动语态，同时还要根据语境考虑用哪种时态。

第三步：要注意主谓一致。

2. 非谓语动词

当句中已有谓语动词又没有并列连词，并且谓语动词与括号中的动词并列，该动词就是非谓语动词。

此时，就要根据非谓语动词的用法确定用具体的某种形式。如作主语或宾语，就用动名词 (表一般意义)或不定式形式(表具体意义)；作目的状语或在形容词后作状语，用不定式；作伴随状语或作定语，要根据与逻辑主语的关系，用现在分词或过去分词；有时也要根据句式搭配来确定，如see/hear/notice sb.do/doing sth., spend...doing sth.等。具体解题技巧如下：

第一步：若句中已有谓语，也不是作并列谓语时，应为非谓语动词。

第二步：根据非谓语动词在句中所作句子成分、句式的特殊要求，或某些词语的特殊要求，确定用哪种非谓语动词形式。如作目的状语一般用不定式，作主语或宾语用-ing形式或不定式，在enjoy、finish等动词后作宾语用-ing形式，在decide、refuse等动词后作宾语要用不定式等。

第三步：确定非谓语动词与其逻辑主语是主动还是被动关系。

第四步：根据非谓语动词的动作与谓语动词的动作发生的先后关系确定用一般式还是用完成式。

3. 形容词和副词的比较级或最高级

主要有形容词作定语、形容词和副词的比较等级或最高级、词义比较等情况。

当括号中所给词是形容词或副词，且空格处需要的仍是形容词或副词时，要根据语境，理解句意，若该词意思不变，逻辑上讲得通，就很可能填该词的比较级(或最高级)；若需要用与该词意义相反的词逻辑才通顺的，就要在该词前加表示否定或相反意义的前缀。注意：要善于分析语境，辨别省略了than...的隐性比较级。具体解题技巧如下：

第一步：分析结构，确定所给词在句子中作定语还是状语。

第二步：根据结构、语境或句子意义确定是填比较级还是最高级。

4. 词类转换

当空格处所需词类与括号中所给词的词类不同时，就需要词类转化。我们可根据以下3条规则顺利解题：①作主语或宾语用名词形式；②作定语、表语或补足语用形容词形式；③修饰动词、形容词或另一副词，作状语，用副词形式。

具体解题技巧如下：

第一步：分析结构，确定要填的词在句中充当哪种句子成分。在名词前作定语、在系动词后作表语、作主语和宾语的补足语，一般要用形容词；修饰动词、形容词或副词，或修饰整个句子，作状语，用副词；作主语或宾语用名词，或者在冠词、形容词性物主代词或名词所有格后，用名词。

第二步：根据构词法将括号中的词变成所需要的词类。

注意：

① 有时不但要注意词性转换，而且还要考虑用表示相反意义的前缀或后缀，其逻辑才通。

② 当所给词的词性与空格处所需词的词性相同时，无需改变词性，就可能是加只改变词义但不改变词性的前缀了。

（二）无提示词题目的解题技巧

无提示词一般考查：冠词、介词、连词、代词、助动词、固定搭配等

无提示词题目指的是“在空格处填入适当的内容（1个单词）”这类题，五年来，这类题只考代词、冠词、关联词和介词。那么什么情况下填代词？何时填冠词？何时填关联词？何时填介词呢？

1. 代词

当句子缺主语或宾语时，填代词：人称代词主格和宾格、指示代词或it。因为充当主语或宾语的应是名词或代词，而在语法填空的纯空格中一般是不要求考生填名词的，所以只要句子缺主语或宾语，就填代词。此时，要根据前后语境，看该空格是指人还是事物，指男还是指女，是单数还是复数。除人称代词外，也有可能是填不定代词等。还有可能是填作形式主语或形式宾语的it，替代后面作真正的主语或宾语的不定式、动名词或从句。解题技巧如下：

第一步：分析句子结构。若句子缺主语，则要填代词主格、指示代词、不定代词或it；若动词或介词后面缺宾语，则要填代词的宾格、指示代词、不定代词或it。如果该宾格与主语是同一人，应用反身代词。

第二步：理解句子意思。根据各个代词的意义和用法，以及句子所需的意义，填入合适的代词。

2. 限定词

在作主语、宾语或表语的名词或“形容词+名词”前，一般要用限定词。

限定词是指冠词、形容词性物主代词，或可以作定语的不定代词等。此时，要根据句子的意思来确定空格外的语境意义，由此来判断具体填什么词。如表示特指，大体相当于“这、这些、那、那些”时用the；表示“一(个、本、座……)”时用不定冠词a或an；表示“某人的”，用物主代词；表示“一些”用some，表示“另一个”用another，表示“其他的”用other等。解题技巧如下：

第一步：分析句子结构。若空格后的名词或者“形容词+名词”前没有形容词性物主代词、不定代词、冠词等限定词时，很可能是填限定词。

第二步：理解句子意思。根据所需意义选择恰当的限定语，如需“一(个、座、次……)”填不定冠词，需“某人的”填物主代词，需“其他的”填other。

3. 介词

当空格后的名词、代词或动名词不是作主语、表语，也不是作动词的宾语时，填介词。因为名词和代词最典型的用法是作主语或宾语，既然不作主语和动词的宾语，就应是作介词的宾语了，所以要填介词。具体填什么介词，由介词与该名词的搭配及其意义来决定，也可能是由动词或谓语与介词的句式搭配来决定。具体解题技巧如下：

第一步：若空格后是名词、代词、动名词或what从句，且它们不是作主语或作动词的宾语时，很可能就是填介词。

第二步：根据具体的语境或空格所在的句子意思来确定填哪个介词。

4. 关联词

当空格前后都是句子(一个主谓关系算一个句子)，且这两个句子之间没有关联词时，填关联词；若并列的两个或几个单词或短语之间没有连词，填表示联合、选择、转折等意义的连词(and/but/so/or)；从属句间常依据句子的属性是名词性从句、形容词性从句还是副词性从句来确定其关联词。具体解题技巧如下：

第一步：分析结构，若两个句子(有两个主谓结构)之间，没有句号或分号，也没有连接词，空格处必填连接词(此处的连接词包括并列连词，如：and, but, or, while, so, for等；引导状语从句的从属连词；引导定语从句的关系代词和关系副词；引导名词性从句的连接代词、连接副词和连词that、if、whether)。

第二步：根据两句之间的意义和逻辑关系，或根据句式结构来确定是并列结构还是某种主从复合句。

第三步：若是主从复合句，要根据从句的特点，结合连词的意义和作用，确定填具体的某个连接词。

五、真题学科素养分析与策略

真题回顾·典例1·2018新课标全国卷Ⅰ

According to a review of evidence in a medical journal, runners live three years __61__ (long) than non-runners.You don't have to run fast or for long __62__ (see)the benefit.You may drink, smoke, be overweight and still reduce your risk of __63__ (die) early by running. While running regularly can't make you live forever, the review says it __64__ (be) more effective at lengthening life __65__ walking, cycling or swimming.Two of the authors of the review also made a study published in 2014 __66__ showed a mere five to ten minutes a day of running reduced the risk of heart disease and early deaths from all __67__ (cause).

The best exercise is one that you enjoy and will do.But otherwise... it's probably running.To avoid knee pain, you can run on soft surfaces, do exercises to __68__ (strength) your leg muscles(肌肉),avoid hills and get good running shoes.Running is cheap, easy and it's always __69__ (energy).If you are time poor, you need run for only half the time to get the same benefits as other sports, so perhaps we should all give __70__ a try.

学科素养分析表

语篇分析	词汇考查	语法考查
说明文 医学报告类 语篇结构 第一段：医学报告内容 第二段：如何跑步	考查词汇变形： 67. causes 68. strengthen 69. energetic	考查语法内容： 61. 副词比较级longer 62. 考查不定式目的状语to see 63. 动名词dying 64. 时态 is 65. 比较句型 than 66. 定语从句 that / which 70. 代词指代 it / running

语篇解读：

本文是一篇说明文。文章讲述了跑步的好处，它可以帮助人们延年益寿。

答案解析：

61. longer 考查副词的比较级。“医学报告显示，经常跑步的人比不跑步的人多活3年。”根据than可知用比较级，故填longer。

62. to see 考查不定式作目的状语。“你不必跑得太快或时间太长就能看到它的好处。”此处不定式作目的状语，故填to see。

63. dying 考查动名词。“你也许喝酒、吸烟或超重，但通过跑步仍然会减少早亡的风险。”此处of是介词，其后用动名词。故填dying。

64. is 考查动词的时态。“医学报告显示，跑步比散步、骑车和游泳更能有效地延长寿命。”这里叙述的是一个事实，故用一般现在时。故填is。

65. than 考查比较句型。“跑步比散步、骑车和游泳更能有效地延长寿命。”根据文章中的more effective可知此处填than。

66. that / which 考查定语从句的关系词。此处a study是先行词，其在定语从句中作主语，故填that或which。

67. causes 考查名词复数。“一项研究表明，仅仅每天5分钟到10分钟的跑步，就能减少各种原因的心脏病和早亡。”根据句意用复数形式。故填causes。

68. strengthen 考查词形变化。“锻炼以增强你腿上的肌肉。”此处to是不定式符号，其后用动词原形。故填strengthen。

69. energetic 考查词形变化。“跑步总是让人充满活力。”根据it's可知，系动词后用形容词作表语。故填energetic。

70. it / running 考查代词或名词的用法。“我们都应该试试跑步。”此处give it a try意为：试试。此处it指running。故填it或running。

名师点睛：

本文比较难的一个题是第70题。短语give it a try学生不容易想出来。give a try试试，give sb. sth.，give sth. to sb. 这些短语学生都很清楚。但give后加it或sth.的形式比较少见。高考复习要尽可能多地复习相关的短语，尤其是用得比较多，而课本中出现较少的短语。

真题回顾 · 典例2 · 2018新课标全国卷II

Diets have changed in China — and so too has its top crop.Since 2011,the country __61__ （grow）more corn than rice.Corn production has jumped nearly 125 percent over __62__ past 25 years, while rice has increased only 7 percent.

A taste for meat is __63__ (actual) behind the change: An important part of its corn is used to feed chickens, pigs, and cattle.Another reason for corn's rise: The government encourages farmers to grow corn instead of rice __64__ (improve) water quality.Corn uses less water __65__ rice and creates less fertilizer（化肥）runoff.This switch has decreased __66__ (pollute) in the country's major lakes and reservoirs and made drinking water safer for people.

According to the World Bank, China accounts for about 30 percent of total __67__ (globe)fertilizer consumption.The Chinese Ministry of Agriculture finds that between 2005—when the government __68__ (start) a soil-testing program __69__ gives specific fertilizer recommendations to farmers—and 2011, fertilizer use dropped by 7.7 million tons.That prevented the emission(排放) of 51.8 million tons of carbon dioxide. China's approach to protecting its environment while __70__ (feed) its citizens "offers useful lessons for agriculture and food policymakers worldwide." says the bank's Juergen Voegele.

学科素养分析表

语篇分析	词汇考查	语法考查
说明文 环保类 语篇结构第一段：中国的饮食改变了，玉米增产量大。 第二段：玉米用水和化肥少，可以减少污染。 第三段：中国使用化肥的数量减少了，二氧化碳的排放也减少了。	考查词汇变形： 63. actually 66. pollution 67. global	考查语法内容： 61. 时态has grown 62. 冠词 the 64. 目的状语to improve 65. 比较句型 than 68. 时态started 69. 定语从句that/which 70. 现在分词 feeding

语篇解读：

本文是一篇说明文。文中讲述了中国为保护环境在农作物种植上做了一些改变，并得到了世界上知名人士的认可。

答案解析：

61. has grown考查时态。since加时间点，主句要用现在完成时。句意：2011年以来，中国种植的玉米比水稻多。故填has grown。

62. the考查冠词。句意：玉米产量在过去25年里增长了近125%，而大米只增长了7%。是特指在过去的25年里。故填the。

63. actually考查副词。句意：对肉的需求实际上是这种变化的背后原因。句子结构完整，用副词修饰句子。故填actually。

64. to improve考查非谓语动词。句意：为了改善水质政府鼓励农民种植玉米而不是水稻。没有连词且谓语动词是encourages，故improve应该用非谓语动词。此处表示目的，故用不定式。故填to improve。

65. than考查连词。句意：玉米比水稻使用的水更少。根据关键词less可知，填比较连词。故填than。

66. pollution考查词性转换。句意：这一转变减少了中国较大的湖泊和水库的污染，使人们的饮用水更加安全。has decreased后跟名词作宾语，故填pollution。

67. global考查词性转换。句意：中国约占全球化肥总消费量的30%。fertilizer consumption是名词短语，故应该用形容词修饰。故填global。

68. started考查谓语动词。句意：在2005年政府开始了一项土壤测试项目。本句是when引导的定语从句，由于时间是2005年，故用过去时。故填started。

69. that/which 考查定语从句关系词。根据空后的谓语动词gives可知，该空缺少主语，指代program并且引导后面的句子。指物用that/which，故填that或者which。

70. feeding考查省略句。句意：中国在养活了中国人民的同时又保护了环境。这一做法为全世界的农业和粮食政策制定者提供了很有用的经验。空格处表示正在进行的动作，while后面省略了China is。省略句的原则：在时间状语从句、条件状语从句、让步状语从句中，如果从句的主语和主句的主语一致且含有be动词时，那么可以把主语和be动词一起省略。故填feeding。

名师点睛：

学会分析句子成分。The Chinese Ministry of Agriculture finds that between 2005—when the government started a soil-testing program which/that gives specific fertilizer recommendations to farmers—and 2011，fertilizer use dropped by 7.7 million tons.这句话中有两个定语从句。一个是关系副词when引导的定语从句，先行词是2005，the government是主语，a soil-testing program是宾语，故此空缺少谓语动词，我们可

以看出时态是一般过去时。另一个是关系代词指代program引导的定语从句，先行词是program，gives是第三人称谓语动词，可以看出是考查关系词。指代物并作主语，关系词要用that/which。

真题回顾·典例3·2018新课标全国卷Ⅲ

I'm not sure __61__ is more frightened, me or the female gorilla（大猩猩）that suddenly appears out of nowhere.I'm walking on a path in the forest in the Central African Republic.Unexpectedly, I'm face-to-face with the gorilla, who begins screaming at __62__ top of her lungs.That makes her baby scream, and then a 400-pound male appears.He screams the __63__ (loud)of all.The noise shakes the trees as the male beats his chest and charges toward me.I quickly lower myself, ducking my head to avoid __64__ (look) directly into his eyes so he doesn't feel __65__(challenge).

My name is Mireya Mayor.I'm a __66__(science)who studies animals such as apes and monkeys.I was searching __67__ these three western lowland gorillas I'd been observing.No one had seen them for hours, and my colleagues and I were worried.

When the gorillas and I frightened each other, I was just glad to find __68__ (they) alive.True to a gorilla's unaggressive nature, the huge animal __69__(mean)me no real harm. He was just saying: "I'm king of this forest, and here is your reminder!" Once his message was delivered, he allowed me __70__ (stay)and watch.

学科素养分析表

语篇分析	词汇考查	语法考查
记叙文 人与动物关系类 语篇结构 第一段：偶遇大猩猩 第二段：故事结果	考查词汇变形： 66. scientist 68. them	考查语法内容： 61. 宾语从句引导词 which 62. 冠词 the 63. 副词最高级loudest 64. 动名词looking 65. 过去分词challenged 67. 介词for 69. 时态meant 70. 目的状语to stay

语篇解读：

本文为记叙文。文章主要讲述了作者在中非偶遇大猩猩，彼此惊恐的经历。

答案解析：

61. which考查宾语从句。句意：我不确定哪一个更可怕，我，还是突然出现的雌性大猩猩。此处为宾语从句，空格处表示选择，所以用which表示“哪一个”。

62. the考查冠词。此处为固定短语at the top of，此处表示以最大的肺活量喊叫。

63. loudest考查最高级。根据后面的of all可知，他声音最大，所以用最高级loudest。

64. looking考查动词。动词avoid后要用动词的ing形式。此处表示避免直接看他的眼睛。用looking。

65. challenged考查非谓语动词。根据语境可知，此处表示不直视他的眼睛，他就不会感到被挑战。feel为系动词，表示“被挑战”，用过去分词challenged。

66. scientist考查名词。根据语境可知，“我”是一名科学家。scientist科学家。

67. for考查动词短语搭配。search for是固定搭配，表示“寻找”，表示“我”在寻找“我”研究的三只西部低地大猩猩。

68. them考查代词。此处作find 的宾语，所以用宾格them。

69. meant考查谓语动词。分析本句的句子成分可知，本句缺少谓语，再根据总体时态可知要用一般过去时，所以用meant。

70. to stay考查非谓语动词。固定短语allow sb. to do允许某人做某事，应该用to stay。

名师点睛：

此题考查固定搭配较多，其中第62、64、67、70都为固定搭配，对于这类题目我们需要熟练掌握动词的固定搭配以及介词短语。而第61题则考查从句，对于从句我们可以通过分析句子成分确定连接词。如本题为宾语从句，宾语从句中缺主语，所以应该从连接代词who、whom、what、which、whose中选择，此外根据句意可判断用which。

六、2019年高考语法填空学科素养主题语境之备考训练

（一）说明文

真题回顾 · Passage 1 · 吉林省长春市2018届高三年级四模

No matter where you are, humans are constantly measuring and checking time.Some of us are good at it—planning and doing things ahead of time, __41__ others are always trying to beat the clock and do things at the eleventh hour.

Tardiness（拖拉）can be serious.If you __42__ (be) one minute late for work, would you resign? It may sound extreme, but that is exactly __43__ occurred in the UK upper chamber of parliament, the House of Lords, in January 2018.International development minister Lord Bates arrived one minute late, and, as a result, was unable to answer a __44__ (schedule) question.Instead of trying __45__ (make) up for lost time, as many might do, he resigned on __46__ spot.He apologized for his discourtesy (无礼) and stated that he was ashamed.His resignation, though, __47__ (reject) by the UK prime minister.

So, how late is too late? Many cultures take punctuality very seriously.In contrast, others seem to view tardiness __48__ just the normal way of things.What is considered acceptable is based on culture. That is, if you don't mind waiting, it might be best to attend your __49__ (appoint) in good time.And if the worst comes to the worst, remember the old English proverb, "__50__ (well) late than never."

真题回顾·Passage 2·湖北省襄阳四中2018届高三5月四模

China, which takes pride in inventions in ancient times, has once again demonstrated its __61__ (able) to change the world with its "new four great inventions": high-speed railways, electronic payments, __62__ (share) bicycles and online shopping.The "new four great inventions" are all related __63__ China's high-tech innovation（创新）, which has improved the quality of people's lives. "My wallet is no longer in use.I can buy and eat anything __64__ I want simply with a tap of my phone," said Lin Jinlong, __65__ overseas Chinese student from Cambodia, __66__ (add) that "even pancake sellers are using Alipay (mobile payment).We can also order food at home, which is super convenient.If I __67__ (be) at home in Cambodia, I would have to go outdoors."

The bikes themselves are not new, but the operating model of bike-sharing is based on satellite navigation system, mobile payment, big data and other high technologies.It is __68__ (increase) clear that China is innovating and no longer copying Western ideas.This is partly because China skipped over the PC age and went directly to mobile.China has the __69__ (large) mobile use in the world.

In terms of the "new four great inventions", Charlie Dai, principal analyst of American market research company Forrester, said, "These products and services __70__ (improve) the customer experience so far, improving national and global economy at the same time".

（二）记叙文

真题回顾 · Passage 1 · 湖南长沙雅礼中学、河南实验中学 2018届高三联考

Our parakeet（长尾鹦鹉）Chip and Goldie, a stray tortoiseshell kitten we took in, __41__ (grow) to be best friends, eating and playing together.I was a member __42__ a bird conservation organization at the time, so we often took care of injured __43__ (bird). Goldie helped raise dozens of injured and orphaned native birds, __44__ (act) as a watchful guardian.One day, it was Chip who needed Goldie's supervision.I had left a large bowl of pancake batter（面糊）__45__ (cover) in the kitchen.But while I was out of the room, Chip climbed onto the bowl to have __46__ taste but soon fell in and sank. __47__ (luck), Goldie was on hand and stuck her face in the bowl to fish Chip out.She cleaned his face and beak so he could breathe before running to alert me with a loud meow.I followed Goldie, __48__ was also covered in batter, back into the kitchen __49__ found a battered budgie on the floor. After being washed, dried and warmed, Chip made a full __50__ (recover).Bowls were always covered in future and Goldie and Chip remained the best of friends.

真题回顾 · Passage 2 · 山西省太原市2018届高三第二次模拟

In 1940, four teenage boys and their dog were walking through woodland close to Lascaux, when their dog suddenly disappeared.The boys searched all around.They came to a cave and looked into the cave __41__ could see nothing.

A few days later, the boys returned to the cave.They could hardly believe __42__ eyes.In the weak lamplight, the boys saw red horses and cows, and black bulls and deer charging across the walls of the cave, which looked so __43__ (frighten) that the boys jumped back in fear.Little did the boys know that they had made one of the most important __44__ (discover) of that century.

The Famous Lascaux Caves consist of a large hole and __45__ series of connecting caves, with a natural water system.The paintings there were an especially important find because they are so numerous and so well preserved.After a few years, the caves were opened __46__ a tourist attraction, and 1,200 people per day came to the site __47__ (admire) the paintings. __48__ (fortunate), many visitors resulted in changes in the cave's atmosphere, and green algae（水藻）began to grow around the walls.Since then, the caves __49__ (close) to the public in an effort to conserve the fragile paintings in this precious underground site.

Today, the caves have computer-controlled air-conditioning and are inspected daily. Scientists hope that these precautions will prevent any __50__ (far) damage to the paintings.

（三）议论文

真题回顾 · Passage 1 · 河南郑州2018届高三下学期三模

Throughout modern history, perhaps there has never been a scientist as iconic（偶像的）as Stephen Hawking.

Whether he __41__ (educate) the world with his knowledge of the universe, or making fun of himself in TV shows, it is hard to imagine what the world will be like now Hawking is no longer in.

On March 14, 2018, the British physicist passed away in Cambridge.Since then, many people have expressed their condolences（哀悼）on social media, including British computer scientist Tim Berners-Lee, __42__ invented the World Wide Web. "We have lost a great mind and a wonderful spirit," Berners-Lee wrote.

Hawking was an icon for many reasons, but he will be best remembered __43__ his work in the field of science.

Building on German scientist Albert Einstein's work, Hawking explained his belief that space __44__ (start) with the Big Bang, and will end with black holes.

"This complete set of laws can give us the __45__ (answer) to questions like 'How did the universe begin?'" Hawking wrote in his 2010 work *The Grand Design*. "Where is it going and will it have an end? If so, how will it end?"

Besides his work in science, he also managed to overcome many difficulties in his personal life.While __46__ (study) at Cambridge University, he was diagnosed with motor neuron（运动神经元）disease at the age of 21.His __47__ (ill) left him paralyzed and he was told he only had a short time to live.However, he went on to become one of the __48__ (great) minds the world has ever known.

"I felt it was unfair.Why should this happen to me?" he once recalled. "At the time, I thought my life was over and that I would never realize the potential I felt I had. But now, 50 years later, I can be satisfied with my life."

Hawking left behind a great legacy（遗产）. His signature book *A Brief History of Time: From the Big Bang to Black Holes*, __49__ (publish) in 1988, became one of the world's best-selling science publications.And in 2014, UK actor Eddie Redmayne played

Hawking in the movie *The Theory of Everything*, which tells the tale of the physicist's life.

He may no longer be with us, __50__ Hawking will continue to inspire the world for generations to come.As he once said himself, "Look up at the stars and not down at your feet!"

真题回顾 · Passage 2 · 皖西南名校2018年高三联考

Like most people, I was brought up to look upon life as a getting.It was not until in my later thirties __41__ I made this important discovery: giving away things __42__ (make) life so much more exciting.One discovery I made about giving away is that it is almost __43__ (possibility) to give away anything in this world without getting something back, though the return often comes in __44__ unexpected form.One Sunday morning the local post office delivered a letter to my home, though it __45__ (address) to me at my office.I wrote the postmaster a note of __46__ (appreciate). More than a year later I needed a post office box for a new business I was starting.I was told at the window that there were no boxes __47__ (leave), and that my name would have to go on a long waiting list.As I was about to leave, the postmaster appeared in the doorway.He had overheard our conversation. "Wasn't it you that wrote us a letter a year ago about __48__ (deliver) a special delivery to your home?" I said yes. "Well, you are __49__ (certain) going to have a box in this post office if we have to make one for you.You don't know __50__ a letter like that means to us.We usually get nothing but complaints.

参考答案

（一）说明文

真题回顾 · Passage 1 · 吉林省长春市2018届高三年级四模

41. while 42. were 43. what 44. scheduled 45. to make
46. the 47. was rejected 48. as 49. appointment(s) 50. Better

语篇解读：

这是一篇说明文。文章主要讨论了不同文化中人们对迟到的不同看法。

答案解析：

41. 考查连词。该空的前一句说"我们中的一些人擅长提前计划和做事情"，后一句说"其他的人总是试图在最后一刻赶时间做事情"，两句话之间是对比关系，所以这里应该填连词while。

42. 考查虚拟语气。本句是if引导的条件状语从句，即非真实条件句。表示的是假设或实际可能性不大的甚至不可能发生的情况，故采用虚拟语气。句意：如果你上班迟到一分钟，你会辞职吗?

43. 考查连接代词。本句是表语从句，从句中缺少的成分是主语，这里的主语指代的是事情，所以用what。

44. 考查形容词。在冠词a和名词question之间应该用形容词，所以把schedule变成形容词形式scheduled（预定的）。

45. 考查动词不定式。固定搭配try to do sth.（试图干某事），所以这里填to make。

46. 考查定冠词。固定短语on the spot（在现场）。句意：他并没有像许多人那样，试图弥补失去的时间，而是当场辞职。所以这里应该填定冠词the。

47. 考查时态和语态。根据本段时态和句意可知，主语resignation和reject为动宾关系，故用过去时的被动形式。句意：尽管他的辞呈被英国首相拒绝了。故用was rejected。

48. 考查介词。固定搭配view... as... 意为“把……看作……”。句意：相比之下，其他人似乎认为迟到是正常的事情。所以这里填as。

49. 考查名词。形容词性物主代词后面应该跟名词。句意：如果你不介意等的话，最好在合适的时间去参加你的约会。所以这里填appointment(s)。

50. 考查副词比较级。英语谚语“Better late than never”（迟做总比不做好）。所以这里应该填Better。

真题回顾·Passage 2·湖北省襄阳四中2018届高三5月四模

61. ability　62. shared　63. to　64. that　65. an

66. adding　67. were　68. increasingly　69. largest　70. have improved

语篇解读：

本文介绍中国的新四大发明。

答案解析：

61. 考查名词。此处its是形容词性物主代词，后面应该用名词形式，able是形容词，故答案为ability（能力）。

62. 考查过去分词作前置定语。“被分享的自行车”，此处share和bicycle之间是被动关系，作前置定语，故答案为shared。

63. 考查固定搭配。be related to与……有关，故答案为to。

64. 考查定语从句。此处anything是先行词，不定代词，指物，且后面的定语从句缺少引导词和宾语，不定代词作先行词，后面的定语从句用that引导，故答案为that。

65. 考查不定冠词。“林金龙说，一位来自柬埔寨的中国海外留学生。”overseas以元音音素开头，故答案为an。

66. 考查现在分词。此处林金龙和add之间是主动关系，所以用现在分词作伴随状语，故答案为adding。

67. 考查虚拟语气。句意：如果我在柬埔寨的家里，我就得去户外。根据主语的谓语动词would have可知此处是if引导的虚拟语气，与现在的事实相反，从句用一般过去时态，be动词的过去式用were，故答案为were。

68. 考查副词。clear是形容词，副词修饰形容词，故答案为increasingly。

69. 考查形容词最高级。句意：中国拥有世界上最大的移动手机的应用。定冠词the用在最高级前面，故答案为largest。

70. 考查时态。根据so far可知句子用现在完成时态，These products and services是句子主语，复数形式，故答案为have improved。

（二）记叙文

真题回顾 · Passage 1 · 湖南长沙雅礼中学、河南实验中学2018届高三联考

41. grew　42. of　43. birds　44. acting　45. uncovered

46. a　47. Luckily　48. who　49. and　50. recovery

语篇解读：

Chip在碗里被Goldie捞了上来。它们成为最好的朋友，一起吃饭，一起玩耍。

答案解析：

41. 考查时态。句意：我们的长尾小鹦鹉Chip和Goldie，我们收养的一只龟甲色的流浪猫，后来成为最好的朋友，一起吃饭，一起玩耍。讲述过去发生的事情用一般过去时态，故答案为grew。

42. 考查介词。句意：当时我是一个鸟类保护组织的成员，所以我们经常照顾受伤的鸟类。此处表示所有关系，“……的”，故答案为of。

43. 考查名词复数。句意：当时我是一个鸟类保护组织的成员，所以我们经常照顾受伤的鸟类。此处用名词复数，故答案为birds。

44. 考查现在分词。句意：Goldie帮助饲养了几十只受伤的和孤立的本土鸟类，充当了一名警惕的守护者。此处Goldie和act之间是一种主动关系，作结果状语，故答案为acting。

45. 考查过去分词作宾语补足语。句意：我在厨房里留了一大碗露在外面的煎饼面糊。根据后文Chip偷吃面糊可知，面糊是没盖，故用uncover，再根据与pancake batter是被动关系，故用过去分词作宾语补足语，故答案为uncovered。

46. 考查不定冠词。句意：Chip爬上了碗，尝了一口，但很快就掉进去并沉了下去。结合句意，可知答案为a。

47. 考查副词。句意：很幸运，Goldie就在身边，把脸贴在碗里把Chip捞上来。此处是副词修饰整个句子，故答案为Luckily。

48. 考查定语从句。句意：我跟着Goldie回到厨房，他也被弄上了面糊，在地板上发现了一个弄脏了的小鹦鹉。此处Goldie是先行词，拟人手法，后面的非限制性定语从句缺少引导词和主语，故答案为who。

49. 考查并列连词。句意：我跟着Goldie回到厨房，他也被弄上了面糊，在地板上发现了一个弄脏了的小鹦鹉。此处是并列的谓语，故用连词and。

50. 考查名词。形容词修饰名词，再根据前面的a，可知此处用名词单数，故答案为recovery。

真题回顾 · Passage 2 · 山西省太原市2018届高三第二次模拟

41. but 42. their 43. frightening 44. discoveries 45. a

46. as 47. to admire 48. Unfortunately 49. have been closed 50. further

语篇解读：

这是一篇记叙文。文章讲述了著名的Lascaux Caves被发现的经过、重要意义和作为景点之后对其采取的保护措施。

答案解析：

41. 考查连词。此处指男孩们进洞寻找他们的狗，但什么都没找到。前后句是转折关系，故填but。

42. 考查代词。“男孩们不敢相信他们的眼睛。”这里表示“男孩们的”用物主代词their，故填their。

43. 考查形容词。男孩们看到的洞穴内的图画是如此令人恐惧。修饰物，表示“令人恐惧的”，故填frightening。

44. 考查名词。此处运用了one of+复数名词，表示“……之一”。此处指那个世纪最重要的发现之一，故填discoveries。

45. 考查冠词。此处指著名的Lascaux Caves包括一个大洞和一系列连接洞穴组成，表示“一系列的”是a series of，故填a。

46. 考查介词。此处指几年后，这些洞穴作为一个旅游景点开放，表示“作为，当作”。故填as。

47. 考查动词不定式。“每天有1200人来到这个景点来欣赏这些画。”表示目的用动词不定式，故填to admire。

48. 考查副词。“大量游客导致洞穴内空气的变化和绿藻的生长。”此处指游客造成的不良影响，表示“不幸地”，单独作状语用副词，故填Unfortunately。

49. 考查时态语态。句中时间状语Since then 和现在完成时连用，主语the caves和动词 close是被动关系，指洞穴已经被关闭，故填现在完成时的被动语态have been closed。

50. 考查形容词比较级。“科学家们希望这些预防措施能阻止对这些画更深层的损害。”此处指和现在相比更深层的损害，有比较的意思。故填further。

（三）议论文

真题回顾 · Passage 1 · 河南郑州2018届高三下学期三模

41. was educating　42. who　43. for　44. started　45. answers

46. studying　47. illness　48. greatest　49. published　50. but / yet

语篇解读：

本文为夹叙夹议文。文章讲述了英国科学家霍金去世的事情，并高度评价了他对人类的伟大贡献及对世界的影响。

答案解析：

41. 考查谓语动词。分析句子可知，根据or后面的“making”可知，本句要用进行时，但由于是讲霍金生前的事，故用过去进行时was educating 。句意：不管他是用宇宙知识教育世界，还是在电视节目中取笑自己，很难想象现在没有霍金的世界会是什么样子。

42. 考查定语从句的关系词。分析句子... British computer scientist Tim Berners-Lee, __42__ invented the World Wide Web.可知，本句中的Berners-Lee后被一个定语从句修饰，而先行词Berners-Lee在从句中作主语，指人要用关系词who。故填who。

43. 考查介词。句意：霍金成为人们的偶像有很多原因的，但他将因为在科学领域的成就被人们铭记。for在此表示“因……而被记住”。故填for。

44. 考查谓语动词。句意：Hawking解释了他相信宇宙是从宇宙大爆炸开始的，并将以黑洞结束。本文是讲述霍金过去的事，故要用一般过去时，因此本题填started。

45. 考查名词复数。根据后面的“(answer) to questions”可知，是许多问题的答案，所以要用复数形式answers。

46. 考查省略句。分析句子While __46__ (study) at Cambridge University, he was diagnosed with motor neuron (运动神经元) disease可知，本句中的While __46__ (study) at Cambridge University, 是省略句，这是因为主从句主语一致时，从句的主语可以省略而变成非谓语形式。而study的逻辑主语是he，与动词study二者是主动关系，故用动词的-ing形式，即studying。

47. 考查名词作主语。分析句子可知，空格处在句子中作主语，形容词不能作主语，所以要用其名词形式，故填illness。句意：他的病使他瘫痪了，而且被告知他的生命只有很短的时间。

48. 考查形容词最高级。句意：然而，他后来成为世界上最伟大的人物之一。分析句子可知，他是最伟大的人物之一，根据前面的one of...，可知要用最高级greatest。

49. 考查非谓语动词。《时间简史——从“大爆炸”到“黑洞”》，在1988年（被）出版时，成为世界上最畅销的科学出版物之一。分析句子His signature book *A Brief History of Time: From the Big Bang to Black Holes,* 49 (publish) in 1988, became one of the world's best-selling science publications.可知，谓语动词是became，而 49 (publish) in 1988是修饰主语“书”的，要用非谓语形式。书是被出版的。故填published。

50. 考查连词。句意：他也许不再和我们在一起了，但霍金将继续激励世界上的一代又一代人。前后两句是转折关系，故填but / yet。

真题回顾 · Passage 2 · 皖西南名校2018年高三联考

41. that　42. makes　43. impossible　44. an　45. was addressed
46. appreciation　47. left　48. delivering　49. certainly　50. what

语篇解读：

文章主要讲述了作者通过一件事明白了给予让生活更令人兴奋。

答案解析：

41. 考查强调句。句意：直到我三十多岁的时候，我才有了这个重要的发现。It was not until... that... 直到……才……，根据题意填that。

42. 考查动词时态。句意：给予让生活更令人兴奋。“giving away things”动名词作主语，谓语动词使用第三人称单数。根据题意，故填makes。

43. 考查形容词作表语。句意：我的一个发现是，在这个世界上，给予别人东西不可能没有任何回报。形容词作表语，“it is impossible to do”，根据题意，故填impossible。

44. 考查不定冠词。句意：我的一个发现是，在这个世界上，给予别人东西不可能没有任何回报。根据题意，故填an。

45. 考查被动语态。句意：一个星期日的早晨，当地邮局给我家送了一封信，尽管那封信上的地址是我的办公室。be addressed to在（信封和包裹）上写姓名、地址；致（函）。根据题意，故填was addressed。

46. 考查名词。句意：我写了一封感谢信给邮局局长。介词of后使用名词。根据题意，故填appreciation。

47. 考查过去分词作定语。句意：在窗口我被告知没有箱子了。boxes与leave之间是被动关系，故使用过去分词作定语。根据题意，故填left。

48. 考查动名词。句意：是不是你一年前给我们写了一封关于给你家特殊邮寄的信？介词about后使用动名词。根据题意，故填delivering。

49. 考查副词。句意：嗯，如果我们必须为你做一个，你肯定会在这个邮局里有一个盒子。副词修饰动词。根据题意，故填certainly。

50. 考查宾语从句。句意：你不知道那封信对我们意味着什么。由what引导宾语从句。根据题意，故填what。

专题六 短文改错

一、《新课标》与考纲要求

高考中的短文改错题型主要是最新课标学科素养中的语言知识的考查。理清语言知识的细目，以语篇为依托，对语法和词汇知识进行全面复习，做到心中有数。

高考短文改错题是给出一篇约100词的短文，文中有10处错误，要求考生对每个句子进行判断，如有错误将其改正。错误类型包括词法、句法、行文逻辑等方面的错误。每句中最多有两处错误仅涉及一个单词的增加、删除或修改。

高考短文改错着重考查考生的语言基本功和正确使用英语进行表达的能力。此题型不仅要求考生牢固掌握一定的词汇和语法知识，还要求考生具有一定的阅读理解和逻辑推理能力。它针对考生平时学习英语过程中，尤其是在写作中常犯的错误而设计，考生在平时写作中常出现的错误是短文改错考查的重点。

二、命题分析

2016—2018年新课标卷高考英语短文改错试题分析

年份	试卷类型	体裁	词数	考点分布
2018年	新课标卷I	记叙文	113	冠词；动词时态；不定代词；副词；名词复数；定语从句；非谓语动词；形容词；介词；连词
	新课标卷II	记叙文	108	名词；名词单复数；冠词；非谓语动词；情态动词；代词；固定搭配；介词；时态；宾语从句的连接词
	新课标卷III	记叙文	102	时态；非谓语动词；连词；固定搭配；代词；固定结构；比较级；主谓一致；副词
2017年	新课标卷I	记叙文	114	数词；冠词；连词；时态；名词单复数；非谓语动词；固定句型；副词；形容词；介词
	新课标卷II	记叙文	92	不定代词；冠词；形容词；定语从句；副词；动词搭配；连接词；名词；时态；非谓语动词
	新课标卷III	记叙文	110	介词；动词时态；连词；非谓语动词；动词时态；限定词；定语从句；形容词；形容词最高级；代词

续 表

年份	试卷类型	体裁	词数	考点分布
2016年	新课标卷I	记叙文	93	定语从句；连词；时态；词性；连词；非谓语动词；介词；冠词；代词；副词
	新课标卷II	记叙文	106	特殊结构；情态动词；并列结构；连词；冠词；代词；名词单复数；虚拟语气；时态；代词
	新课标卷III	说明文	108	名词复数；形容词最高级；冠词；反身代词；so/such的用法；时态；形容词；非谓语动词；介词；状语从句

三、题型解读

一般来说，短文改错的语言材料通常来自考生习作或类似于考生习作的文章。所选材料篇幅较短，约100词左右，10～12个句子；难度不大，基本上无生僻的词汇和语法结构。短文改错的话题较常见，通常是叙述一件事情或说明一个事物。从体裁上看，历年高考试题中的短文改错以记叙文和应用文为主，兼顾说明文和议论文。通常从词法、句法和行文逻辑三个角度设题，错误类型有多词、缺词和错词三种，比例一般为错词：多词：缺词=8：1：1。

四、解题策略与技巧

（一）错误类型：错词、多词、缺词

错词、多词和缺词三者的比例大致为8：1：1。其中，错词主要针对实词，多词和缺词主要针对虚词。实词包括动词、名词、代词、形容词、副词；虚词包括冠词、介词、连词。

1. 错词

（1）冠词：固定搭配、序数词、最高级等 。

（2）名词：单复数、所有格等。

（3）代词：代词指代不一致的错误。代词的指代一致性包括数、格和性三方面的统一;连接代词、疑问代词、关系代词的误用等。

（4）谓语动词：时态、语态、语气、情态动词、固定搭配、主谓一致等。

（5）非谓语动词：现在分词与过去分词、不定式之间的用法区别，非谓语动词的时态语态误用等。

（6）形容词、副词两种词性的混用；比较等级及修饰语的误用。

（7）介词：固定搭配的误用。

（8）连词：关联词的误用。 包括并列连词（and, but, or, so, when）和从属连词

（各种从句的引导词）。

2. 多词

（1）冠词：名词前是否多了冠词。

（2）谓语动词：及物动词后是否多了介词。

（3）不定式：不定式符号to是否应该省略掉。

（4）形容词、副词：比较级构成是否重复。

（5）介词：状语前、关系副词前、及物动词后是否多了介词。

（6）连词：主从复合句中的because与so连用、although与but连用。

（7）固定搭配：按照惯用法看，是否多词，如（was）used to do。

3. 缺词

（1）冠词：名词前是否缺冠词。

（2）不及物动词：其后是否缺介词。

（3）不定式：是否少了不该省略的to。

（4）动词：动词(如被动语态)、助动词、情态动词是否被遗漏。

（5）固定搭配：按照惯用法，是否少词。

（二）实词错误规则

1. 动词

关于动词，首先要根据句子的结构分清该用谓语动词还是非谓语动词。要明确不作谓语的动词必须用非谓语形式，而究竟用哪种非谓语动词是由非谓语动词的句法功能决定的。

第一步：分析句子结构——作状语的非谓语动词，可以是分词，也可以是不定式。

第二步：表示目的——只能是不定式。

（1）谓语动词的常见错误类型。

① 时态、语态错用；

② and前后动词形式不一致；

③ 第三人称单数形式错用；

④ 主谓不一致；

⑤ 易混动词的用法错误；

⑥ 缺少动词，特别是be动词；

⑦ 主动语态和被动语态错用；

⑧ 动词的固定搭配错误等。

（2）非谓语动词的常见错误。

① 动词与非谓语动词混用；

②三类非谓语动词之间的混用；

③不定式符号to的有无；

④并列结构连接的不定式或动名词前后不一致（尤其距离较远时）；

⑤介词后用了动词原形而不是动名词作宾语；

⑥某些动词后要求接动名词或不定式作宾语，容易混淆。

2. 名词

名词的常见错误主要是单复数及所有格的错误使用。

（1）区别名词的可数与不可数。

（2）根据名词前面的修饰语或谓语动词的单复数来判断用单数还是复数。

（3）记住常考的一些不可数名词：advice, fun, progress, information, furniture, equipment等。

3. 代词

常考的代词包括人称代词、指示代词、反身代词、不定代词、关系代词及疑问代词等。

对于短文中出现的每一个代词都要注意它所指代的内容及在句中的作用，注意其“数”“格”“性”是否正确和前后是否一致。

数：I — we　　him — them

格：she — her　　my — mine

性：he — she　　him — her

4. 形容词和副词

（1）形容词和副词的混用：除了be之外，多数系动词后要用形容词作表语。

（2）词性的误用：形容词主要作定语修饰名词；副词主要作状语修饰动词、形容词、副词等。

（3）形容词和名词等其他词类的混用。

（4）比较级、最高级的误用以及一些固定搭配如as... as的误用。

（5）固定搭配：固定搭配指与动词、形容词、副词等有关的短语，平时要多注意积累。

（三）破解虚词之错

1. 冠词

（1）误用a和an：根据单词的第一个音素来判定。

（2）误用 a 和 the。

（3）多冠词或缺冠词。

2. 介词

主要考查介词在固定短语中的误用、多用或者漏用，这些短语包括介词与动词、形容词、名词等连用。

3. 连词

为使文章结构严谨，在行文中要用到各种连词。在并列句中，我们要从上下文来判断句与句之间的关系是并列、转折、选择、递进还是其他关系。在复合句中，应根据主从句之间的关系来判断连词的使用是否正确。

（1）并列连词的误用。

主要涉及and, but, or, so等几个表示并列、转折、选择、因果等关系的词语。严格来说，这类错误主要是行文逻辑的错误。

（2）从句引导词的错误。

主要涉及引导词的错用、误加与漏用，有时候将不是从句的成分误认为是从句而误加引导词。这就需要考生弄清词性以及句子之间的关系。

另外，还要注意一些连词的固定用法：either...or, neither...nor, not only...but also, not...but等，要注意它们的搭配。

（四）把握“三”“四”“五”，共12个考点

1. 三个必考点

名词的单复数；介词的误用、多用或少用；动词时态不一致。

2. 四个常考点

连词的误用、多用或少用；冠词的误用、多用或少用；词语辨析；词性误用。

3. 五个考点

代词；非谓语动词；情态动词；主谓一致；形容词的比较级和最高级。

（五）关注词法、句法和行文逻辑

1. 词法

介词、冠词、连词的多用、少用或误用，词性误用，非谓语动词，各类词缀，如否定前缀，名词、形容词、副词后缀。

2. 句法

主谓一致，时态一致，名词的单复数一致，代词的格和数一致。

3. 行文逻辑

并列句中两个简单句的关系，因果、转折、选择、并列关系等。

（六）解题步骤

总体步骤：浏览全文，掌握大意；分句阅读，逐行找错；由易到难，各个击破；检查核对，注意方法。

做短文改错题通常遵循以下几个步骤：通读文章，了解大意；逐句分析，行中找错；再读短文，检查漏洞。即按照“文章→句子→行→文章”的顺序。

1. 通读全文，了解大意

短文改错是考查考生在理解的基础上对语篇整体的识错、纠错能力，必须从全篇考虑，而不能只顾一句或一行。要理解文章的谋篇布局，弄清楚整篇文章的意思。在阅读过程中，要注意行文逻辑、文章的时态以及人称等。

2. 逐句分析，行中找错

尽管短文改错是以行设置错误的，但语言毕竟是以句子为完整意义单位的。所以，可以逐句分析，看看单句是否有错；如果有错，有几处错误，是什么错误，再看看错误在哪一行。把“短文改错”转化为“单句改错”，然后再在行中找错，这样就会降低难度。

3. 再读短文，检查漏洞

做完以后，再把文章阅读一遍，检查是否有遗漏情况，尤其注意上下句之间的逻辑关系。多读一遍，就有可能把某些不清楚的地方理顺。

五、真题回顾之学科素养分析

真题回顾·典例1· 2018新课标全国卷I

假定英语课上老师要求同桌之间交换修改作文，请你修改你同桌写的以下作文。文中共有10处语言错误，每句中最多有两处。每处错误仅涉及一个单词的增加、删除或修改。

增加：在缺词处加一个漏字符号（Λ），并在其下面写出该加的词。

删除：把多余的用斜线（\）划掉。

修改：在错的词下划一横线，并在该词下面写出修改后的词。

注意：

① 每处错误及其修改均仅限一词；

② 只允许修改10处，多者（从第11处起）不计分。

During my last winter holiday, I went to countryside with my father to visit my grandparents.I find a big change there.The first time I went there, they were living in a small house with dogs, ducks, and another animals.Last winter when I went here again, they had a big separate house to raise dozens of chicken.They also had a small pond which they raised fish.My grandpa said last summer they earned quite a lot by sell the fish.I felt happily that their life had improved.At the end of our trip, I told my father that I planned to return for every two years, but he agreed.

学科素养分析表

语篇分析	词汇错误	语法错误
记叙文 讲述了乡下的巨大变化	1. countryside前加the，考查冠词 3. another改成other，考查形容词的用法 4. here改成there，考查副词及语意理解 5. chicken改成chickens，考查名词复数 8. happily改成happy，考查形容词作表语 9. 删除for，考查介词的用法	2. find改成found，考查动词时态 6. which改为in which或where，考查定语从句的关系词 7. sell改成selling，考查动名词 10. but改成and，考查并列连词的用法

语篇解读：

本文是一篇记叙文。文章主要讲述了作者在去年寒假期间和父亲去乡下看望爷爷奶奶过程中的所见所闻，由此讲述了乡下的巨大变化。

答案解析：

第一处：countryside前加the。考查冠词。“去年寒假，我和父亲去乡下看望爷爷奶奶。”此处特指去的是乡下，故加定冠词the。

第二处：find改成found。考查动词时态。根据文章中的During my last winter holiday可知，事件发生在过去，故用一般过去时。故将find改成found。

第三处：another改成other。考查形容词的用法。“他们住在一个小房子里，院子里有狗、鸭子和其他牲畜。”根据句意可知，将another改成other。

第四处：here改成there。考查副词及语意理解。“去年冬天我又一次去了那里。”故将here改成there。

第五处：chicken改成chickens。考查名词复数。“他们拥有一个大的独立住宅，还养了许多鸡。”根据前文的dozens of可知，其后用名词复数形式。

第六处：which改为in which或where。考查定语从句的关系词。“他们还有一个小池塘，里面养着鱼。”此处a small pond是先行词，其在后面的定语从句中作地点状语，故用in which或where。

第七处：sell改成selling。考查动名词。“去年夏天他们通过卖鱼挣了一大笔钱。”此处介词by后用动名词，故用selling。

第八处：happily改成happy。考查形容词作表语。“他们的生活有了很大提高，我感到很高兴。”此处形容词作表语，故将happily改成happy。

第九处：删除for。考查介词的用法。时间名词有every、each、last等词修饰时，其前不用介词。故删除for。

第十处：but改成and。考查并列连词的用法。“我计划每两年回来一次，他同意了。”此处是并列关系，故将but改成and。

名师点睛：

本文中第九处改错是学生容易忽视的考点。时间名词有every、each、last、this、that等词修饰时，其前不用介词。

例：We are going to fish this morning.

I finished the course last winter holiday.

真题回顾 · 典例2 · 2018新课标全国卷II

When I was little, Friday's night was our family game night.After supper, we would play card games of all sort in the sitting room.As the kid, I loved to watch cartoons, but no matter how many times I asked to watching them, my parents would not to let me.They would say to us that playing card games would help my brain.Still I unwilling to play the games for them sometimes.I didn't realize how right my parents are until I entered high school.The games my parents taught me where I was a child turned out to be very useful later in my life.

学科素养分析表

语篇分析	词汇错误	语法错误
记叙文 文章讲述了作者的个人经历	第一处：把Friday's改为Friday 第二处：把sort改为sorts 第三处：把the改为a	第四处：把watching改为watch 第五处：把to删除 第六处：把us改为me 第七处：在unwilling前加was 第八处：把for改为with 第九处：把are改为were 第十处：把where改为when

语篇解读：

这是一篇记叙文。文章讲述了作者的个人经历。小时候周五晚上家长不允许作者看卡通片，而是让他和他们一块儿玩扑克牌游戏。长大后作者才明白，这些纸牌游戏在后来的生活中很有用。

答案解析：

第一处：考查名词。名词作定语，往往表明被修饰名词的时间、地点、类别、目的、用途、材料或来源等。名词所有格作定语则强调与被修饰的词的所有关系或表示逻辑上的谓语关系。此处表示“星期五晚上”，并不是所有关系，故把Friday's改为Friday。

第二处：考查名词单复数。all表示三者或三者以上，后用名词复数。故把sort

改为sorts。

第三处：考查冠词。这里表示“作为一个孩子”，a用在表示泛指的单数名词前，the表示特指。故把the改为a。

第四处：考查动词不定式。句意：无论我要求多少次要看（卡通片）。用不定式表示目的。故把watching改为watch。

第五处：考查情态动词。would后跟动词原形，故把to删除。

第六处：考查代词。句意：他们会对我说玩纸牌有助于大脑。偷换人称代词，是对“我”说，前面提到的是I，而不是we。故把us改为me。

第七处：考查固定搭配。be unwilling to do sth.意为“不愿意做某事，不情愿做某事”。本文介绍的是过去的情况，故用过去时。所以在unwilling前加was。

第八处：考查介词。play the games with sb.表示“和某人一起玩游戏”，故把for改为with。

第九处：考查时态。根据上下文语境可知此处要用一般过去时。故把are改为were。

第十处：考查宾语从句的连接词。句意：当我是个孩子的时候，父母教给我的纸牌游戏在我日后的生活中证明非常有用。宾语从句连接词并不是表示地点状语，而是时间状语。故把where改为when。

名师点睛：

名词作定语与名词所有格作定语的区别。一般来说，名词作定语通常说明被修饰的词的性质，而名词所有格作定语则强调对被修饰的词的所有（权）关系或表示逻辑上的谓语关系。“the Party members（党员）”中，名词定语表示members的性质；“the Party’s calls（党的号召）”中，Party具有动作发出者的作用，calls虽然是名词，却具有动作的含义。a student teacher实习教师，a student’s teacher一位学生的老师。

真题回顾·典例3·2018新课标全国卷Ⅲ

It was Monday morning, and the writing class had just begin.Everyone was silent, wait to see who would be called upon to read his and her paragraph aloud.Some of us were confident and eager take part in the class activity, others were nervous and anxious. I had done myself homework but I was shy.I was afraid that to speak in front of a larger group of people.At that moment, I remembered that my father once said, “The classroom is a place for learning and that include leaning from textbooks, and mistake as well.” Immediate, I raised my hand.

学科素养分析表

语篇分析	词汇错误	语法错误
记叙文 文章主要讲述了写作课上作者克服恐惧心理主动回答问题的事	第三处：把and改为or 第五处：表示“我的”用my不用myself，或改为定冠词the也可以 第九处：错误不是一个，所以要用复数 第十处：把immediate改为immediately	第一处：begin改为begun 第二处：wait 要用非谓语形式waiting，表伴随 第四处：eager后加to 第六处：be afraid to do害怕做某事，所以that为多余，删掉 第七处：把larger改为large 第八处：that作主语，谓语动词用第三人称单数includes

语篇解读：

本文为记叙文。文章主要介绍了写作课上作者克服恐惧心理主动回答问题的事。

答案解析：

第一处：考查时态构成。根据语境可知，句子用过去完成时，过去完成时的构成是had done，所以begin要改为begun。

第二处：考查非谓语动词。根据句子成分分析，本句谓语为was，而且没有连词，wait与主语是主动关系，所以wait 要用非谓语形式waiting，表伴随。

第三处：考查连词。句意：每个人都沉默了，等着看谁会被要求朗读他或她的段落。一次只能叫一个人，男女两者是选择关系，故把and改为or。

第四处：考查固定搭配。be eager to do sth. 渴望做某事，故eager后加to。

第五处：考查代词。句意：我已经完成了自己的作业。表示“我的”用my不用myself，或改为定冠词the也可以。

第六处：考查固定结构。be afraid to do害怕做某事，所以that为多余，删掉。

第七处：考查比较级。句意：我不敢在一大群人面前说话。这里没有比较的意思，故把larger改为large。

第八处：考查主谓一致。that作主语，谓语动词用第三人称单数includes。

第九处：考查名词单复数。错误mistake不是一个，所以要用复数。

第十处：考查副词。此处要用副词在句中作状语修饰整个句子，故把immediate改为immediately。

名师点睛：

此题中的难点为非谓语动词的考查，如第二处错误。第二处解答时要分析句子结构，根据句中是否有谓语、连词来判断使用谓语还是非谓语，再根据句子主语everyone与wait之间为主动关系，所以要用现在分词waiting。

六、2019年短文改错主题语境之备考训练

(一)记叙文

真题回顾 · Passage 1 · 山西省太原市2018届高三第二次模拟

Do you believe love is the most important? In the early twenty century, homeless people were often brought up in orphanages, in that they received little love.At one time, Dr.Skeels took twelve children from art orphanage or had a young girl look them each day.He also studied another twelve children who are left in the orphanage all day long.He followed these children not until they grew up, and the results were shocked.The children staying all day in the orphanage were either dead or suffering from serious illnesses. However, the twelve children loved by the girl were all healthy and independently.The only difference between the life of these children—the love, made a great difference to us.

真题回顾 · Passage 2 · 山东省泰安市2018届高三第二次模拟

Last week, my friends invited me go camping to see the sunrise. I felt so exciting and asked for my parents'permission. Luckily, he agreed. We got to the mountain top that we would stay for a whole night. We were singing together while one of my friends were playing the guitar. The next morning, we wake up at about five o'clock. We could not wait to see the sun to come up. After a while, we saw the red color light up the sky gradual. It was so amazing scenery. The beauty in nature impressed me at that moment.

真题回顾 · Passage 3 · 河南省洛阳市2018届高三第三次统一考试

The photo was taken during the sixty anniversary of our school.The elderly man on the picture attended our school 50 years ago, shortly after it founded.It was the first time he has been back to our school from he graduated and he was deeply impressed by its look.Once a young student, the elderly man now has gray hair or wrinkles, while our school has a new and more modern look.After all these years, he's still emotional when talking about that how proud he is of once being a student of our school.I was great touched by the scene.I know someday I'll have a same feeling as this lovely man.

（二）议论文

真题回顾·Passage·河北省石家庄市第二中学2018届高三仿真模拟一

Dear Mr. Li,

I'm Wangtao.I'm written to tell you my opinion about employing a foreign language teacher.

They are two factors to take into consider.For a thing, the sense of humor is necessary for a teacher, who makes his class interesting and lively. For another, ensure efficiency in teaching and learning, the foreigner's ability to speak Chinese matters much, so only with the help of Chinese can they communicate with each other smoothly.

Various of activities out of class, such as English Evening and English Corner, should be organized by the foreign language teacher, which brings the students more chances to communicate with the teacher and improve his oral English.

（三）说明文

真题回顾·Passage 1·湖南长沙雅礼中学、河南省实验中学2018届高三联考

Many of us were raised with the saying “Waste not, want not” .None of us, therefore, can completely avoid waste in our lives.

Any kind of waste was thoughtless, whether we waste our potential talents, our own time, our limited natural resource, our money, or other people's time.Each of us can become more aware of and careful.The smallest good habits can make the big difference. It's a good feeling to know in our hearts we are doing our best in a world what is in serious trouble.By focusing on oil, water, paper, food or clothing, we are playing a part in cutting down on waste.

We must keep reminding us that it is easier to get into something than it is to get out of it.Actually, severe damage done to our land is fair recent in the history of our evolution. It's time for us to say no to waste so that our grandchildren's children will able to develop well.

真题回顾·Passage 2·安徽省六校教育研究会2018届高三第二次联考

Stockholm, the capital of Sweden, hopes to stop using fossil fuel (化石能源) completely by 2040.Now the city wants larger lorries what cause more pollution to use bio-fuel, which are produced from waste.Stockholm is also working with Fortum, an energy company, to take advantage a city-wide heating system, use waste heat from supermarkets and stadiums to supply heat for homes.However, the city is trying to change people behavior, step by step.On one newly built estate (庄园), people are providing with tablets that show its real-time energy usage.This is to help them good understand how they use and waste gas, water and electricity.

真题回顾·Passage 3·安徽省滁州市2018届高三9月联合质量检测

An opening week held in our school last week so that we could show a great achievements we made in art education.

The art works exhibition went on from Monday to Friday,exhibit the excellent art works,such as paper cuts, paintings and flower arrangements.Both of the art works were created by the students of our school.That attracted the public most was the singing and dance performances in Friday afternoon.All these activities draw the close attention of the public and the parents as well,receiving high praises from the public.

Through these activity,the public has a better understanding of our school.As a result of,we all think that the opening week was of great successful.

参考答案

(一) 记叙文

真题回顾·Passage 1·山西省太原市2018届高三第二次模拟

语篇解读：

这是一篇记叙文。文章讲述了Dr.Skeels通过跟踪记录在孤儿院长大的孩子和从孤儿院领养长大的孩子的不同，告诉我们爱在生活中的重要性。

答案解析：

第一处：twenty→twentieth考查数词。表示第几世纪要用序数词，故twenty改为

twentieth。

第二处：that→which考查定语从句。句中包含定语从句，先行词是orphanages指物，在定语从句中作状语，指物时介词in后用关系代词which，故that改为which。

第三处：or→and考查连词。此处指Dr.Skeels从孤儿院领出了12个孩子，还有一个年轻女孩照顾他们。前后句是并列关系，不是转折，故or改为and。

第四处：look后面加after。考查动词短语。此处表示“照顾”，用look after，故look后面加after。

第五处：are→were考查动词时态。此处指被留在孤儿院的另外12个孩子，故事发生在过去，所以用一般过去时的被动语态，故are改为were。

第六处：删除not。考查句意。until“直到……时”，not until“直到……才”，此处指他追踪这些孩子直到他们长大。根据语境，这里是表示“直到……时”，用until，删除not。

第七处：shocked→shocking考查形容词。shocked“震惊的”，常修饰人；shocking“令人震惊的”，用来修饰物。此处表示结果是“令人震惊的”，用shocking。故shocked改为shocking。

第八处：independently→independent考查形容词。此处作系动词were的表语，和and前的形容词healthy并列也用形容词，故independently改为independent。

第九处：life→lives考查名词。此处指这些被调查的孩子们的生活，用复数形式。故life改为lives。

第十处：us→them考查代词。此处指代these children，表示他们的生活，用they的宾格，故us改为them。

真题回顾 · Passage 2 · 山东省泰安市2018届高三第二次模拟

语篇解读：

本文是一篇记叙文。本文主要讲述了上周，作者和朋友一起去野营观看日出美景的经历。

答案解析：

第一处：考查固定句型。invite sb.to do sth.邀请某人做某事，是固定句型，所以第一句中go 前面加上to。

第二处：考查v.-ed形式。v.-ing修饰物，而v.-ed修饰人，这里修饰人，所以第二句中exciting 改成 excited。

第三处：考查代词。指代前面的“我的父母”，是两个人，所以he 改成 they。

第四处：考查定语从句。where we would stay for a whole night作定语，修饰前面的the mountain top，所以where we would stay for a whole night是一个定语从句，

关系词在从句中作地点状语，所以第三句中that 改成 where。

第五处：考查主谓一致。"one of + 可数名词复数"表示"……之一"，作主语时谓语动词用单数，所以第五句中were 改成 was。

第六处：考查时态。作者在回忆往事，表示发生在过去的事情，用一般过去时，所以wake 改成woke。

第七处：考查固定用法。句意：我们迫不及待地想看到太阳升起。感官动词see, watch, observe, notice, look at, hear, listen to, smell, taste, feel + do表示动作的完整性、真实性；上述动词+doing 表示动作的连续性、进行性。这里表示太阳升起，是表示完整的动作"升起"，故去掉come前面的to。

第八处：考查副词。修饰动词短语light up，用副词，所以第八句中gradual 改成gradually。

第九处：考查so与such用法的区别。so修饰形容词，而such修饰名词，这里修饰名词scenery，所以第九句中 so 改成 such。

第十处：考查介词。句意：在那一刻，自然的美景令我非常感动。表示"……的"，所以第十句中 in 改成 of。

真题回顾·Passage 3·河南省洛阳市2018届高三第三次统一考试

语篇解读：

本文是一篇记叙文。学校六十年校庆时，拍下一张照片，照片上的老人是五十年前的学生。这是他毕业后第一次回来，谈起学校他仍然很激动，人老了而学校更新、更现代化。

答案解析：

第一处：考查序数词。这张照片是在我们学校六十周年纪念日拍摄的。序数词前用定冠词the，这里应该用序数词，故把sixty 改为 sixtieth。

第二处：考查介词。"在照片里"应该用介词in，故把on 改为 in。

第三处：考查语态。此处found和it之间是被动关系，又是指过去的事，所以这里用一般过去时的被动语态，故在it后加was。

第四处：考查固定句式。It was the first（second...） time that 主语+过去完成时态，意为"某人第几次做某事"，故把has 改为 had。

第五处：考查连词。这是他自从毕业后第一次回到我们学校。这里是since（自从……以来）引导的时间状语从句，故把from改为 since。

第六处：考查并列连词。"这位老者，曾经的年轻人，现在有灰白的头发和皱纹。"此处是并列的递进关系，故把or 改为 and。

第七处：考查比较级。"我们学校有了更新、更现代化的外貌。"根据后面的

more可知此处用比较级，故把new 改为 newer。

第八处：考查宾语从句。“他谈到自己曾经因为是我们学校的学生而感到自豪时，他仍然很激动。” talk about后面是how引导的宾语从句，故把that去掉。

第九处：副词修饰过去分词，故把great 改为 greatly。

第十处：考查固定结构。“我知道有一天我会和这个可爱的男人有同样的感觉。” the same... as...意为“与……相同”，故把a 改为 the。

（二）议论文

真题回顾 · Passage · 河北省石家庄市第二中学2018届高三仿真模拟一

语篇解读：

这是一篇议论文。本文主要介绍了作者对关于聘请外语教师的意见。

答案解析：

第一处：考查动词。句意：我正在写信说一说关于聘请外语教师的意见。与主语I是主动关系，时态用现在进行时，故written改为writing。

第二处：考查名词。名词opinion是可数名词，在下文中谈到了几种意见，所以此处要用复数形式，故opinion改为opinions。

第三处：考查固定句型。句意：这里有两个因素要考虑。固定句型：There be...（有……），故They改为There。

第四处：考查名词。固定短语：take into consideration（考虑），故consider改为consideration。

第五处：考查固定句型。固定句型：For one thing ... for another（一方面，另一方面），故a改为one。

第六处：考查关系代词。who makes his class interesting and lively是定语从句，关系代词作主语，指代上文中的the sense of humor（幽默感），指物，所以要用which，故who改为which。

第七处：考查不定式。句意：为了确保教与学的效率，外国人说汉语的能力很重要。要用不定式作目的状语，故在ensure前加to。

第八处：考查连词。句意：另一方面，为了保证教与学的效率，外国人说汉语的能力非常重要，因为只有借助汉语，他们才能顺利地进行交流。后半部分是原因，故so改为because/as。

第九处：考查词的用法。Various（各种各样的）是形容词，可以直接修饰名词，所以要去掉of；或者把Various换成名词Varieties，构成Varieties of（各种各样的）修饰后面名词，故去掉of或 Various改为Varieties。

第十处：考查代词。此处是指提高“学生们”的口语，所以应该用人称代词

their，故his改为their。

（三）说明文

真题回顾 · Passage 1 · 湖南长沙雅礼中学、河南省实验中学2018届高三联考

语篇解读：

本文讲述的是关于生活中的浪费问题及应该采取的措施。

答案解析：

第一处：考查连接副词。句意：我们中的许多人都是这样说的“不浪费，不需要”。然而，我们没有人能完全避免生活中的浪费。前后句是一种转折关系，故把therefore改成however。

第二处：考查时态。句意：任何一种浪费都是轻率的，无论我们是在浪费我们的潜能，我们自己的时间，我们有限的自然资源，我们的金钱，还是其他人的时间。这里在讲述一种客观事实，所以句子用一般现在时态，故把was改成is。

第三处：考查名词复数。句意：任何一种浪费都是轻率的，无论我们是在浪费我们的潜能，我们自己的时间，我们有限的自然资源，我们的金钱，还是其他人的时间。resource（资源），是可数名词，这里要用名词复数形式，故把resource改成resources。

第四处：考查形容词作表语。句意：我们每个人都能变得更加清醒和谨慎。become是连系动词，后面用形容词作表语，故把of去掉。

第五处：考查固定搭配。固定搭配：make a big difference产生很大的不同，有很大影响。故把the改成a。

第六处：考查定语从句。句意：在我们的心中，我们在一个陷入严重困境的世界里尽了最大的努力，这是一种很好的感觉。此处a world是先行词，指物，后面的定语从句缺少主语和引导词，故把what改成that/which。

第七处：考查并列连词。句意：通过关注石油、水、纸张、食品和服装，我们在减少浪费方面发挥了作用。此处表示并列关系，故把or改成and。

第八处：考查反身代词。句意：我们必须不断提醒自己，进入某件事比摆脱它更容易。这里是“提醒我们自己”，用反身代词作宾语，故把us改成ourselves。

第九处：考查副词。副词修饰形容词，故把fair改成fairly。

第十处：考查固定结构。固定搭配：be able to do sth.能做某事；will后跟动词原形，故在will后面加be。

真题回顾·Passage 2·安徽省六校教育研究会2018届高三第二次联考

语篇解读：

一座城市使用新能源的理念，正在悄悄改变人们的行为，改变人们的环保理念。

答案解析：

第一处：考查冠词。句意：斯德哥尔摩，瑞典的首都，希望到2040年完全停止使用化石能源。“the capital of Sweden”是Stockholm的同位语，作同位语时，capital前不加冠词，故应将the去掉。

第二处：句意：这座城市想让造成更多污染的大卡车使用生物燃料。分析句子结构，“what cause more pollution”是定语从句，修饰larger lorries，引导词在从句中作主语，指物，故该从句要用关系代词which/that引导。what不能引导定语从句。

第三处：考查主谓一致。“which are produced from waste”是定语从句，修饰bio-fuel，which指代bio-fuel，根据主谓一致原则，谓语动词应用第三人称单数形式is。

第四处：考查介词。take advantage of意为“利用……”，是固定短语，故要在advantage和a之间加of。

第五处：考查非谓语动词。句意：斯德哥尔摩和一家名为Fortum的能源公司合作来利用全市供热系统，利用来自超市和体育馆的余热为家庭供暖。“use waste heat from supermarkets and stadiums to supply heat for homes”是方式状语，主句主语和use之间是主动关系，故要用现在分词作状语。

第六处：考查副词。句意：这座城市正在努力地逐步改变人们的行为。该句和上一句（斯德哥尔摩和一家名为Fortum的能源公司合作来利用全市供热系统，利用来自超市和体育馆的余热为家庭供暖）之间是并列关系，不是转折关系，故应将However改为“Besides/Moreover”。

第七处：考查名词所有格形式。句意：这座城市正在努力地逐步改变人们的行为。根据句意，修饰behaviour要用名词所有格形式，故应将people改为people's。

第八处：考查被动语态。句意：一个新建的庄园，给人们提供了平板电脑。tablets和provide之间是被动关系，故该句应用被动语态，将providing改为provided。

第九处：考查代词。一个新建的庄园，给人们提供了平板电脑，这些平板电脑可以显示人们实时的能源使用情况。该处指人们的能源使用情况，故应将its改为their。

第十处：考查比较级。句意：这有助于他们更好地了解他们如何使用水、电、气。结合句意，应将good改为better。

真题回顾·Passage 3·安徽省滁州市2018届高三9月联合质量检测

语篇解读：

作者对上星期自己学校举办的开放周活动进行了介绍。

答案解析：

第一处：考查语态。An opening week与hold之间是被动关系，用被动语态，所以held前面加was。

第二处：考查冠词。特指“我们在美术教育中取得的巨大成绩”，所以a改成the。

第三处：考查非谓语动词。The art works exhibition 与 exhibit 之间是主动关系，用现在分词，所以exhibit改成 exhibiting。

第四处：考查代词。句意：所有的这些作品都是由我们学校的学生创作的。both表示两者，all表示三者或三者以上，所以Both改成All。

第五处：考查主语从句。这里含有一个主语从句，引导词在从句中作主语，所以That改成What。

第六处：考查固定用法。表示“星期五下午”，要用on。

第七处：考查时态。发生在过去的事情，要用一般过去时。所以draw改成drew。

第八处：考查名词。句意：通过这些活动，公众对我们的学校有一个更好的了解。“这些活动”是一个复数概念，所以activity改成activities。

第九处：考查固定短语。句意：结果，我们所有人都认为这次开放周活动非常成功。As a result是固定短语，意思是“结果”，所以去掉of。

第十处：考查固定短语。of great success是固定短语，意思是“非常成功”，所以successful改成success。

专题七 书面表达

一、《新课标》与考纲要求

1. 考试大纲及《考纲说明》要求

众所周知，考试大纲是高考命题的规范性文件和标准，是考试评价、复习备考的依据，是推进考试内容改革的切入点。要求考生根据提示进行书面表达，考生应能清楚、连贯地传递信息，表达意思；有效运用所学语言知识。

写作是四项语言技能中不可分割的一个重要部分，更是语言生成能力的重要表现形式。要求考生根据提示进行书面表达。考生应能准确使用语法和词汇；使用一定的句型、词汇，清楚、连贯地表达自己的意思。任何一篇文章都需要有一个主题，作者应该围绕该主题，借助一些句型、词汇等，清楚、连贯地表达自己的思想。

试题设置总是遵循“高起点，低落点”的原则。试题多为半开放式，给考生一定的提示的同时，也给考生提供了更为广阔的思维空间，使考生有很大的自由发挥的余地，从而考查学生的写作能力。

2. 新课标学科素养相关要求

全国新课标卷命题从不跟风，最新时尚的话题从不出现在考卷中。一些所谓跟风的新原创试题，一般不会出现在高考书面表达中。全国卷总是从平凡的接近学生生活实际的题材入手，于平凡中见深度。

落实立德树人的根本任务，凸显高考的思想性和育人功能：语言是知识与文化的载体，也是思维方式的体现。融入中国优秀传统文化，通过“讲好中国故事”引导、增强文化自信。

从近几年高考写作的体裁形式看，全国卷总是以应用文的形式呈现，尤其是书信和电子邮件。这体现了高考重在考查学生的语言能力，形式以实用的应用文为主。

二、试题分析

近三年新课标全国卷高考英语书面表达考查情况一览表

项目＼卷别		体裁	命题形式	话题
2018	全国卷Ⅰ	应用文（电子邮件）	提纲式	给外国朋友回复邮件，内容为合适的礼物及餐桌礼仪
	全国卷Ⅱ	应用文（通知）	提纲式	写通知，请大家观看一部英语短片 *Growing Together*
	全国卷Ⅲ	应用文（回信）	提纲式	给外国朋友介绍你校体育运动情况
2017	全国卷Ⅰ	应用文（电子邮件）	提纲式	告知英国朋友上课计划（时间、地点、学些唐诗、了解唐朝历史）
	全国卷Ⅱ	应用文（邀请函）	提纲式	邀请外教朋友参观中国剪纸艺术展
	全国卷Ⅲ	应用文（邀请函）	提纲式	邀请朋友加入校乒乓球队
2016	全国卷Ⅰ	应用文（求助信）	提纲式	请外教帮你修改求职信
	全国卷Ⅱ	应用文（邀请信）	提纲式	邀请英国朋友参加国际中学生摄影展
	全国卷Ⅲ	应用文（道歉信）	提纲式	因故不能赴约给好友写道歉信

综观近三年新课标全国卷的高考书面表达题可知，体裁主要为应用文，以考查书信和电子邮件为主，话题贴近考生的生活实际。这种考查方式不仅体现了高考重视对考生英语能力的考查，而且也引导考生关注英美国家的文化和社会生活，关注中国传统文化和社会主义核心价值观。

三、题型解读

（一）提纲类作文

1. 提纲作文特点

提纲作文是近几年高考英语书面表达的热点题型。命题者通常把提纲作文与其他常用文体形式(如书信、电子邮件、报道、通知、日记等)有机结合在一起进行考查，使该类书面表达综合性越来越强。提纲作文的特点为：

提纲作文就是把文章的情景和内容要求分成块，以短文提示、要点提示和表格提示三种形式呈现，要求考生据此进行写作，这实际上是对考生思路和文章写作范围所做的明确限定，写作内容贴近学生的生活实际。因此，提纲中所列举的要点要全部涉及，一个也不能遗漏。这类作文主要考查的内容有：说明主题、分析原因或解释做法。作文题目中一般会提供：标题、提纲、起始句。标题限定短文的基本发展方向，提纲规定短文的基本框架，起始句则提供短文的起点。考生应紧扣主题，并根据提纲提示的思路和要点展开段落。

为了提高文章档次，考生应在保证内容要点齐全的同时进行合理而又紧扣主题的发挥。因此，该类型的书面表达具有一定的灵活性，能较好地体现考生的英语思维和运用能力。

2. 提纲作文的解题思路

（1）深挖题干，明确要求

提纲作文最基本的特征就是内容信息明确和写作要求具体。只有充分利用已给的信息，才有可能写出合格的作文。首先我们要从与内容相关的信息中提炼出具体要写的要点，这基本上决定了文章的主题和所要采用的体裁。题干中所给的其他要求则从规范方面对写作提出了要求。找出了要点、明确了要求，那么写作也就有了方向。

（2）分析要点，构建框架

从性质、重要性及关联度这几点出发，对提炼出的要点进行排序和重新整合，并在结合主题的情况下安排文章的大致脉络，也就是确定文章的段落，使要点在排列的次序上符合逻辑和人们的认知规律。要点的性质、重要性及关联度决定了哪些要点要放在一个段落中去呈现。对于英文写作，鉴于词数的限制，段落并不会太多，通常在第一段和第三段之间变化。对于三个段落的书面表达，首段通常为引入段；第二段一般为中心段落，需要呈现的要点基本上都集中在第二个段落；而第三段一般为结论段或总结段。

（3）要点齐全，量力表达

若要文章有一个基本的、稳定的得分，首先要做到的就是题干所要求的要点要齐全，并且要保证表达上没有明显的低级错误。这两点是最基本的要求。100多词的提纲作文，把要点用英语词汇和句式表达出来就能基本达到这个要求。

想要在分数上有所突破，就不能只是在要点齐全上做文章，还需要在原有要点的基础上进行题干要求之外但又在情理之中的发挥，也就是说增加一些细节信息；其次，还需要在表达上有所提升，也就是说采用一些比较高级的词汇和结构，比如特殊句型、非谓语结构等。当然，这些需要建立在考生对自己的表达能力比较有信心的基础上，跳过格式，注重风格。

英语书面表达常常和应用文结合起来，内容/主题不同，所采用的文体一般也不同。而不同的文体都有着属于该文体的语言风格，比如，议论文的语言通常比较有说服力，说明文的语言比较讲究科学性和准确性。当然，语言风格属于较高层次的要求。但如果能很好地把握文章的语言风格，它自然会成为文章的一个亮点。否则，还是考虑比较稳妥的方式为好。

3. 提纲作文类型

（1）感谢信 (Letter of Thanks)

感谢信的写法没有固定的格式，目的是为他人给予自己的帮助、安慰、款待以及赠送礼物等表示感谢。感谢信最主要的特点是真诚。缺乏真挚的感情而答谢他人，收信人将对你的谢意产生怀疑，感谢的目的也就失去了。因此，写感谢信首先得真心诚意。感谢信的另一个特点是具体。写感谢信切忌泛泛而谈，而应着重于具体的感谢事由。

真题回顾·典例1·2017陕西一模

假如你是李华，在过去一周你在英国参加中学生文化交流活动，其间，一直住在你的英国好友Peter家，现在已经回国，请你根据以下要点给他写一封感谢信。要点包括：

1. 表达感激之情；
2. 回忆各种收获；
3. 发出邀请。

____

____

____

____

____

____

写作指导：

书面表达考查考生运用已有的知识和技能来进行思想交流,完成特定的交际任务的能力。本篇书面表达所设置的情景是感谢在英国参加中学生文化交流活动期间Peter对你的帮助，为应用文中的感谢信,是书面表达中常见的考查类型。写作时宜用第一人称，时态以过去时和将来时为主。感谢信的语言要真诚，感谢的事由要具体。根据题干的要点提示，本篇书面表达的正文部分可分三段来写：

第一段：开门见山，说明写信的目的——表达谢意。

第二段：简述收获，表达谢意。准确明了地写出对方对自己的帮助或付出并表示感谢。

第三段：发出邀请。合乎礼节，情真意切。重申对对方的感激之情并希望给予回报。

范文赏析：

Dear Peter,

I am writing to convey my gratitude for your kind help and care during my stay in your country, without which I wouldn't have enjoyed it so much.

Guided by you, I had a chance to visit some places of interest in England and experience such unique culture as well as beautiful scenery.Thanks to your generous help, I do believe that I have a better understanding of your country and culture.What's more, during the week, the comfortable room, delicious meals and especially your friendly family made me feel at home.

I will be more than pleased if I have the opportunity to repay your kindness.I will show you around in China.I am looking forward to your coming.

Yours,

Li Hua

（2）道歉信 (Letter of Apology)

日常生活中难免会出现一些差错，如失约、损坏东西等。遇到这种情形，应及时写信致歉，以消除不必要的误解，维系正常的关系。道歉信除应及时写之外，还必须写得诚恳，歉意应发自内心，决不可敷衍塞责。再则，事情的原委要解释清楚，措辞应当委婉。

真题回顾·典例2·2016新课标全国卷III

假定你是李华，与留学生朋友Bob约好一起去书店，因故不能赴约。请给他写封邮件，内容包括：

1. 表示歉意。
2. 说明原因。
3. 另约时间。

注意：

1. 词数100左右。
2. 可以适当增加细节，以使行文连贯。

写作指导：

写作分三步走：第一步，表示歉意；第二步，说明具体原因、提出补救办法;第三步，再次致歉，希望得到理解。

在写作过程中，尽可能提供比较合理的理由。如果违反生活常识将导致扣分。在解释完原因后，尽量提供一个合适的补救办法，使行文更加完满。

范文赏析：

Dear Bob,

I'm sorry to say that I cannot go to the bookstore with you on Friday afternoon.I have just found that I have to attend an important class meeting that afternoon.I hope the change will not cause you too much trouble.

Shall we go on Saturday morning? We can set out early so that we'll have more time to read and select books.If it's convenient for you, let's meet at 8:30 outside the school gate.If not, let me know what time suits you best.I should be available any time after school next week.

Yours,

Li Hua

（3）邀请信 (Letter of Invitation)

写作注意事项：盛情邀请参加聚会、共度假期或游览某地等；建立密切联系，加强感情交流；拓展相关内容，激发他人的兴趣。

写作方法：首段要开门见山说明写作目的；主体方面要做到三点：首先，具体交代邀请原因；其次，邀请内容包括活动性质、时间、地点、日期；最后，表达有关要求和希望；尾段要再次盛情邀请并希望尽快答复。

真题回顾 · 典例3 · 2017新课标全国卷Ⅰ

假定你是李华，想邀请外教Henry一起参观中国剪纸（paper-cutting）艺术展。请给他写封邮件，内容包括：

1. 展览的时间、地点；

2. 展览内容。

注意：

1. 词数100左右；

2. 可以适当增加细节，以使行文连贯。

____

____

____

____

____

____

写作指导：

邀请信分为发出的邀请信和回复别人的邀请信。邀请信的结构：

Beginning：invitation

Body：when，where，why，how...

Ending: expectation，gratitude

范文赏析：

I'm Li Hua, one of your students in your cultural class.I know you're interested in one of Chinese traditional art forms—paper-cutting.So I invite you to attend an exhibition of it.

It'll be held from June 10 to July 10 this year and the opening time is from 9：00 a.m. to 7：00 p.m. from Monday to Saturday and the place of the exhibition is at the City Gallery, which is located at 118, Jian Guo Road, Hai Dian District.Shall we go there together this Friday afternoon? I will meet you at 2：00 p.m. at the teaching building gate if you like.

You know we Chinese have a lot of traditional art forms, of which paper-cutting is one of the most popular.In the exhibition, you will enjoy many special kinds of paper-cuttings.Maybe you can learn one or two skills of the cutting.

Looking forward to your early reply.

Regards,

Li Hua

（4）建议信 (Letter of suggestion)

建议信的写作目的是提出建议或忠告，不是投诉信。观点要合情合理，注意礼貌当先。

首段：简介自己，不要啰唆；说明目的，注意语气。

主体：提出具体建议；首先肯定优点，再写改进内容，否则会变成投诉信；经常进行交流，注意对方的感受，时时提到你和我，否则容易跑题写成议论文。

尾段：总结建议，注意礼貌，使对方易于接受。

写作流程图如下所示。

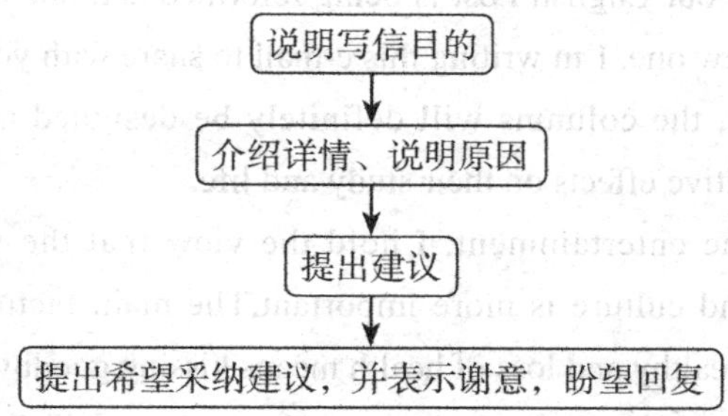

真题回顾·典例4·2014年上海

学校英语报正在酝酿改版，拟从现有的三个栏目（健康、娱乐、文化）中去除一个，并从三个备选栏目（时尚、职业规划、读者反馈）中挑选一个纳入该报。假设你是该校学生程飞，给校报编辑写一封电子邮件，表达你的观点。邮件须包括以下内容：

1. 你建议去除的栏目及去除的理由。
2. 你建议增加的栏目及增加的理由。

____

____

____

____

____

____

写作指导：

这篇书面表达属于提纲类范畴，这篇作文要求就校英语报改版的事情给校报编辑写一封电子邮件，表达自己的观点。邮件须包括以下内容：①你建议去除的栏目及去除的理由；②你建议增加的栏目及增加的理由，根据自己的建议选定栏目的设置并以邮件方式表达自己的观点。考生在写作过程中要确定切题且符合英语写作逻辑的篇章结构。确立邮件文体之后，要弄清要点，围绕要点展开，条理要清晰，理由要充分。在写作的过程中，要注意人称、时态语态和常见的语法问题，文章尽量简洁，在文章中尽可能多地使用“高大上”的词汇，遵循短语优先原则，再配以特殊句型和复合句，让文章更上档次。

范文赏析：

Dear Editor,

I've learned that our English Post is being reformed and one of the three columns is to be replaced by a new one. I'm writing this e-mail to share with you my opinions.

Needless to say, the columns will definitely be designed according to students' interest and have positive effects on their study and life.

Compared to the entertainment, I hold the view that the value of the columns concerning health and culture is more important.The main factor is that it is of great significance to keep healthy and loss of health means kissing goodbye to life.Consequently, more knowledge of how to keep fit can improve the quality of life.In addition, the progress in acquiring cultures contributes to broadening one's horizons, which in turn is beneficial to one's study and the establishment of philosophy of life.

Furthermore, the career planning should be taken into account in the school English Post. On one hand, it covers one's career development a great deal. On the other hand, it makes a great difference to one's career success in the future.

What has been mentioned above is my personal ideas.Here I am in the hope that my advice will add a brilliant touch to the improved version of our school English Post.

Yours sincerely,

Cheng Fei

（5）通知(Notice)

① 口头通知

要注意以下几点：第一，要有称呼用语。如：在正式场合用的Ladies and gentlemen,对学生用的Boys and girls 等。第二，要有开头语。常用的开头语有：

May I have your attention, please?

Be quite.There is something important I have to tell you.

You need to know.

I have something to tell you.

时态问题:口头通知是要告诉大家即将进行的活动，因此要以一般将来时为主。

人称问题:口头通知常用第二人称表示被通知的对象。

要有结束语,常用的结束语有：

That's all.Thank you.

Any questions? Does everyone understand?

② 书面通知

书面通知具有以下特点：

书面通知的正文上面的正中有NOTICE或ANNOUNCEMENT 标题。

在正文最后的右下角要写上发通知的单位或组织者的姓名。

真题回顾·典例5·2018新课标全国卷Ⅱ

你受学生会委托为校宣传栏“英语天地”写一则通知，请大家观看一部英语短片*Growing Together*，内容包括：

1. 短片内容：学校的发展；
2. 放映时间、地点；
3. 欢迎对短片提出意见。

注意：

1. 词数100左右。
2. 可以适当增加细节，以使行文连贯。

____

____

____

____

____

____

试题分析：

2018年高考英语书面表达体裁为通知，替学校的“英语天地”邀请学生看英文短片*Growing Together*。继2015年、2016年、2017年连续三年考查写信之后，全国Ⅱ卷考查了应用文中的另一典型体裁，内容为邀请看电影相关的时间、地点的通知。学生对该题材和内容熟悉，对词汇的要求也相对基础。

纵观全国II卷英语书面表达，从题材上来讲，除了2014年考查了记叙文，十年中有九年均考查了应用文，应用文占90%。所以考生在高考英语写作的准备中应当把重心放在应用文上，熟练掌握英语应用文写作的几个相关专项，并且熟识高考英语基础词汇。

2009—2018年高考英语新课标卷II书面表达

年份	命题形式	文体	内容
2009	文字提纲	信件——回信	写信介绍改建后前门大街的情况
2010	文字提纲	信件——去信	给笔友写信告知招聘广告信息

续 表

年份	命题形式	文体	内容
2011	文字提纲	信件——祝贺信	写信向学校辅导中心求助
2012	文字提纲	信件——申请信	申请参加国际中学生新加坡夏令营
2013	文字提纲	信件——去信	请笔友代卖自己制作的中国结
2014	文字提纲	短文	十年后的我
2015	文字提纲	信件——邀请信	邀请外教一起去敬老院陪老人过重阳节
2016	文字提纲	信件——邀请信	邀请英国朋友Peter参加摄影比赛并提供摄影作品
2017	文字提纲	信件——邀请信	写信邀请外教参加剪纸展览
2018	文字提纲	通知	通知观看英语短片

写作点拨：

英语书面通知的时态应该以一般将来时为主，多使用被动语态、简单句。在通知中不应当过度使用较复杂的词语和读起来拗口的句子。

另外，层次一定要清晰，一个层次要表达一件事情，使人看起来一目了然。

满分范文：

Boys and girls,

May I have your attention, please? Recently, an outstanding movie will be shown in our campus.Welcome to join us and enjoy it! Here are some relevant details about it.

To begin with, the name of the movie is *Growing Together*, which is about the development of our beloved school; as a result, it will be not only meaningful but also interesting.Besides, it will be in the library from 2:00 to 4:00 in the afternoon on June 9th. What's more, everyone of you will be welcome to take part in it, enjoying the movie, having a heated discussion afterwards and giving your own comments.

Hopefully, you would make it to our activity.I have the confidence that you will have a great time.

The Student Union

（二）开放类或半开放类作文

给出很少的提示或近乎命题作文，这种题要求考生发挥想象把文章的内容合理地表达出来。也有的是给出漫画、一句话或一种情景，让考生根据自己的理解写作文，即给出漫画、主题或两三点提示，由考生去发挥、构思。

（半）开放作文形同于书面表达，但又不等同于书面表达,这种题型只给出主题，也就是说只告诉你正在或将要发生什么事情，至于事情发生的过程、结果则完全由考生自己去发挥，考生的思维完全可以发散。所以，考生的思路不同，写出的作文就会是千人千面。

常见的(半)开放式作文命题形式：

1. 标题式

标题式(半)开放作文的命题形式往往是要求考生围绕一个特定的话题去写作。标题式(半)开放作文实际上相当于汉语的命题式作文，考生只要围绕题目中所给的特定的话题说明、叙述、举例，再谈谈自己的感想或发表自己的看法就可以了。

2. 漫画式

漫画式(半)开放作文以北京高考为代表。命题形式往往是要求考生围绕一幅漫画去写作。然而，相对于“标题式”(半)开放作文而言，“漫画式”(半)开放作文的写作难度更大。

“(半)开放作文”只要求你做两件事情，一件是描述图画（describe the following picture），另一件是阐述你对图画理解和看法（explain how you understand it）。相应地，你只需要写两个段落，一段是“描述段”，另一段是“议论段”。

不必过深地挖掘图画信息，只需用简单的英文，表达平易的道理。换句话说，只要你能用正确的英文表达你的感想，便赢得了胜利。

3. 图画类作文

图画作文是近年来高考书面表达考查的热点题型之一。它是指根据某幅图画所提供的图像信息写一篇短文或叙述一个故事；或通过几幅相关的图画说明某个问题或得出某个结论。体裁多样，可以是记叙文、议论文或说明文等。

根据图画内容及体裁的不同采用不同的段落发展方式。图画作文可以当作三段式的提纲作文来写：第一段描述图画并揭示其寓意（寓意一般用一句话来概括），第二段分析原因，最后一段发表评论或提出建议。其中第二、三段是写作的重点。叙事型图画作文（通常会涉及多幅画，要求对某一事件的发生、发展进行描述）可根据图画的数目和具体内容来确定段落。

4. 图表类作文

图表作文要求将图表形式的信息转化成段落文字信息。信息以图表的形式呈现出来，需要弄清所给的图表、数据、标题及文字说明等各种信息之间的关系，通过分析、研究提炼和确定文章的中心思想，得出令人信服的结论。图表作文中所说的图主要有曲线图、饼状图和柱状图等；而表则一般是统计表。

图表作文可分为三个段落来写。第一段点明调查/统计对象并进行图表信息的转换，转换过程中需要注意的是信息的取舍和详略程度。第二段主要是根据信息总结出规律或找出问题出现的原因。 第三段主要是建议的提出或解决方法的提出。其中第一段和第二段是重点段落，第三段可根据题干要求进行取舍。

真题回顾·典例6·2017江苏卷

请认真阅读下面有关我国电影票房收入（box-office income）的柱状图及相关文字，并按照要求用英语写一篇150词左右的文章。

Saturday Afternoon.In a Shopping Centre.

Li Jiang: Hi, Su Hua.Which movie shall we see?

Su Hua: Whatever.We've got so many choices, *Kung Fu Yoga*, *Journey to the West*... Each sounds great!

Li Jiang: Yeah! And some movie stars are fantastic.

Su Hua: And the high-tech!...

Li Jiang: Perfect! Let's get some food first.We only have 20 minutes left.

Su Hua: No hurry.The cinema is on the same floor.

One Day in **2016**.At Home.

Son: Mum, shall we go and see a film tonight?

Mother: Why bother? We can stay at home and watch films online.It's convenient with our new and faster network.

Son: But it feels good in a cinema.

Mother: And the price... We have to pay 50 yuan a ticket.

Son: Only 10 yuan more than last year.

Mother: But still we cannot get the money's worth.Some films are just boring...

写作内容：

（1）用约30个单词概述柱状图信息的主要内容。

（2）我国电影票房收入变化的原因有哪些，简要谈谈你的看法（上述对话仅供参考，原因不少于两点）。

（3）谈谈你对我国电影票房收入走向的看法，并简要说明理由。

写作要求：

（1）写作过程中不能直接引用原文语句。

（2）作文中不能出现真实姓名和学校名称。

（3）不必写标题。

评分标准：

内容完整，语言规范，语篇连贯，词数适当。

写作指导：

此类作文对考生的能力要求极高。首先考生要以30词左右概述短文内容。接下来要分析票房收入变化的原因并给出自己的看法，并谈谈自己对票房走向的看法。作文以第三人称和一般现在时为主。①概述：中国电影票房在2012—2016年间呈现不断增长的趋势，但是2016年的增长相比于前几年很缓慢。②分析原因：票房增长与人们生活水平的不断提高息息相关，人们有了多余的钱，才可能消费、娱乐；另一方面，电影的制作技术日臻成熟，许多优质的电影不断上映；再者，互联网的普及无疑起到了很大的宣传作用。③看法和理由：票房增速将会小幅上涨或有所回落。只要给出恰当的理由，对票房看涨或是看落皆可。

写30词左右的概述时，语言要简练、不拖沓。遣词造句要符合英语的表达习惯，尽量用上定语从句、状语从句和非谓语动词与倒装句等语法和句型。同时注意语句的连贯性。

范文赏析：

Possible version one：

The box-office income of Chinese movies witnessed a constant increase from about 17 billion yuan in 2012 to over 40 billion in 2015.However, that increase slowed down in 2016.

The reasons behind this are various.The fast economic development before 2016 was probably the most powerful engine driving the constant growth in the box-office income. The application of new technologies and the wide appeal of movie stars could also account for the increase.However, China saw a decline in its economic growth rate last year.And the Internet increased options for movie lovers.Consequently, some viewers began to turn away from cinemas, leading to a slower growth.

China’s economy is expected to grow at a medium speed in the coming years, so an increase is possible in the investment in the movie industry and the number of quality movies.Therefore, its box-office income will probably enjoy a slight increase.

(150 words)

Possible version two：

As is indicated in the graph, the box-office income of Chinese films increased constantly from 2012 to 2015, but its growth, for one reason or another, slowed down in 2016.

The increase in the box-office income can be attributed to a number of factors. The quality of life has improved and watching films is regarded as a good means of entertainment.Besides, filming technology has advanced and more quality films are on offer.Moreover, the Internet plays an important part.On the Internet, people can seek information about their favorite stars and buy tickets at a discount as well, which is both time-saving and economical.

However, the film market may witness a slowdown in the near future.Cinemas have gradually given way to the rise of the Internet and cellphones, and the ticket price is on the increase.Therefore, the film industry should make greater efforts to attract more viewers.

(150 words)

四、2019年高考学科素养主题语境分类写作之备考训练

（一）人与社会

1. 文化交流

真题回顾 · Passage 1 · 了解中国文化 · 洛阳龙门石窟 · 开放类 · 书信应用文

假设你是李华，你的美国笔友高二学生Tom对中国的龙门石窟艺术很感兴趣，今年暑假他打算到中国来，准备从北京到龙门参观石窟。请你给Tom写一封电子邮件，告知他如下内容：

1. 简单介绍龙门石窟；
2. 介绍从北京到龙门石窟的乘车方式；
3. 介绍景点的服务条件。

参考词汇：龙门石窟Longmen Grottoes 词数：100词左右。

选题理由：

洛阳龙门石窟是世界石雕艺术的典范，是中国呈现给世界的瑰宝，许多外国人到龙门参观石窟。学生在历史书中都学过相关的知识，因而学生对此很熟悉。本题符合高考命题趋势：有传播中华优秀文化的意识，能够用英语讲述中国故事，展示学生的爱国情怀，增强文化自信。

构思点拨：

先从整体上构思文章的结构：很高兴收到Tom的电子邮件，对其对龙门石窟感兴趣表示赞赏；介绍从北京到龙门的乘车方式；介绍景点的服务条件；希望早日见到笔友Tom。

参考范文：

Dear Tom,

I'm very happy to know that you are interested in Longmen Grottoes in your e-mail. Longmen Grottoes, which is truly a large museum of stone sculpture, were inscribed in the World Heritage List by the World Heritage Committee of UNESCO in November of 2000. I prefer you to take high-speed railway to arrive at Longmen station because it is convenient and fast. After you get to the station, you can take a taxi or bus to go to the Grottoes.The scenic area provides good service. You can enjoy the delicious food there and have a good rest in the hotel. I'm sure you will have a good time there.

I'm looking forward to meeting you in China as soon as possible.

Yours,

Li Hua

附：写作素材

1. 范文亮点

（1）从句：①定语从句： which is truly a large museum of stone sculpture；②宾语从句that you are interested in Longmen Grottoes in your e-mail；③状语从句because it is convenient and fast。

（2）短语：be interested in；prefer ... to ...; look forward to; as soon as possible。

2. 拓展素材

（1）词汇：treasure珍宝；unique独一无二的；ancient古代的；convenient方便的；well-preserved保存完好的；attract吸引。

（2）短语：be proud of因……而自豪；be famous for以……而闻名；be made of由……制造的；the wonders in the world世界奇观；be well known for以……而闻名；place of interest名胜古迹；green hills and clear waters 青山绿水；famous mountains and great rivers名山大川；natural scenery/attractions自然景观；arrive at/in到达；be located in位于。

（3）①句型：not only... but also... 不但……而且……；Only in this way can we... 只有这样，我们才能……；Words can't describe my feelings at that time.语言无法表达我当时的感受；It is said that... 据说……。②中国京剧（让世界了解中国文化遗产）——［提纲类］［书信应用文］。③中国剪纸文化（让世界了解中国的风俗习惯）——［提纲类］［书信应用文］。

2. 节假日活动

真题回顾·Passage 2·2018日照市高三校际联考·开放类·书信应用文

假如你是李华，打算邀请你的朋友英国交换生Julie在端午节那天到你家做客。请根据以下内容用英语给她写一封电子邮件。

1. 乘坐26路公交车到人民广场站下车。

2. 跟妈妈学习包粽子(zongzi)。

3. 去东湖公园看龙舟比赛(dragon boat races)。

注意：

1. 词数100左右。

2. 可适当增加细节，以使行文连贯。

选题理由：

高中生要理解和鉴赏中外优秀文化，培育中国情怀，坚定文化自信，拓展国际视野，增进国际理解，逐步提升跨文化沟通能力、思辨能力、学习能力和创新能力，形成正确的世界观、人生观和价值观。

参考范文：

Dear Julie,

How are you recently? We are going to have a pleasant holiday this Friday, because Dragon Boat Festival is coming! So I'm earnestly inviting you to come to my home.

Just take No. 26 bus and get off at People's Square Station, where I'll be waiting for you and we'll go home together.Then my mother will prepare tasty food for our lunch, including zongzi. We'll learn how to make it with our own hands, and you'll learn how this traditional Chinese food came into being.

When lunch is over, we'll go to East Lake, where we'll enjoy watching wonderful dragon boat races.Interesting, isn't it?

I can't wait to see you soon!

Yours,

Li Hua

3. 公益活动（志愿和支援）

真题回顾·Passage 3·公益活动·提纲类·通知

3月12日是“植树节”(Tree Planting Day)，某校学生会要组织全体学生参加植树活动。

1. 植树日期：3月12日；
2. 植树地点：云蒙山；
3. 集合地点、时间：学校操场，早晨7时；
4. 要求：全体学生参加，每班带5～6个水桶作浇水用，乘校车前往。

请根据上述内容，以学生会名义拟一份英语口头通知，以便在学校广播站的“English for Today”节目中播放。

注意：

1. 不要逐字翻译所给的汉语说明；
2. 字数100左右；
3. 语句连贯，意思准确。

____

____

____

____

____

____

选题理由：

学生参与公益活动是学生接触社会的一项重要活动，可以肯定地说，每个学生在学校都参加过公益活动。因此，此话题贴近学生生活，让学生有话可写。

参考范文：

Comrades,

Attention, please! March the twelfth is our Tree Planting Day.

We have decided to go to the Yun Meng Hill and plant trees there that day.All the students in our school are asked to take part in the activity, which is meaningful to us.In order to water young trees , each class must take five or six buckets with you.We are going to meet on the sports ground at seven on the morning of March 12.And then, we will take our school bus to go there.

That's all.Thank you!

4. 人际关系

真题回顾·Passage 4·半开放类·书信应用文

假设你是李华，你们学校进行了英语教学改革，请你给你的美国朋友Peter用英语写一封英语信介绍一下你们学校现在的英语学习情况。内容必须包含以下三个方面：

1. 以前的学习方法。
2. 合作学习的好处。
3. 谈谈你的感受。

注意：

1. 词数100词左右。
2. 文章的开头和结尾已经给出，不计入总词数。
3. 可适当增加细节，以使行文连贯。

Dear Peter,

____

____

____

____

____

____

Yours,

Li Hua

选题理由：

该试题贴近考生实际生活，话题涉及校园和睦相处关系的内容，属于半开放性话题，故需要自由发挥的地方较多。

参考范文：

Dear Peter,

In the past in our English class, the teacher only forced us to remember many dull English words, drills and grammar rules, which was aimed at exams. And this maked us lose interest in learning English.

But now, in our English class, our teacher creates chances for us students to work together in groups to communicate with each other in English.In this way, we share the enjoyment of learning language and we feel the happiness of communicating.Learning in groups arouses our hunger for understanding, sharing, cooperating and knowledge.

In my opinion, learning in cooperation is a good way to learn English.

Yours,

Li Hua

5. 人物介绍

真题回顾 · Passage 5 · 人物 · 图表类 · 人物介绍

请根据下表的提示写一篇英语短文。

霍金资料

霍金	1. 1942年1月8日，出生在英国牛津	
	2. 1962年毕业于牛津大学，而后进入剑桥大学攻读博士学位	
	3. 1963年被诊断出渐冻症。他忍受病痛40多年。 4. 1988年写下《时间简史》，霍金死于2018年，享年76岁。 5. 霍金的精神激励了全世界的人们	
你能向他学点什么？		

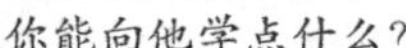

注意：

1. 词数：100词左右。

2. 可适当增加细节，以使行文连贯。

提示词：ALS俗称渐冻症。

选题理由：

霍金是热点新闻人物之一，学生也比较熟悉他的成就，有话可说，写起来会比较得心应手。本文是一篇人物介绍型记叙文，是历年高考常考的一种写作文体，符合新课标高考命题思想。

构思点拨：

这是一篇人物介绍，属于记叙文的范畴。在写作的时候，要使用一定的复杂句型和过渡词，保持行文流畅。写作时注意要点的整合。

本文为记叙文类书面表达，文章主要是关于人物方面的描述。写作之前要认真审题，要确保写作内容的完整，尤其是一开始的信息材料。接着对于表格里的信息要适当展开处理，采用一定的句型句式。最后发表个人观点，需要对前面的内容加以总结，整篇文章对学生的语言表达能力有一定的要求。

参考范文：

Stephen William Hawking was born in Oxford, England, on Jan.8, 1942. He graduated from Oxford in 1962 and did well enough on his final exam to earn admission to the University of Cambridge to pursue a doctorate.In 1963, he was diagnosed as ALS and he suffered from the serious disease for over forty years.He wrote the book *A Brief History of Time* in 1988.He is one of the famous scientists in this century.He died at the age of 76 in 2018.Personally, he has set a good example to us students and we can learn a lot from him. Not only his perseverance and persistence but also his optimism are what we can benefit from.

6. 科技与人

真题回顾 · Passage 6 · 共享单车 · 提纲类 · 书信应用文

假定你是李华，你的美国朋友Tom在给你的邮件中提到他对中国新近出现的一种共享单车“mobike”很感兴趣，并请你做个简要介绍。

注意：

1. 词数100左右。

2. 可以适当增加细节，以使行文连贯。

____

____

____

____

____

____

选题理由：

共享单车话题越来越普遍，这也是生活中的一个话题。此话题为学生所熟知，能够激发学生的想象力，符合新课标理念下的命题方向。

构思点拨：

写此类英语作文时，首先要发挥自己的想象力，写出符合逻辑的内容，最后要写出自己的看法。语句要通顺流畅，尽可能地避免语法错误，将语义表达清楚。

参考范文：

Dear Tom,

I am more than delighted to know you show great interest in shared bikes which have received increasing attention home and aboard.It is my pleasure to introduce them to you.

When you spot a shared bike, what you need to do is just scan the QR code of the bike to unlock it and enjoy your trip. Not only are shared bikes environmentally friendly and convenient, but also they charge low rates and can be parked almost anytime and anywhere, which have given them advantages over other means of public transport.

With Mobike entering the UK, I can't help but wonder about its situation there.Could you please be kind enough to tell me something about that?

Yours sincerely,

Li Hua

附：写作素材

1. I am more than delighted to know you show great interest in shared bikes which have received increasing attention home and aboard.

2. When you spot a shared bike, what you need to do is just scan the QR code of the bike to unlock it and enjoy your trip.

3. Not only are shared bikes environmentally friendly and convenient, but also they charge low rates and can be parked almost anytime and anywhere, which have given them advantages over other means of public transport.

4. With Mobike entering the UK, I can't help but wonder about its situation there.

5. ... which have received increasing attention home and aboard... which have given them advantages over other means of public transport.

6. Not only are shared bikes environmentally friendly and convenient, but also they charge low rates and can be parked almost anytime and anywhere.

7. What you need to do is just scan the QR code of the bike to unlock it and enjoy your trip.

8. 采用高级词汇，如more than（非常）， show great interest in...， home and aboard，given sb. advantages over...，other means of public transport，can't help but do...，be kind enough to do...等。

7. 社会热点

真题回顾·Passage 7·开放类·书信应用文

假定你是李华，你校将于3月25日上午8:30到10:30在学校礼堂二楼举行主题为“关爱地球”的英语演讲比赛。请你给你班的外教怀特先生（Mr. White）写一封电子邮件，邀请他前来担任评委并做总结发言。

注意：

1. 词数100左右。

2. 可适当增加细节，以使行文连贯。

选题理由：

关爱地球是学生们非常关注的话题，让每个人都有东西可写，符合高考的命题要求。

参考范文：

Dear Mr. White,

How are you going? I am writing to invite you to serve as the judge of our English speech contest, whose topic is “Love the Earth”. It is expected that the contest will last 2 hours, from 8:30 a.m. to10:30 a.m. on March 25th on the second floor of our school hall.

We will be very grateful if you could set aside some time and attend the contest.As an honored guest, you are expected to make a speech at the end of the contest.We are looking forward to seeing you that day.

Please contact me if you have any questions.

Yours sincerely,

Li Hua

（二）人与自我

1. 语言学习

真题回顾·Passage 1·东北三省三校2018年高三第一次模拟·开放类·书信应用文

假设你叫李华，你的澳洲朋友Devin参加汉语水平考试（HSK）未能通过，请你写一封信，安慰一下你的朋友。内容包括：

1. 对考试失利的安慰。

2. 对汉语学习提出建议。

注意：

1. 词数100左右。

2. 可以适当增加细节，以使行文连贯。

3. 开头语已为你写好，不计入总词数。

Dear Devin,

I am sorry to hear that you failed to pass HSK.

____

____

____

____

____

____

Yours sincerely,

Li Hua

选题理由：

语言学习是学生学校生活中最重要的活动之一，也是高考的命题热点。本话题贴近高中生的生活实际，而且具有一定的开放性，使得每个学生都能够有话可说。这符合高考的命题方向。

参考范文：

Dear Devin,

I am sorry to hear that you failed to pass HSK.I hope that the unexpected failure will not let you down, for I have still been amazed by the excellent Chinese you spoke when we first met.

As we know, language learning is never an easy task, but needs painstaking efforts and patience.Personally, I think you'd better pay close attention to the formal use of Chinese words and expressions, which really count.Meanwhile, you may as well watch more Chinese materials as much as you can afford.More importantly, you should learn from the mistakes that you have made.Anyhow, you've already made great progress in your learning of Chinese. Good luck next time.

Yours,

Li Hua

2. 健康饮食

真题回顾 · Passage 2 · 健康饮食 · 提纲类 · 说明文

假设你是艾玫，你的美国笔友Alice来信说她打算在暑假节食减肥，想听听你的意见。请根据以下要点，给她写一封电子邮件谈谈节食的利弊和你的看法。

要点：

1. 她想节食减肥的心情可以理解。

2. 适度节食减肥有益于健康；过度节食减肥有损健康。

3. 你的节食减肥建议。

注意：

1. 词数为100左右；

2. 参考词汇：节食be on a diet；

3. 电子邮件的开头和结尾已为你写好（不计入你所写词数）；

4. 已给出的电子邮件的开头和结尾不得抄入答题卡。

Dear Alice,

I'm very glad to have received the letter you sent me two weeks ago.

____

____

____

____

____

____

Yours truly,

Ai Mei

选题理由：

健康饮食以及节食话题也是高考的命题热点。本话题贴近高中生的生活实际，而且具有一定的开放性，使得每个学生都能够有话可说。这符合高考的命题方向。

构思点拨：

根据写作要求，首先描述现状；然后分条给出建议，第一条写饮食方面；第二条写锻炼方面；最后提生活习惯方面的建议。注意提建议一定要有条理。

参考范文：

I'm very glad to have received the letter you sent me two weeks ago.In your letter you say you are going to be on a diet in the coming summer, hoping to look more attractive, which is understandable. I'd like to share with you my ideas about it.

Undoubtedly, a proper diet can not only help you lose ugly fat, but can also help you keep it off and lead a more active, happier and healthier life.However, a too strict diet can do more harm than good to health.

Everyone longs for beauty, but in my opinion, natural beauty is real beauty.Wish you to develop good eating habits and follow a healthy way of life so as to keep fit.I firmly believe you will make it.

Yours sincerely,

Li Hua

3. 体育健身

真题回顾 · Passage 3 · 开放类 · 书信应用文

假如你是李华，你的美国笔友Alice给你发了一封电子邮件，想了解关于你慢跑的一些情况。请你根据以下要点给她回邮件。内容包括：

1. 开始慢跑的时间：2014年。

2. 慢跑带来的益处：睡眠好，白天精力充沛；身材苗条，皮肤越来越好，更积极、自信。

3. 以后还将继续坚持。

注意：

1. 词数100左右。

2. 文章的开头和结尾已经给出，不计入总词数。

3. 可适当增加细节，以使行文连贯。

Dear Alice,

I am very happy to receive your e-mail.

____

____

____

____

____

____

Yours sincerely,

Li Hua

选题理由：

慢跑是校园的主要活动之一，也是学生强健体魄的最重要的方式之一。此话题为学生所熟悉，符合高考的话题要求。

参考范文：

Dear Alice,

I'm very happy to receive your e-mail.Since 2014, I have been jogging.It is jogging that gives me a lot of benefits.First of all, I have a good sleep and more energy during the day. Therefore, I can study efficiently and have made great progress.In addition, not only do I have slim body shape but also my skin is better and better.I am more positive and confident than before.

I'm proud of myself that I can keep running for over 2 years.What's more, I won't quit easily like before.Instead, I have made up my mind to insist on jogging longer than before.

Yours sincerely,

Li Hua

4. 校园生活

真题回顾 · Passage 4 · 齐齐哈尔2018届高三第一模 · 开放类 · 书信应用文

假定你是李华。本周六是你十八岁生日，家人将在光明饭店为你举办一次生日宴会。请你给朋友John写一封信，邀请他参加。内容包括：

1. 提出邀请。

2. 十八岁生日的意义。

3. 宴会情况。

注意：

1. 词数100左右。

2. 可以适当增加细节，以使行文连贯。

Dear John,

____

____

____

____

____

Yours,

Li Hua

选题理由:

写书信是高考英语全国卷比较固定的模式。本文是邀请信，是高考常考的形式之一。去饭店过生日的话题越来越普遍，这也是生活中的一个话题。此话题为学生所熟知，能够激发学生的想象力，符合新课标理念下的命题方向。

参考范文:

Dear John,

I'm writing this letter to invite you to my 18th birthday party this Saturday.

An 18th birthday is unusual for every child in China, because it means that a teenager who has been an adult becomes more mature and wiser.So my family is determined to hold a big party at Guangming Hotel.Many friends and relatives are invited to the party. The hotel band will play amazing music, and a variety of Chinese food will be served.If you take part in the party, you will definitely enjoy the atmosphere and have a good time with us.

Look forward to your coming.

Yours,

Li Hua

5. 感恩教育

真题回顾 · Passage 5 · 开放类 · 书信应用文

假设你是李华，你高中毕业后被北京外国语大学录取，在教师节到来之际，你给你的英语老师王老师写了一封信，信的内容包括：

1. 感谢他三年来对你的关怀和照顾。
2. 感谢他对你英语学习的指导。
3. 祝老师身体健康、工作顺利。

注意：

1. 词数100左右。
2. 可适当发挥，写一个具体事例。

选题理由：

感恩是每个人都应该具备的一种品质，感谢恩师是一个熟悉的话题，使学生有话可说，符合高考的要求。

参考范文：

Dear Mr. Wang,

The Teachers' Day is around the corner.At this moment, I want to express my gratitude to you.

Looking back on my senior campus life, you encouraged me many times and built up my confidence whenever I met with difficulties.I used to be poor at my English, and there was a time when I decided that I wanted to give it up.It was your advice that made me interested in English.Without your care, I wouldn't have been admitted into Beijing Foreign Studies University.

Words can't express my thanks to you.Here I sincerely hope that you are in good health and work happily every day.

Yours,

Li Hua

（三）人与自然

1. 环境与保护

真题回顾 · Passage 1 · 文明校园 · 开放类 · 邮件

假定你是学生会主席李华，为响应学校建设文明校园(civilized campus) 的号召，倡导同学们争做文明学生，请给校报英语专栏的编辑写封邮件，内容包括：

1. 列举不文明行为。
2. 提出改进措施。

注意：

1. 词数100 左右。
2. 可以适当增加细节，以使行文连贯。
3. 开头和结尾已给出，不计入总词数。

Dear Editor,

Yours,

Li Hua

选题理由：

校园环境与每个学生都息息相关，建设文明校园是每个人的责任。此话题贴近学生生活，使学生有话可说，符合高考的命题要求。

构思点拨：

本篇书面表达属于提纲类作文，提纲是文章的总体框架，要在提纲的范围内进行分析、构思和想象；要依据提示情景或词语，按照一定逻辑关系来写；本文写作时可以按照所给要点的顺序写。根据要表达的内容确定句子的时态、语态，注意使用高级词汇和句式，以增加文章的亮点。

参考范文：

Dear Editor,

As the chairman of the Students' Union, I'm writing to draw your attention to some improper behaviour among us students: littering and scribbling.It makes our campus dirty and unpleasant, which does great harm to the image of the civilized campus.Besides, I always feel ashamed whenever I see this.

It is clearly not appropriate for a student to litter and scribble about.I wonder if the school could place more dustbins around and set up specific rules against such behaviour. At the same time, students should be encouraged to develop good habits and better behave themselves.

I believe that with the joint efforts of students and teachers, our school will become a more enjoyable place in the near future.

Yours,

Li Hua

附：写作素材

1. It makes our campus dirty and unpleasant, which does great harm to the image of the civilized campus.

2. I always feel ashamed whenever I see this.

3. I wonder if the school could place more dustbins around and set up specific rules against such behaviour.

2. 旅游和交通

真题回顾 · Passage 2 · 郴州市2018届高三第一次质检 · 开放类 · 书信应用文

假定你是李华，你的美国朋友Ben寒假想来北京旅游，请你帮他做一个旅游计划。请你根据以下要点用英语给他写一封信。内容如下：

1. 时间：20天(2018年2月1日—2018年2月20日)；

2. 活动：参观北京的一些知名旅游景点，欣赏中国国粹京剧，在北京胡同和当地人一起欢度春节；

3. 你的建议。

参考词汇：京剧Beijing Opera，胡同Hutong

注意：

1. 词数100左右，文章的开头已为你写好，不计入总词数；

2. 可以适当增加细节，以使行文连贯。

Dear Ben,

I'm glad that you are coming to Beijing for your winter vacation.

____

____

____

____

____

____

Best wishes!

Yours,

Li Hua

选题理由：

本文把旅游和中国文化结合在一起，突出了学生熟悉的两个内容。在当今社会，每个人都有旅游的经历。有关旅游的话题是每个人都熟悉的话题，使学生有话可说，符合高考的要求。

参考范文：

Dear Ben,

I'm glad that you are coming to Beijing for your winter vacation.I'd like to make a travel plan for you.

I think the best time to experience Chinese customs is the Spring Festival, which falls on February 15 next year, so you can arrange your trip in February, from 1st to 20th.If you want to know how we Chinese celebrate the Spring Festival, I advise you to live with a local family in Beijing Hutong.And you can't miss Beijing Opera, which is an important part of Chinese culture and attractive for most travelers to Beijing.Apart from the Chinese culture, there are many places of interest in Beijing and you will find it very worthwhile to visit them, such as the Palace Museum, the Forbidden City and the famous Great Wall.

I have some more suggestions for you.In order to enjoy yourself in Beijing, you'd better invite a friend who can speak very good Chinese to travel with you, which will be very helpful and convenient for you.Hope you'll have a good time in Beijing.

Best wishes!

Yours,

Li Hua

3. 美丽乡村

真题回顾 · Passage 3 · 家乡巨变 · 提纲类 · 电子邮件

假如你是李华。你有一位美国笔友Tom,他想了解你的家乡近几年的变化。请根据下面表格中的内容，用英语给他写一封信，介绍家乡的情况。

家乡情况

过去	现在
路少且窄，堵车；公园少； 空气污染严重	路多而宽，畅通；新建许多公园； 空气质量提高

注意：

1. 词数100左右。
2. 可以适当增加细节，使短文连贯。
3. 开头和结尾已给出。
4. 短文应包括所有内容要点，但不可逐字翻译。

Dear Tom,

I am happy to share my opinion about my hometown.

____

____

____

____

____

____

Yours,

Li Hua

选题理由：

感受家乡的变化是每个人都熟悉的话题，使学生有东西可写，符合高考的要求。

参考范文：

Dear Tom,

I am happy to share my opinion about my hometown.Great changes have taken place here in recent years.

In the past, my hometown was not as beautiful as it is.The traffic was very heavy and roads were narrow.There used to be few parks.The air was polluted seriously.But now, everything has changed! My hometown takes a new look.The old streets have been broadened and more roads have been constructed.Many new parks have been built, where people can take exercise, sing songs and play games.The air is fresher than before.We can enjoy the blue sky and white clouds all the year round.

My hometown has become a modern place, whose tomorrow will be better!

Yours,

Li Hua

4. 自然与环境

真题回顾 · Passage 4 · 环境污染 · 提纲类 · 应用文

假如你是一名高中生李华，由于几年来雾霾天气越来越严重，严重地影响了人们的健康和生活，请你用英语写一篇文章向学校报刊投稿，写作内容如下：

1. 说明雾霾情况及危害。

2. 提出应对措施。

注意：

1. 上下文连贯，行文流畅。

2. 词数100左右（开头和结尾已经给出，不计入总词数）。

参考词汇：雾霾天气the haze weather

Dear editor,

Recently, the haze weather has become a daily one right here in large parts of China, ______

______

______

______

______

______

Best regards.

Yours,

Li Hua

选题理由：

空气污染与每个人都息息相关，保护环境、防止空气污染是每个人的责任，中学生也不例外。此话题贴近学生生活，使学生有话可说，符合高考的命题要求。

参考范文：

Dear editor,

Recently, the haze weather has become a daily one right here in large parts of China, which has done great harm to our daily life. Traffic accidents and the delay of flights frequently happen because of the haze weather.More and more people have to go to see the doctor because of the serious disease caused by the haze.A great number of people have to stay at home to avoid the haze, even affecting students' normal classes.

In my opinion, strict measures on environmental protection should be taken.We should call on people to form the habit of using green products and saving energy as much as possible. What's more, we have to do more to raise people's awareness of environmental protection.Only in this way can we expect to have more sunny days.

Best regards.

Yours,

Li Hua

5. 走进大自然

真题回顾 · Passage 5 · 踏青 · 图画类 · 日记

假设你是中学生李华。下面四幅图记录了周日你在中山公园踏青的经历。根据图用英语写一篇日记。

注意：词数100左右。

Sunday, May 4 Fine

____

____

____

____

____

____

选题理由：

“自然与环境”是高中新课程标准24个话题之一，亦是高考英语常考话题。这些话题与学生的生活息息相关，联系密切。通过对这些话题的学习以及高考英语对这些话题的考查，可以让学生多注意身边的人和事、关注社会环境、树立环保意识、学会与大自然和谐相处。

构思点拨：

这是一篇看图写作，一共四幅图。做题时应注意以下几点：第一，认真看图；第二，初步构思，考虑用词、短语、句型和时态;第三，连词成句，然后再连句成文，尽可能地充分利用所学的短语或句型来表述具体的内容;第四，反复检查，修改错误;第五，注意所给的汉语提示，一般来说，看图写作中的汉语提示往往给定了有关的时间、地点、人物等相关的信息，还有参考词汇都是有用信息。在把握了文章的中心后，应在内心构思一个基本的框架，并考虑使用恰当的词语、短语和句型，以充分地表达文章的内容，这是体现自身能力的重要环节。然后再将各图串连起来。串连时，要注意使用适当的连接词语或过渡性语句，不至于让读者觉得文章中出现跳跃现象，更使上下文的衔接紧凑、自然。

参考范文：

Sunday, May 4 Fine

It was a sunny day today and I went to Zhongshan Park for a spring outing.The moment I entered the park, a variety of beautiful flowers and green trees came into sight. Attracted by the beauty, I couldn't stop taking photos.As I wandered along the path, enjoying the beautiful view, I noticed something unpleasant.Two schoolgirls jumped over the fence to pick flowers and climb the tree.Obviously they didn't realize that their behavior had done great damage to the beauty of the park.Without hesitation, I went up and stopped them politely.Quite embarrassed, the two girls came out immediately.Then they took pictures outside the fence.Seeing that, I smiled and everything looked nicer in my eyes.

附：写作素材

1. The moment I entered the park, a variety of beautiful flowers and green trees came into sight.

2. Attracted by the beauty, I couldn't stop taking photos.

3. As I wandered along the path, enjoying the beautiful view, I noticed something unpleasant.

4. Obviously they didn't realize that their behavior had done great damage to the beauty of the park.

5. Quite embarrassed, the two girls came out immediately.

6. Seeing that, I smiled and everything looked nicer in my eyes.